Comparative youth culture

05

Comparative youth culture
The Sociology of Youth Cultures and Youth Subcultures in America, Britain and Canada

Michael Brake

London and New York

2

First published in 1985
by Routledge & Kegan Paul Ltd
Reprinted 1987

Reprinted in 1990, 1993
by Routledge
11 New Fetter Lane, London EC4P 4EE

Simultaneously published in the USA and Canada
by Routledge
29 West 35th Street, New York, NY 10001

Set in 10 on 11 point Times
Printed and bound in Great Britain
by Butler and Tanner Ltd
Frome, Somerset

British Library Cataloguing in Publication Data
A catalogue record for this book is available from the British Library.

Library of Congress Cataloging in Publication Data
Brake, Michael

Comparative youth culture.
Bibliography: p.
Includes index.
1. Youth–United States. 2. Youth–Great Britain.
3. Youth–Canada. 4. Subculture. I. Title.
HQ796.B687   1985   305.2'35   84–27633

ISBN 0–415–05108–8

Contents

Preface   ix

1   **The use of subculture as an analytical tool in sociology**   1
Subcultural analysis and sociology   1
Culture, class and ideology   3
Subcultures and style   11
Subcultures, social reality and identity   15
The development of an analytical framework for
     the study of subcultures   18
Youth becomes a social problem – the
     development of subcultures as a concept in
     delinquency, and the rise of youth culture   21
   1 Respectable youth   23
   2 Delinquent youth   23
   3 Cultural rebels   23
   4 Politically militant youth   23
Conclusion   27

2   **Street-wise. The delinquent subculture in sociological theory in the United States**   30
The Chicago school and the social ecology of the
     city   34
Criticisms of the social ecology model. The
     problems of pluralism – class, conflict and
     power   37
Youth culture and class   39
The statistical presence of delinquency in the
     working-class neighbourhood   43
Differential identity in the deprived
     neighbourhood   46

Contents

Anomie theory and its influence on subcultural
  studies   48
The influence of American naturalism. Matza
  and the drift into and from delinquency   53
Conclusion   57

3   Just another brick in the wall. British studies of
    working-class youth cultures   58
The social ecology of the British working-class
  neighbourhood   59
Education: anti-school culture and leisure   60
Societal reaction and labelling: moral panics, folk
  heroes and folk devils   63
Contemporary British ethnographic studies   64
The new wave of British subcultural theory   65
No future – a brief history of British working-
  class subcultures and their styles   72
  Teddy boys – 'gonna rock it up – gonna rip it
    up'   73
  Mods – 'the kids are all right'   74
  Rockers – 'leader of the pack'   75
  Skinheads – 'violence on the terraces'   75
  Glamrock and glitter   76
  Punks – 'white riot'   76
The 'youth riots' of 1981   80

4   The trippers and the trashers – bohemian and
    radical traditions of youth   83
The cultural rebels – bohemian and middle-class
  delinquency   83
  The emergence of youth counterculture in the
    United States   85
  The beat generation   87
  Hippies, freaks and heads – the counterculture   90
  The structure of the counterculture   93
Religious imperialism – the rise of the cults   103
The radical tradition – political militancy and
  protest movements   105

5   Hustling, breaking and rapping – black and brown
    youth   116
Black people, culture and the economy   116
In the ghetto – formal and informal economies   120
Black on blues – black culture and youth   124
'Los vatos locos' – Hispanic youth culture in the
  barrio   129

'Inglan is a bitch' – black and brown youth in
    Britain 132
'Dread in Babylon'. Rude boys and
    Rastafarians – Afro-Caribbean youth culture
    in Britain 133
Asian youth in Britain 139
Black and brown girls 140
'Let the power fall' – racism and its effect on youth 142

6   **'Take off eh!' – Youth culture in Canada** 144

7   **The invisible girl – the culture of femininity versus
masculinism** 163
Love and marriage – escape into romance 166
Girls and delinquency 170
Girls in male-dominated subcultures 171
Punk women 176
The celebration of masculinism 178

8   **No future? Subcultures, manufactured cultures and
the economy** 184
Manufactured cultures and the economy – the
    relationship of production and consumption 184
Youth culture and identity 189
Youth and the future 191
No future? Youth and unemployment 192

Bibliography 199

Index 225

Preface

In this book I have developed an examination of much of the disparate work on youth culture, subcultures and delinquency which has been a subject of research since the early 1930s. One major theme which is noticeable is that if the young are not socialised into conventional political, ethical and moral outlooks, if they are not programmed into regular work habits and labour discipline, then society as it is today cannot continue. What is central to any examination of youth culture is that it is not some vague structural monolith appealing to those roughly under thirty, but is a complex kaleidoscope of several subcultures, of different age groups, yet distinctly related to the class position of those in them. My argument is that subcultures arise as attempts to resolve collectively experienced problems resulting from contradictions in the social structure, and that they generate a form of collective identity from which an individual identity can be achieved outside that ascribed by class, education and occupation. This is nearly always a temporary solution, and in no sense a real material solution, but one which is solved at the cultural level. Youth cultures interact with manufactured popular cultures and their artefacts but I would argue against manufactured cultures being deterministic in the sense that they are uninfluenced by their consumers. On the whole, youth cultures and subcultures tend to be some form of exploration of masculinity. They are therefore masculinist, and I have tried to consider their effect on girls, and one distinct sign of the emancipation of young girls from the cult of romance, and marriage as their true vocation, will be the development of subcultures exploring a new form of femininity. Given the material place of women in society today, this is likely to take some time.

One of the most worrying signs of friction and alienation in contemporary society is the problems that racial minorities have to face. Their harassment by law and order personnel, the use of the conspiracy laws and their isolation from their white peers suggest that a whole generation feels betrayed. The present crisis in capitalism, and the high unemployment rate which particularly affects ethnic minorities and women, make the situation seem pessimistic. If we are to have a culturally plural society, then we need to develop a socialist culture which retains the progressive elements of the different subcultures that have been developed, and which counteracts the reactionary traditional elements that manifest themselves most clearly in racism and sexism. This obviously involves not only a cultural struggle but also being involved in a class struggle against the oppression in our present society. Economic exploitation develops an oppressive culture which alienates and brutalises large sections of our society. The class struggle necessarily involves not only the way forward to a material revolution, but also a cultural revolution.[1]

In this book I have attempted to go beyond my original work on British youth culture, *The Sociology of Youth Cultures and Youth Subcultures* (1980). My publishers wanted more American material, so I reconstructed the book so that it became a comparative study of youth culture in Britain, Canada and the United States, still looking at minority youth and girls. This is plainly an impertinence from a foreigner who did not grow up in those countries. However, I have lived and worked in them, and when one travels in North America its familiarity makes one realise how influential North American popular culture is. The British are ambivalent to North America; they are disdainful, but are fascinated and obsessed by it. It is both familiar and yet completely foreign. These ambivalences will doubtless show in this book.

I would like to thank Jim Albert, Bob Gaucher, Paul Nesbitt Larking and Ian Taylor for their help and comments on Canada. Peter Hopkins was an encouraging editor. There are many people to thank, but especially Nicola Hewitt, who encouraged both books and was a careful editor and support person beyond the call of friendship. This book is dedicated to her.

Chapter 1

The use of subculture as an analytical tool in sociology

Subcultural analysis and sociology

Culture has several, often contradictory meanings and its ambiguity, conceptually, can be located in its differing uses throughout
history. Williams (1961; 1973) has seen this in the context of the
culture and society. Two basic, familiar definitions have arisen historically. Firstly, the classical perspective of using a cultural setting
as a standard of excellence, a yardstick of sensitivity, intellect and
manners developed in the bourgeois world, and this can be encap-
sulated in the notion of 'high culture'. The other view which has
its roots in anthropology is seen by Williams (1961, p. 57) as a

> particular way of life which expressed certain meanings and
> values not only in art and learning, but also in institutions and
> ordinary behaviour. The analysis of culture, from such a
> definition, is the clarification of the meanings and values
> implicit and explicit in a particular way of life, a particular
> culture.

This is the conceptualisation of 'low culture' as a form of consciousness, of a way of life, and one which is central to the development of subculture as an analytical concept. It involves the 'study
of relationships between elements in a whole way of life' (Williams,
1961, p. 57). In the United States, theories concerning mass society
and mass communications obfuscated the point made by Swingewood that 'consumer capitalism, rather than creating a vast, homogeneous and culturally brutalised mass, generates different levels
of taste, different audiences and consumers. Culture is stratified, its
consumption differential' (Swingewood, 1977, p. 20). Culture was
seen as a reified object, and its scholars tended to respond with
suspicion to the synthetic culture of the mass media. Debra Clarke
(1980) makes the point that there are many cultures and many

cultural forms, and some of these may be appropriated by class linked groups. However, it is important to remember that if culture indicates a relation to a way of life, this is intimately bound up not with consumption in the social relations of capitalism, but in the social relations of production. Implicitly this leads the relation of culture firmly back to the set of social relations most predominant in society – class relations. Clarke criticises the simplistic assumptions of mass society and mass communication studies in the United States for three reasons. Firstly, they fail to examine the historical transformations in society which influence popular culture, in particular the artistic and cultural commodities that transform the media into a feature of class domination. Secondly, there is absent any sophisticated, or indeed often any mention of a model of social class, and thirdly, the moralism which she argues taints the analysis. This ranges from the left criticism that communication is one-sided, from elites to the masses, to the conservative argument familiar from the celebration of 'high culture' which romanticises the past and decries the vulgarity of synthetic popular culture.

The earliest use of subculture in sociology seems to be its application as a subdivision of a national culture (Lee, 1945; Gordon, 1947). Culture is seen here as learned behaviour emphasising the effects of socialisation within the cultural subgroups of a pluralist society. There are again anthropological influences as, for example, Tylor (1871, p. 10), who argues that culture 'taken in its wide ethnographic sense, is that complex whole which includes knowledge, belief, art, morals, law, custom and many and any other capabilities and habits acquired by man as member of a society'. Firth (1951, p. 27) states that 'Culture is all learned behaviour which has been socially acquired'. This emphasis on culture as a socialising influence on subgroups is useful to subculture. Kroeber and Kluckhohn (1952, p. 2) synthesise a definition of culture empirically drawn from analysing 160 definitions of culture taken from different social sciences and conclude that

> Culture consists of patterns, explicit and implicit of symbols, constituting the distinctive achievements of human groups, including their embodiments in artefacts; the essential core of culture consists of traditional (i.e. historically derived and selected) ideas and especially their attached values; culture systems may, on the one hand, be considered as products of action, and on the other as conditioning elements of further action.

Ford (1942) offers the view that culture is a 'traditional way of solving problems', a 'learned problem solution', a view which was to be taken up by A.K. Cohen who saw a major determinant of

2

subcultures among youth as 'What people do depends upon the problems they contend with' (Cohen, 1955, p. 51).

Whilst culture is a cohesive force binding social actors together, it also produces disjunctive elements. To argue that culture is merely cohesive is to take an ahistorical, idealist view. In any complex society culture is divisive merely because the presence of several subcultures indicates a struggle for the legitimacy of different subgroups' behaviour, values and life styles against the context of the dominant culture of the dominant class. Swingewood (1977) puts this well,

> Throughout the major social institutions (the family, religious, educational, political and trade union organisations), cultural values, norms and aspirations are transmitted, congealing into largely nonconscious routines, the norms and customs of everyday experience and knowledge. At the level of popular consciousness, culture is never simply that of the 'people' or region or family or subordinate class. Culture is not a neutral concept; it is historical, specific and ideological.

We are born into social classes, themselves complexly stratified with distinct 'ways of life', modified by region and neighbourhood. This local subculture into which we are first socialised is that parochial world against which we measure social relations that we meet in later life, and in which we begin to build a social identity. Our social identity is constructed from the nexus of social relations and meanings surrounding us, and from this we learn to make sense of ourselves including our relation to the dominant culture.

Culture, class and ideology

Contemporary theories of youth culture, especially in Britain, have been influenced by Marxist thought. History is not neutral, but a perpetual disclosure and working out of contradictory and conflicting class relations, which include ethnic relations where racial minorities are an underclass, and the relations between the sexes influenced by patriarchal cultures. The social production of material necessities generates sets of social relations both between and within classes. In this sense, what is called in Marxism the mode of production (a form of social organisation which links human labour to the environment and transforms raw materials into goods), creates the social relations of production, that is the various social relations of those people involved in production. Classical Marxism sees this as owners, managers and workers, but obviously the situation is more complex than this, and includes those on the periphery of the work force, such as youth or the elderly, as well as working men and women, the latter being involved in domestic as well as occupational work. In *Capital* Marx argues a historical, materialist theory of ideology, distinguishing between reality as it appears in everyday life, and reality which is revealed by a more scientific analysis. We are, however, unaware of the ideological nature of social relations just because our awareness is organised by ideology itself to obscure the real relations of bourgeois society. Our response to our culture is a response to history of which Marx (1951, p. 251) reminds us:

> Men make their own history, but they do not make it just as they please; they do not make it under circumstances chosen by themselves, but under circumstances directly encountered, given and transmitted from the past.

The theory of ideology in *Capital* reveals that the conditions for the production of mystificatory beliefs in capitalist society lie in that disjuncture between what the real relations of production are and their appearance. Marx, however, firmly grounds his theory of ideology in the arena of class struggle (1970, p. 39).

> ... the ideas of the ruling class in every epoch are the ruling ideas ... the class which is the ruling force in society is at the same time its ruling intellectual force. The class which has the means of material production at its disposal has control at the same time over the means of mental production, so that thereby, generally speaking, the ideas of those who lack the means of mental production are subject to it. ...

Developing the disjuncture between the real and apparent relations of production, Althusser (1971, p. 162), influenced by the psychoanalyst Jacques Lacan, argues that 'Ideology represents the "imaginary" relationship of individuals to their real conditions of existence'. This relationship is 'imaginary' just because ideology does not correspond to the real relations in society. It represents a distorted relation to those real relations, but its attraction is that it is one which is lived. Ideology in Althusser has a material existence, it is not free-floating but constitutes what he describes as ideological state apparatuses (ISAs) such as the family, mass media, the churches, education, law and politics. Ideology is for Althusser beneath consciousness; in this sense it is unconscious. It is firmly sedimented in common sense which conceals its ideological nature. Hall *et al.* (1978) puts this well:

> It is precisely its 'spontaneous' quality, its transparency, its 'naturalness', its refusal to be made to examine the premises on

The acceptance of — a very rare, a very different style of sub-c, in a climate which wasn't changed — so who then?

which it is founded, its resistance to change or to correction, its effect on instant recognition, and the closed circle in which it moves which makes common sense, at one and the same time, 'spontaneous', ideological and unconscious. You cannot learn, through common sense, how things are; you can only discover where they fit into the existing scheme of things.

In a society such as in the United States, for example, where black workers form, by and large, a subproletariat, racist ideology is reproduced in material form at the economic level. Because they are over-represented in the lower economic incomes, because of poor educational advantages and over-representation in unemployment, they are structurally subordinate to white workers. The evidence of material structure, welfare and unemployment statistics and educational achievement records produces support for the racist assumptions that black workers take white workers' jobs, live on welfare, do not work in school and so forth. What is concealed is the real underlying mechanisms of racism. These include the use of black workers when there is a shortage of semi-skilled labour, the structured nature of employment in modern low labour-intensive industry, the lack of funding to poor black neighbourhoods.

Gramsci (1973) has suggested that ruling social groups can exert social authority over subordinated classes by not only winning, but shaping, consent to their authority. In his division of the state into political and civil society he argues that it has a dual task: to maintain domination and to produce consent to this domination. This consent which the ruling class obtains from its subordinate classes is called 'hegemony' by Gramsci, and it holds in abeyance the 'armour of consent' or coercion by the state through force. The authority of a fraction of a dominant class is extended through to the spheres of civil society, so that an apparent universality emerges. Dominant class ideas appear as common-sense explanations. Subordinate groups may offer resistance or alternatives, but these are always negotiated within a cultural context which emerges from ruling class (or a fraction of its) ideas. The cultures and subcultures of subordinate classes are constantly accommodated, and the arena of class struggle is viewed not just over social production and profit but also over hegemony. Because the support of the dominated classes is never permanent, hegemony is conceptualised as having a 'moving equilibrium' and class fractions have to shift their alliances to sustain it. This opens up, as in the work of Hall and his associates (Hall and Jefferson (eds), 1976), an interesting analysis of subcultures engaged in a struggle over cultural 'space'. Indeed, Hall argues that youth subcultures attempt to solve problems which they are only able to do in an 'imaginary' way, because they are never able, given the peripheral class position of youth, to tackle the fundamental problems of class access to education and occupation.

In any complex, stratified society there are several cultures which develop within the context of a dominant value system. The dominant value system is never homogeneous; instead there are constant modifications and adaptations of dominant ideas and values. The major cultural forms are class cultures, and subcultures can be conceptualised as subsets of these larger cultural configurations. Subcultures, then, share elements of larger class cultures (sometimes called the parent culture by writers), but are also distinct from it. Working-class, black subcultures, for example, share elements both of urban or rural working-class culture, but also have the distinctive elements of black culture. To be black and working-class is not the same as being white and working-class. Subcultures also have a relationship to the overall dominant culture which, because of its pervasiveness, in particular through the mass media, is unavoidable. Membership of a subculture necessarily involves membership of a class culture and the subculture may be an extension of, or in opposition to, the class culture. Parkin (1971) has suggested that what he calls 'subordinate value systems' reflect the ways of life and material conditions of existence of subordinate classes so that the cultures of the subordinate are not alternatives but negotiations of the dominant value systems. In this way subordinate cultures are different from dominant cultures, and form a 'pragmatic acceptance' of hegemony, as the result of a class struggle in ideas. For Parkin, a 'corporate' culture emerges as a result of a series of negotiations, qualifications and limited situational variants, either within or against the hegemonic culture. Hall *et al.* (1978, p. 155) put this as

> The difference between 'corporate' and 'hegemonic' cultures
> emerges most clearly in the contrast between general ideas
> (which the hegemonic culture defines) and more contextualised
> or situated judgements (which will continue to reflect their
> oppositional material and social base in the life of the
> subordinate classes). Thus it seems perfectly 'logical' for some
> workers to agree 'the nation is paying itself too much'
> (general) but only too willing to go on strike for more wages
> (situated).

Groups, then, hold mixed values, generally in relation to dominant values, but they may be situated in relation to the groups' specific class context or subgroup problems. This means that for youth subcultures, as Murdock and McCron (1976) found, many members took over styles either 'situated' in the family or neighbourhood or 'mediated' from the synthetic culture of the teenage entertainment industry. As such they were expressions and extensions of the dominant meaning system, rather than deviant from, or in opposition to it. Most youth subcultures, unless they have an articulated political element, are not in any simple sense oppositional. They may be rebellious; they may celebrate and dramatise specific styles and values, but their rebellion seldom reaches an articulated opposition. Even where it does, as it did with the counterculture of the 1960s (more accurately the period between 1964 and 1972), or in black and Hispanic youth cultures, it becomes accommodated and contained, although in the latter case the exploitation is less easily accommodated.

Downes (1966, p. 9) has suggested that one must distinguish between subcultures which emerge in positive response to the demands of social and cultural structures, e.g. occupational subcultures, and those which emerge in response to these structures as in the delinquent subcultures. He also argues that those subcultures originating from within a society can be differentiated from those that originate from without, such as with immigrant groups or traditions. This particularly holds true for ethnic or minority cultures. Membership of a subculture necessarily involves membership of a class culture, and the subculture may be an extension of, or in opposition to, this. It may form a miniature subworld of its own, or it may merge with the dominant class culture. There may be a clear subculture with distinct 'focal concerns'. These are described by Miller, W.B. (1958, p. 6) as 'areas and issues which command widespread and persistent attention and a high degree of personal involvement'. This introduces the important aspect of different values, and these may significantly deviate from middle-class norms. If we use these criteria, then we can begin to distinguish some form of analysis of subcultures which are distinguished by age and generation, as well as by class, and which consequently generate specific focal concerns. Miller suggests that working-class youth is concerned with toughness, trouble, smartness, excitement, fate and autonomy, arguing that between 40 and 60 per cent of the United States' total population are significantly influenced by the major outlines of the working-class cultural system. These are further mediated, as Cohen, P. (1972) suggests, by family, the neighbourhood and the local economy. By the use of these variables we can develop a concept of youth or youthful subcultures which has been popularly subsumed under the term 'youth culture'. This has often been loosely applied to some sort of structural monolith of all those under thirty, regardless of class, age group, ethnicity or even gender. There is, as we shall see, a complex kaleidoscope of several adolescent and youthful subcultures appealing

7

to different age groups from different classes, involving different life styles. These subcultures appeal to different self-images, values and behaviour and they bear a close relation to their parent class culture. There is a symbiotic relationship between myth and reality in these subcultures.

Culture, then, may be seen as containing a source of signs or potential meaning structures which actors inherit and respond to. Subcultures, by their very existence, suggest that there are alternative forms of cultural expression reflecting a cultural plurality in a culture, which often seems, on superficial examination, to dominate the members of a society. Culture has several levels: the historical level of ideas, the level of values, the level of meaning and the consequent effects on art, popular culture, sport, signs and symbols. There are also the effects of the process of material production, and the symbolic and material effects of artefacts and mass media on cultures. Finally, there is the dynamic, subjective element of human action and the way it is interpreted between actors. Subcultures exist where there is some form of organised and recognised constellation of values, behaviour and actions which is responded to as differing from the prevailing sets of norms. It also serves as a function, summarised by Downes (1966, p. 7) who argues that subcultures emerge 'where there exists in effective interaction with one another, a number of actors with similar problems of adjustment for whom no effective solution as yet exists for a common, shared problem'. This use of the subculture as a 'collective solution' to commonly experienced problems has its tradition in the work of A.K. Cohen, and is addressed in Cloward and Ohlin, as we shall see later. Its application to include wider structural contradictions has been taken up by Murdock, Hall and Birmingham University's Centre for Contemporary Cultural Studies, and by Brake. This approach goes beyond Cohen's view of working-class youth's attempt to deal with status problems caused by the 'middle-class measuring rod' of the education system. It allows us to define subcultures as meaning systems, modes of expression or life styles developed by groups in subordinate structural positions in response to dominant meaning systems, and which reflect their attempt to solve structural contradictions arising from the wider societal context. As such a subculture has to develop new group meanings, and an essential aspect of its existence is that it forms a constellation of behaviour, action and values which have meaningful symbolism for the actors involved.

Subculture as a concept has much to offer sociological understanding of human interaction against a cultural and symbolic background. It takes role-play and reconstructs it as an active ingredient in a dialectical relation between structure and actor. At the structural level it indicates how culture is mediated to and generated by a collectivity of social actors, and at the existential level it indicates how meanings are taken from a subculture, used to project an image and hence an identity. This has an effect on the internal labelling element of identity, and uses external symbols to develop a self-image which has a cultural and an existential reality to the actor. Subcultures negotiate between the interpersonal world of the actor and the dynamics of the larger elements of social interaction. However, as a concept it is not without problems. Clarke (1974) looks at the formal and substantive elements of sub-culture, and argues that if the term was introduced today it would be rejected. It has 'spongy' aspects, which reveal its vagueness over areas such as the cultural and structural elements of the concept, the definitions of subcultural boundaries, and the genesis, mainten-ance and change of subcultures. Subculture has two complementary perspectives which often become confused. There is the empirical evidence of what constitutes membership of a subculture, which is abstracted from the social structure. There is also the hermeneutic aspect of cultural analysis – what the subculture 'means'. Subcul-tural analysis involves examining an organised set of social rela-tions, as well as a set of social meanings. A subculture is not the same as a subcommunity, so problems arise as to why one subcom-munity and not another creates a subculture. These are problems of empirical and interpretative method, however, rather than prob-lems in the use of the concept.

Fischer (1975) suggests that subculturisation is the result of ur-banism. He sees a link between community and urbanisation (Fischer, 1972). The concentration in urban areas of large hetero-geneous populations leads to the weakening of interpersonal ties, primary social structures and normative consensus. Dynamic popu-lation density leads to a complex, structural differentiation with consequences of alienation, social disorganisation, deviant be-haviour and anomie. This may have some truth for those who migrate from the rural areas to the towns but the evidence of Gans (1962), Lewis (1952), and Willmott and Young (1957) finds that there are close-knit communities within towns with long traditions of social support and closeness. Liebow (1967) finds similar pri-mary groups existing for unemployed men in the ghetto. Fischer, however, argues that urban groups are more likely to deviate from the traditional norms of society. The more urban the setting, argues Fischer, the more variety there is of subculturisation. Subcultures develop which generate subsystems of a social nature that can protect and foster the subcultures against external threats. Uncon-ventional elements of a subcultural origin become diffused into mainstream culture. This argument romanticises urban tolerance

9

towards the emergence of subcultures, but it does suggest that in specific urban areas, usually metropolitised cities (for example, Amsterdam, San Francisco or London) the diversity of urban population creates the atmosphere for the generation of various subcultures. In a metropolis there is usually a downtown or bohemian area which contains a neighbourhood where various outsiders, such as drug addicts, inter-racial couples, students, artists, minor criminals, immigrants, a gay community and so forth make up a form of bohemian, lumpenproletariat underworld. Two things occur if subcultures flourish. An informal grapevine recruits outsiders from other areas into the subcultures. This has an effect on the subcultural boundaries, which may harden over time, especially if subjected to stigmatisation which may give spurts to their collective life, or they may be assimilated and absorbed into mainstream culture. The boundaries of subcultures remain a problem, even when clearly delineated as with exogenous subcultures such as those generated by immigrant groups. As these become part of metropolitan life they develop endogenous subcultures as, for example, with young Rastafarians in the London West Indian subculture. The other effect of a multiplicity of subcultures is their diffusion into mainstream culture. This clarifies why a 'value stretch', as Rodman (1965) called it, occurs in society. This is a commitment to norms, values and cultural themes which seems ambiguous, ambivalent and contradictory. Because of cultural differences from the assumed consensus, people may hold at least two sets of values. The 'value stretch' bridges the discrepancies between consensual public values (or the central value system as structural-functional sociology calls it) and privatised variance from these. We can see that a situation of apparent consensus on appropriate, respectable values and behaviour exists, but because of class differences in culture and subcultural deviation there can emerge, especially in an urban setting, a situation of pluralistic social realities. Matza and Sykes (1961) suggest there is a fundamental contradiction present in societal values. Coexisting with respectable values are a series of 'subterranean values' which are permitted expression during certain periods, usually officially approved moments of leisure, carefully differentiated from times of work. An actor, then, may not only hold values of security, routinisation and hard work, but also values involving a search for excitement, adventure and hedonistic, morally disapproved behaviour.

Young (1971) suggests that certain subcultural groups do not hold subterranean values in abeyance until the prescribed time, but actually stress and accentuate them instead of more official respectable values. Yinger (1960) has argued that where subcultural norms are developed which are countervalues and central to the subculture and which bring it into conflict with the larger society, a subculture can be designated as a 'contraculture'. Yinger wants to differentiate as a contraculture the emergent norms of a group in a conflict situation, retaining subculture to describe more traditional forms of subsocieties which have developed particular local norms (e.g. the subculture of the American Southlands). Empirically, no study seems to suggest that there is a pure contraculture, except perhaps in a political subcultural context (such as the Black Panthers). Although oppositional norms may be developed in direct contrast to respectable norms, a subculture which exists in direct conflict with the prevailing society cannot survive for long. There are politically militant elements of subcultures among minority groups, gay people and feminists, but their success and continuation depends on a series of strategies which involve avoiding direct confrontation, but often waging systematic, cultural, guerrilla raids on the dominant morality. A struggle develops over what is and what is not permitted. This illustrates Erikson's (1966) suggestion that deviancy has the function of boundary definition maintenance for what is and what is not permitted in a society.

Subcultures and style

It has been argued above that structural conditions, especially persistent, structural contradictions, often experienced as class problems, are a basic generating force for subcultures. Cultural traditions, particularly those generated by social class, may interact with the apparent middle-class consensus and, when assisted by neighbourhood traditions and specific historic circumstances, act in shaping the cultural form of a subculture. One cultural form common in a subculture is its 'style'. Cohen (1965), in an interesting article which raises the question of the relationship of social structure to social interaction, notes that an important aspect of a reference group such as a distinct subcultural group is the symbolic use of a style.

> An actor learns that the behaviour signifying membership in a particular role includes the kinds of clothes he wears, his posture, his gait, his likes and dislikes, what he talks about and the opinion he expresses. (Cohen, 1965, p. 1)

Several important indicators are raised by style. It expresses a degree of commitment to the subculture, and it indicates membership of a specific subculture which by its very appearance disregards or attacks dominant values. Style I shall define as consisting of three main elements:

11

a 'Image', appearance composed of costume, accessories such as hair-style, jewellery and artefacts.
b 'Demeanour', made up of expression, gait and posture. Roughly this is what the actors wear and how they wear it.
c 'Argot', a special vocabulary and how it is delivered.

An important aspect of style is the differentiation of work and leisure. Thompson (1969) has suggested that the values of leisure have been traditionally feared by employers because they present a counterthesis to work – in order to preserve industrial discipline, as for example the work habit, working schedules, the commencement of the working day, all of which were paced and planned by the worker in the traditional crafts. Work and leisure were strictly separated, so that leisure became channelled into acceptable by-products of the work ethic. Holidays involving hedonistic carousal were seen as an anarchistic attack on work discipline, and the values of austerity, thrift and production were emphasised. One off-spin of mass production and consumption is the creation of a semi-mythical, popular elite, promoted by the mass media and advertising, which the purchase of clothing and artefacts brings within reach of the average consumer. In this situation Burns (1967), drawing on the work of Italian sociologists Pizzorno (1959) and Alberoni (1964), suggests there is an attachment to this mythical elite by the imitation of style and clothing to an identity which stands outside traditional class definitions. The working-class girl imitating cultural heroines such as Marilyn Monroe feels she is part of a specific 'classless' group of other girls who look like Monroe. This can obviously be extended into subcultures which have definite imagery and style. Indeed, style is usually a predominant defining feature of youthful subcultures. The precious gains of working life, money and leisure become invested in dramaturgical statements about self-image, which attempt to define an identity outside that ascribed class, education and occupational role, particularly when the latter is of low status.

A parallel may be drawn between the use of style and fashion in subcultures by considering certain forms of analysis in linguistic theory. It has been argued that there is a general science of signs – semiology (Saussure, 1960). Language is the most sophisticated form of semiology but gesture, music and images can all be analysed. Saussure's work has been fruitfully used by the Birmingham School who have also drawn upon Barthes whose work is also extended into popular culture. For Barthes, 'myth is a type of speech', and he attempts to uncover the hidden sets of rules and conventions that produce meanings peculiar to powerful groups in society which are then rendered universal and 'given' for society in

12

general. The ideological core of these meanings has been exposed to the rhetoric of common sense and turned into myth in Barthes' (1972) exposition of semiotics. There are two systems in Barthes' analysis, for example, he sees a photograph in a French journal of a black soldier saluting the French flag, firstly as a gesture of loyalty, and secondly symbolising France as a great empire under whose flag all her sons serve without colour discrimination. The latter system suggests a meaning derived from the bourgeois and distorted myth of France's egalitarianism. Saussure (1960) differentiates between a systemised set of linguistic conventions called 'langue' (language) and 'parole' – the selection and actualisation of language – speech. Hjelmslev (1959) elaborates this further by distinguishing between the formal standard usage of language and its regional use. The formal set of syntax becomes transformed by social usage. We can also see that subcultural use of fashion is a rhetorical usage of formalised styles, a sort of slang or argot of the 'standard English' of fashion. Style ceases to be merely informative or taxonomic (pointing to a cultural system which indicates membership of class or subculture), and becomes open to interpretation of what it means both subjectively for the actor, and objectively in its statement about the actor's relationship to his world. A hermeneutic interpretation is possible in Ricoeur's (1972) sense of the meaning of cultural documents, in this case style. Style, then, is used for a variety of meanings. It indicates which symbolic group one belongs to, it demarcates that group from the mainstream, and it makes an appeal to an identity outside that of a class-ascribed one. It is learned in social interaction with significant subcultural others, and its performance requires what theatre actors call 'presence', the ability to wear costume and to use voice to project an image with sincerity. Indeed, this form of performance skill may well be tested out by other subcultural members.

Willener (1970) has shown that in certain changing social circumstances actors can transform, invent and juxtapose imagery to create new cultural styles. The symbolism of appearance has been illustrated in the subculture by Willis (1970):

> The dress ... was not primarily a functional exigency of riding
> a motor cycle. It was more crucially a symbolic extension of
> the motorbike and amplification of the qualities inherent
> within the motorbike ...

The complexities of the use of costume have been well analysed by Carter (1967):

> The nature of our apparel is very complex. Clothes are so
> many things at once. Our social shells, the system of signals

with which we broadcast our intentions, are often the projection of our fantasy selves ... clothes are our weapons, our challenges, our visible insults ...

We may use clothing to challenge dominant norms, but we also make statements about our environment.

For we think dress expresses ourselves, but in fact it expresses our environment, and like advertising, pop music, pulp fiction and second feature films, it does so at a subliminal, emotionally charged non-intellectual, instinctual level. (*Ibid.*)

Style also indicates a life style, and as such has an appeal to subterranean values which combine to make a visual challenge at both a structural and an existential level.

and in the Neanderthal way, the Hell's Angels are obeying Camus' law – that the dandy is always a rebel, that he challenges society because he challenges mortality. The motor cycle gangs challenge society because they challenge mortality face to face, doing 100 m.p.h. on the California freeway in Levis and swastikas, no crash helmets and a wide-awake hat, only a veneer between the man and his death ... (*Ibid.*)

Briefly, then, style at a subcultural level acts as a form of argot, drawing upon costume and artefacts from a mainstream fashion context and translating these into its own rhetoric. The difference between conventional costume and imagery is deliberate. American street talk in the black ghetto has taken the language of the dominant white culture, altered its rhythm by introducing African pitch and tempo, and confused the outsider by a complex set of metaphors drawn from the black subcultures. In many ways this is what subcultural style has done. Clarke, Hall, Jefferson and Roberts (1976) illustrate this:

Thus the 'Teddy Boy' expropriation of an upper class style of dress 'covers' the gap between largely manual unskilled near-lumpen real careers and life-chances, and the 'all-dressed-up-and-nowhere-to-go' experience of Saturday evening. Thus in the expropriation and fetishisation of consumption and style itself, the 'Mods' cover the gap between the never-ending-weekend and Monday's resumption of boring dead-end work.

Objects and artefacts (both of a symbolic and a concrete form) have been reordered and placed in new contexts so as to communicate fresh acts of meaning. This is called 'bricolage' by Clarke (1976b) drawing upon the anthropologist Lévi-Strauss. Where there is a reassemblage of styles into a new subcultural style, as with

14

nostalgic revivals such as the Teddy boys, the assemblage must not look as though it is carrying the same message as the previously existing one. A new style is created by appropriating objects from an existing market of artefacts and using them in a form of collage, which recreates group identity, and promotes mutual recognition for members. There is also, as Willis (1972) suggests, a fit or 'homology' between objects, the meaning of these and behaviour. There is, he argues, a homology between intense activism, physicality, externalisation, a taboo on introspection, a love of speed and early rock music in such groups as motorbike boys (or bikers). There is a homology between structurelessness, introspection and loose group affiliation and progressive West Coast rock music in hippies. This is near to the concept of focal concerns, but extends the analysis into the cultural elements of the subculture and its style. The analysis is now extended below the conscious level to consider the meaning of the symbolism. This approach offers a valuable extension to more traditional empirical findings which will be discussed later.

Subcultures, social reality and identity

It has been suggested that subcultures offer, on the one hand, solutions of a 'magical' (that is they appear to be solutions rather than are) rather than of a real nature to inherent contradictions in the socio-economic system experienced at some level by the actor. With youthful subcultures this is perceived and responded to by the actor as a generational problem. On the other hand, the style of the subculture allows an expression of identity through a deliberate projection of a self-image, which claims an identity 'magically' freed from class and occupation. The subjectivistic perception and interpretation of structural problems is personalised, and is limited by the parochial locale of the actor's social class position. In addition, these problems are further mediated by the community in which the actor lives. Thus, for the actor, there is an apparent range of voluntaristic selections of subcultures to choose from. Entrance to the subculture, as we shall see from the empirical evidence, is, however, limited by opportunities related to class and education. Empirically, clusters of subcultural groups are found in specific locations of the social class structure, with a common experience in terms of background, class, education and neighbourhood. The degree of articulation of subcultural life style, and commitment to it varies considerably.

The relation of subcultures and age is important, because adolescence, and the period of transition between school and work,

15

and work and marriage is important in terms of secondary socialisation. Berger and Luckman (1966, p. 77) have suggested that patterns of behaviour are legitimised and habitualised in socialisation through what they see as a basic confidence trick of cultural relativism:

> In primary socialisation there is not a problem of identification. There is no choice of significant others. Society presents the candidate for socialisation with a predefined set of significant others whom he must accept with no possibility of opting for another arrangement. Hic Rhodus – hic salta. ...
> The child does not internalise the world of his significant others as one of many possible worlds. He internalises it as the world, the only existent and conceivable world, the world tout court. ...

Children, then, perceive the world without any idea of the plethora of alternative social realities present, and internalise attitudes mediated to them from emotionally charged social interaction with their parents, or similar significant others. Social institutions are seen as part of a symbolic totality which Berger and Luckman call the 'symbolic universe'. Everything in the world makes sense in relation to the hegemonic apparatus; the received world is experienced as the only world. It is used as a paradigm of experiential explanation which assumes that the symbolic universe is social reality whose subjective features become transformed into objective reality. This is the way we resist chaos in perception and cognition, and impose some form of order upon the world. Central to this stemming from hegemony is an idea about how things are and how they should be. But, argue Berger and Luckman, because the universe is not tidy, apparent anomalies and contradictions have to be avoided. One of the functions of culture, the anthropologist Mary Douglas (1970, p. 102) reminds us, is to categorise the symbolic universe into publicly recognised patterns:

> Culture in the sense of the public, standardised values of a community, mediates the experience of individuals. It provides in advance some basic categories, a positive pattern in which ideas and values are tidily ordered. And above all, it has authority, since each is induced to assent because of the assent of others. But its public character makes its characters more rigid.

Consequently, Douglas, M. (1972) argues that an anomaly is relegated to the categories of good or evil, and may therefore be rejected, ignored, abhorred, venerated or respected. This is why morality as Douglas, J.D. (1972) notes, has an object-like charac-

16

teristic in Western society which makes the rules of morality seem apparently independent of free choice. They contain essential properties which make them necessary to all individuals, who attribute to them some form of eternal, universal absolutism. They become perceived as part of social reality, unproblematic and absolute. This is why Scott (1972) argues that deviancy has a dissident side; it challenges the clarity of the symbolic universe. Deviants are seen either as outsiders, recognised as having left the communal, symbolic universe, or else, as with immigrants, they are ascribed to as outsiders who participate in another symbolic universe which originated in a different culture. This group, as Berger and Luckman (1966, p.91) remind us, 'raise the question of power, since each symbolic universe must now deal with the problem of whose definition of reality will be made to stick'.

A subculture, then, may give an ideology and a form to deviancy which threatens the apparent consensus of the symbolic universe. The subculture makes sense to the potential recruit because of this challenge to the symbolic universe, and the would-be subcultural member identifies with the subculture. The recruit uses the values and imagery of the subculture to alter his own self-image. Glaser (1966) calls this differential identification.

> The image of behaviour as role-playing, borrowed from the theatre, presents people as directing their actions on the basis of their conceptions of how others see them. The choice of another from whose perspective we view our own behaviour is the process of identification. It may be with immediate others, or with distant and perhaps abstractly generalised others of our reference groups. ... Acceptance by the group with which one identifies oneself and conceptions of persecution by other groups are among the most common and the least intellectual bases for rationalisation by criminals. ...

Actors, then, attracted by subcultural reference groups, select those within the parameters set by the social structure which contain an attractive self-image, and an apparent solution to structural problems. In this way actors enter into subcultural interpretations of the dominant hegemony, which presents them with a different perspective of social reality, or sometimes a different social reality. As such they are important agents of secondary socialisation. They introduce the values of the world outside work and school.

We have noted that the symbolic universe is not only a concrete form of social reality, but also a moral paradigm. Subcultures which confront or threaten the symbolic universe mean that the moral paradigm used to explain social reality has to be developed and adapted to deal with any anomaly. Subcultures tend to be

giving heroin addicts Methadone
- brought on by Aids debate.

17

deviant anomalies within the symbolic universe. They usually accept its definition of reality, but nevertheless are anomalies within it.

The development of an analytical framework for the study of subcultures

Becker (1963) has suggested that a fruitful way of considering deviancy is by the means of a 'moral career', by a processual analysis. He argues:

> All causes do not operate at the same time, and we need a model which takes into account the fact that patterns of behaviour develop in orderly sequence ... we must deal with a sequence of steps, of changes in the individual's behaviour and perspectives in order to understand the phenomenon. (Becker, 1963, p. 23)

This is obviously useful to the study of subcultures. However, Lemert (1951) indicates that we need to use this model in a wider context. We need to consider the following points:

1 nature of the deviation, which includes information on the ways in which the deviant and the non-deviant differ, the subculture's relationship to the larger society, and the patterns of interaction within the subculture.
2 Societal reaction to the deviant. This involves the general reaction of public opinion to the deviant, and in particular the reaction of the mass media. This means also considering the effects of these on the subculture. Is it accepted, rejected or stigmatised?
3 The natural history of the deviant, including his socialisation and the reaction of significant others to his subculturisation. This means recording crisis points in the deviant career, such as changes in self-concept.
4 Social participation of the deviant, including his occupational status and income, and the effects on these that deviancy has.

Any theoretical framework needs to consider the process of becoming a member of a subculture, as well as the relationship the subculture has with society and the complex social and cultural relationships the two have. Cultural symbols are important, as Denzin (1970, p. 93) notes: 'Central to understanding behaviour is the range and variety of symbols and symbolic meanings shared, communicated and manipulated by interacting selves in shared situations.' De la Mater (1968) suggests that a study of deviance also needs to consider the genesis of a deviant role or actor and how that is maintained, the reasons why an actor engages in the deviant role, and the maintenance of an actor's commitment to a deviant act. This introduces several social psychological processes. Taylor *et al.* (1973) indicate that a theory of deviance needs to consider both structural and social psychological levels. Such a theory needs to consider the wider origins and determinants of deviance found in wider societal conflicts, as well as immediate origins of a particular deviance. Only against this background can the nature and setting of particular deviant actions be considered. It is also necessary to consider the immediate and wider origins of societal reaction, and the effect this has on the individual's commitment and actions within the subculture. Bearing in mind De la Mater's and Lemert's suggestions, and applying the critique of Taylor *et al.*, the following analysis is suggested for considering subcultures:

1   The nature of the subculture
    a   The historical development of a subculture and its relationship to the structural problems of the wider socio-economic structure needs to be analysed.
    b   The style and imagery of the subculture need a hermeneutic perspective which considers the meaning these may have for potential recruits. The problems 'solved' by the subculture are important at this point.
2   Societal reaction to the subculture. An analysis is needed of mass media mediation of the nature of the subculture. The immediate effects of this in terms of significant others is necessary, as well as wide societal reaction in terms of moral entrepreneurs and public and official guardians of moral order.
3   A natural history of the moral career of the subcultural member needs to be constructed, in particular paying attention to Glaser and Strauss's (1971) 'status passage'. That is, that any moral career needs to be considered in sequences or stages, which have contingencies and problems affecting the actor.

Glaser and Strauss suggest several properties affecting status passage, such as how central it is to the actors. The degree of association and identification is important because subcultural attachment may be part time or full time. Where it is the former it is important to socialise its young urban work force adequately. The young have to be socialised into sets of values involving their place in the work force, the encouragement of

19

an early family, marital life to assist in the reproduction of that work force, and conventional political and moral outlooks concerning the world and their place in it. If this does not occur, then the young work force is not programmed into regular work habits, with values suitable to strictly separated schedules of work and leisure. The young have to be bound into society first by values, and then by the responsibilities of maintaining dependants, and finally by financial commitment which means that the situation can take care of itself. One reason why the majority of people in a work force are docile is that whilst ultimately they may not have a great deal to gain by the prevailing social, economic structure, they have invested in it to the degree that they may have a great deal to lose if there is a sudden disruption of that system. This helps us to understand why the majority of young people pass through adolescence without any particularly long-term, overtly deviant behaviour. They have invested a considerable part of themselves in the prevailing system, and as such to deviate overtly or to oppose it strongly would be of no advantage to them in terms of their immediate situation.

Young (1973) has argued that: 'Deviant behaviour ... is a meaningful attempt to solve the problems faced by a group or isolated individual – it is not a meaningless pathology.' The same argument can be made for collective deviant behaviour in the form of subcultures. In a complex society one needs to know how other non-subcultural elements of an actor's life are dealt with. Important variables therefore are entrance into, and exit from, the subculture, participation in, and commitment to, it and the effects of societal reaction at the individual level. The social visibility and the deviant or respectable nature of the subculture has a distinct effect upon self-image. Negative reactions from a public source can lead to a series of effects such as legal restriction to stigma, depending on the degree of negative societal reaction.

4   The social organisation of the subculture. This involves two levels: the subculture's relation to the structure, and the effects this has on the social interaction within the subculture. The values, norms, symbols, imagery and behaviour of the subculture need to be considered in terms of their organisation.

5   The persistence of discontinuance of the subculture. The subculture is unlikely to remain unaltered, and the altering boundaries of the subculture as well as its changing form need to be considered. One interesting element is the way in which

subcultures may continue thematic focal concerns, yet reconstruct imagery so that the contemporary subculture addresses new interpretations of perennial problems, but with a totally different style which reflects specific problems of a particular generation.

Youth becomes a social problem – the development of subcultures as a concept in delinquency, and the rise of youth culture

One problem facing complex industrial societies is how different forms of cultural plurality can coexist. A plurality of culture does not mean that various cultural groups have equal access to political power or to imposing their cultural patterns on society. The rise of interest of subcultures in the United States, can be traced to the fact that, historically, the United States was faced with the problem of an immigrant labour force. Disparate groups from different ethnic origins, speaking different languages, with different cultural backgrounds were not conducive to the development of a common class-consciousness. The ruling American elite, white Anglo-Saxon Protestants, attempted to impose their own culture. The immigrants, wishing to find a new identity in a new country, were happy to absorb much of this culture, but as successive generations came up against structural contradictions, the Americanisation of low status groups failed. The way in which this process failed among the descendants of African slaves in the ghettos is discussed by Valentine (1968), and the development of African culture in America, in particular in jazz, is discussed by Keill (1966), Hannerz (1969) and Jones (1971). The exogenous immigrant subcultures certainly helped to make the pluralism of the United States one of the most complex in the world, and this had an effect on the development of endogenous subcultures. Subcultures call into question the adequacy of the dominant cultural ideology. For example, what does the 'British way of life' offer to a black unemployed teenager, born in South London, whose experience of the country he was born in is framed in overt and covert racism? Youth itself, then, is not a problem, although certain of its subcultures may be seen as a threat. There are problems for youth, however, created for example by the conscription of the majority of them into the lower strata of a meritocratic educational system which then trains them for occupations which are meaningless, poorly paid and uncreative.

The young are subject to the impact of occupational, educational and economic changes at particular times in history. These are experienced not only in class terms but also in generational terms. For these reasons, most subcultures of a distinctly deviant nature

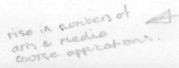
rise in numbers of arts & media course applications.

21

have been working-class, youthful subcultures. This is the group most vulnerable to economic changes. These changes amplify contradictions in the structure which are experienced not only in class terms but also in generational terms. What may be in fact a traditional problem of class is experienced differently by the new generation. These differences may be small or large, but each generation has to work them through against the cultural background of its own generational peer group and its particular received subculture. Cohen, P. (1972, p. 7) suggests that

> You can distinguish three levels in the analysis of subcultures: one is the historical ... which isolates the specific problematic of a particular class fraction, secondly the sub-systems, and the actual transformations they undergo from one subcultural 'moment' to another ... thirdly ... the way the subculture is actually lived out by those who are its bearers and supports.

The solution offered by the subculture is necessarily 'imaginary', argues Cohen. It is an ideological attempt to solve 'magically' real relations which cannot be otherwise solved. The particular time in a young person's life that a subculture has an impact is also notable. It occurs in the period between, or near to, the end of the school career, usually at a point when education is perceived as meaningless in terms of a young person's work prospects, and lasts until marriage. Working-class subcultures in particular infuse into the bleak world of the working-class adolescent a period of intense emotion, colour and excitement during the brief respite between school and the insecurities of the early days of working and settling down into marriage and adulthood. It is left to the personal life of marriage to provide the emotional element of adult life after the brief encounter of a peer group subculture. For the middle class the subculture may last longer, because subcultures for them are often, as Berger, B. (1963b) comments, 'youthful' in the sense that they are the domain of the young in outlook rather than merely the chronologically young.

It is proposed to consider the growth of subcultures in terms of their traditions. Matza (1962) suggested that youth is a time of rebelliousness, and that three particular forms that are attractive to youth are delinquency, radicalism and bohemianism. These modes of rebellion also accentuate subterranean values Matza (1961) suggests. However, he fails to differentiate important intra-group differences in these traditions. In the next chapter we will consider subcultures in terms of the following traditions and themes. The study of youth can be subdivided into four main areas.

1 Respectable youth

Obviously, youthful rebellion is relative and, as Berger (1963b) suggests, most young people manage to pass through life without being involved in any teenage culture, or at least those aspects of it seen as deviant. They may be involved in fashions, but not necessarily life styles. This group is seen by deviant subcultures as a negative reference group, the conformists, or straight youth.

2 Delinquent youth

Barnard (1961) has pointed out the important fact that teenagers reflected the class cultures of their parents, and that class pervaded all aspects of the teenage world in terms of its cultural elements. E.A. Smith (1962) also stressed this in his study of American youth culture. Delinquent subcultures studied have tended to be working class, usually affecting young adolescent males. Males have usually been involved with illegal activities such as theft or violence or vandalism, and females with sexual misbehaviour which has been used by courts to take them under legal protection orders. The bulk of empirical studies are concerned with this group.

3 Cultural rebels

This group tends to be involved in subcultures in the fringes of the bohemian tradition. They are on the periphery of the literary-artistic world, being adherents to it rather than artists. They tend to be middle class, and where young subcultures are involved they tend to have middle-class educations.

4 Politically militant youth

This group is in the radical tradition of politics. The scope of politics may be vast, from environmental and community politics to direct militant action. They may be factions of political groups or a broad mass movement like the peace movements of the 1950s. They may be ethnic groups, such as the Young Lords or the Black Panthers, broad-based civil rights movements, issue-oriented groups such as the anti-Vietnam war groups, pacifists, student groups, political factions or environmentalists.

These traditions may of course overlap, especially in terms of their tactics and cultural traditions. However, it is proposed to examine these traditions in detail.

To summarise, it is argued that the study of subcultures is useful in the field of collective deviance and that subcultures provide particular functions for the young.

1   They offer a solution, albeit at a 'magical' level, to certain structural problems created by the internal contradictions of a socio-economic structure, which are collectively experienced. The problems are often class problems experienced generationally.
2   They offer a culture, from which can be selected certain cultural elements such as style, values, ideologies and life style. These can be used to develop an achieved identity outside the ascribed identity offered by work, home or school.
3   As such, an alternative form of social reality is experienced, rooted in a class culture, but mediated by neighbourhood, or else a symbolic community transmitted through the mass media.
4   Subcultures offer, through their expressive elements, a meaningful way of life during leisure, which has been removed from the instrumental world of work.
5   Subcultures offer to the individual solutions to certain existential dilemmas. Particularly, this involves the bricolage of youthful style to construct an identity outside work or school. This is particularly employed by young males for reasons I will discuss later, and therefore subcultures have tended to be masculinist subcultures, especially working-class subcultures.

Adolescence and early adulthood is a period for reshaping values and ideas and exploring one's relationship to the world, and is therefore an important source of secondary socialisation. The young can explore, within the parameters of their immediate class situation, certain elements of achieved versus ascribed identity.

Analyses of youth culture and subcultures can be summarised by dividing them into generational and structural explanations. The first analysis is concerned with the continuity/discontinuity of inter-generational values, and the second with the relationship of youth to social class, the mode of production and its consequent social relations. The generational explanation has focused on age as a specific factor, and is basically concerned with functionalist and neo-functionalist explanations about socialisation. As Woods (1977) suggests, generational theories are summed up in the structural-functional models of Eisenstadt and Parsons, and the generation unit model of Mannheim. Society is formed of inter-related subsystems, and the educational system prepares actors for a place in the economic system, which reflects the stratification system, which in turn participates in the political system. Inter-generational conflict (the 'generation gap') is a socialisation dys-function, resulting from weak integration between society and age groups. Age is the basis of social and cultural characteristics of actors. Youth, especially adolescence, is a preparatory stage for an adulthood based on the division of labour. In pre-literate societies adolescence is replaced by rites which mark the end of childhood and the beginning of adulthood, but in industrial societies the tran-sition is complicated. Youth is not central to the economy and has become isolated as a dependent, economic liability. Youth for Ei-senstadt (1956, p. 28) is a 'transitory phase between the world of childhood and the adult world'. Youth groups in the structural-functionalist model appear at moments of 'disintegrating' with a 'reintegrating' function. They do not seek to change society, but to re-enter it. Parsons (1942) has also taken a similar view towards youth culture, seeing it as particular to American society, with an emphasis of a possible dysfunctional nature on having a good time, emphasising 'its recalcitrance to the pressure of adult expectations and discipline'. Mannheim (1952) prefers a generation unit; within a youthful generation are groups which 'work up the material of their common experience in different specific ways' (Mannheim, 1952, p. 304). The collective experience of specific historical moments is more intense during rapid social change. The more rapid the change, the greater the gap between generational sets of consciousness, but for Mannheim, youthful response contains positive and creative qualities. In this sense Mannheim allows for more impact on social change than traditional structural-function-alists. It has also been argued that disadvantaged youth (working-class) is not anti the prevailing social order, but seeks a place within it, whilst middle-class groups actually seek social change (Woods, 1977), and that therefore the Mannheimian perspective has been more useful because it allows for a structural context. A function-alist approach seems to have been implicitly followed by official youth programmes which have appeared in times of crisis. These are not only the Scouts and similar voluntary organisations, but also state schemes, such as the Mobilisation for Youth in the United States, and job creation and youth training schemes in Europe. This latter type of scheme has multiplied as youth un-employment has increased, 'creating jobs for those who would otherwise be unemployed', emphasising jobs 'of value to the com-munity', or subsidising employers to find low paid temporary work for youth.

Elements of Mannheim's historico-political moment and generational experiences are present in class-based explanations. This traces back subcultures and youth cultures to the relation between the class 'parent culture', hegemony and contradictions in the socio-economic structure. This involves a material as well as an ideological dimension. These issues are discussed later, and involve community and the local economic system, class-based cultures and values, and traditional class problems experienced generationally at particular historical moments. Youth is conceptualised as a particular generational response to a wider class problem involved with structural elements such as housing, employment, future prospects and wages. As we shall also see, these problems have other dimensions for subordinate groups which are in addition to class and age, such as sex and colour. These have a potential across class lines, but any collective solution will ultimately be complicated by class.

Not all subcultures are concerned with age, obviously. For the young, however (and of course not all the young are involved in subcultures), subcultures assist them in dealing with both structural and individual problems. Some of them, especially in working-class youth subcultures, are transient solutions to specific problems. Others are of a more enduring nature leading to social change. Subcultures address themselves to structural problems, and implicitly contain a critique of society, admittedly often inarticulate and tangential. This has been explained away, especially in neo-functional models, as the problems of a transitional phase in adolescence.

> The concept of a 'transitional phase' in adolescence is often employed as a palliative for society's functional problems of recruiting and integrating youth and adult worlds; if it is merely 'a stage they're going through', then adults frankly need not confront the problems their behaviour raises, because after all, 'they'll grow out of it'.

as Berger (1963a, p. 407) notes. If, however, some of them are not going to grow out of it but develop a pride in what they are, feeling little in common with the laws of a society they feel alienated from, then there is a serious problem for that society. Subcultures offer something to working-class youth that middle-class youth sought in the university. This is a moratorium, a temporal and geographical space, which can be used to test out questions about their world and their relationship to it. Identities and ideas can be experimented with, and possibilities for social change considered. Subcultures are rebellious, and usually no more than this. But they do contain the seeds of a more radical dissent which could erupt into an action threatening society. It is this which moral entrepre-

26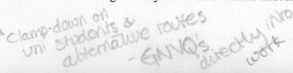

clamp-down on uni students & alternative routes — GNVQ's directly into work

neurs sense. Where this rebellion has a moral edge to it, it threatens the hegemony of the state. The reaction to this is a cry for law and order, and as long as this rebellion can be reduced to a social problem, or an adolescent phase, then it can be successfully excluded from adult society.

Conclusion

Subcultures have been seen to possess not only their own cultural elements, but often a historical response to their subcultural fashions. Each generation attempts to resolve collectively experienced structural problems, and time has passed sufficiently that through mass media records, youth is able to respond to its own subcultural history. Youth experience gaps between what is happening and what they have been led to believe should happen. Murdock (1974, p. 213) sums this up well:

> Subcultures are the meaning system and modes of expression developed by groups in particular parts of the social structure in the course of their collective attempts to come to terms with the contradictions of their shared social situation. More particularly subcultures represent the accumulated meanings and means of expression through which groups in subordinate structural positions have attempted to negotiate or oppose the dominant meaning system. They therefore provide a pool of available symbolic resources which particular individuals or groups can draw on in their attempt to make sense of their own specific situation and construct a viable identity.

In addition to this the strong sense of identification youth has with its peers, neighbourhood, immediate circle of kin, community and locality acts as a divisive force against other groups. Given this it is not hard to explain the respectable youth cohorts. They are those who perceive that they have an investment in the present social structure, and who are then materially reinforced in this investment by work, marriage, dependants and possession of a small amount of property, adopt a conservative stance and an identification with respectability. Conventionality, rebellion or a rejection of some form of respectability (usually a different interpretation of specific aspects of respectability rather than a wholesale rejection of it) is related to the actual age group of young people combined with their class position. Those who have realistically seen school as not related to their future life in routinised labour have different attitudes to those who see a link between education and their future careers. Work is responded to with enthusiasm at first, then disillusionment, usually followed by subcultural work adaptations which help the worker to deal with the work situation. Similar changes can be noted in those who are unattached from emotional relationships, as distinct from those who are engaged, newly married and so forth. These relationships also reflect an investment in society as it is. The transition from school to work, from unattachment to commitment in emotional relationships, from work as peripheral to work as central to existence, and the influence all these have on identity are important in understanding the social relations young people have to production. The reality of violence which runs through young, working-class, male culture needs to be understood not just as the response to brutalising circumstances, but both as a role and an identity in a masculine career structure, and a muffled and semi-articulate form of communication. These all reflect different relations at different 'moments' to the social structure. Close attention needs to be paid to groups of young people at different stages and at different ages. A start has been made with the links traced between girls and the culture of femininity at school, work and at home, and with connections between shopfloor culture and school-resisting culture among adolescent working-class males along the lines of Willis (1977).

Class inequalities are mediated through subcultures, and the degree of oppression involved is not just simply a matter of life chances, the possession of goods and opportunity systems, as suggested in the Weberian and Mertonian models. Materially we can separate young people, but we need also to observe their class location and their social relations to production. For example, materially students, can be separated from other groups of young people. Numerically they are relatively small. Their income is hard to assess, because it is based on grants, loans and parental assistance but it seems much less than the average wage for a comparative working age group. Their cultural capital is considerably higher, and their opportunity to experiment with ideas and life styles, their moratorium from wage labour all place them in a unique and privileged position. The values of certification from higher education fluctuate according to the market, but nevertheless even with graduate unemployment, the embourgeoisement of minor professions such as social work, administration and nursing still give students a favourable weighting towards employment. They may not receive the jobs they have come to expect so easily but they still have a relative advantage over the rest of the population.

Finally, it must be emphasised that two major forms of response in youthful subcultures are either rebelliousness or coolness. Whilst both celebrate masculinity, the former can take the form of cultural rebellion, violence, delinquency or criminal activities, whilst the latter manifests itself in various forms of detachment or disaffiliation distancing the actor from his surroundings. The archetype of this is the cool cat of the late 1950s. Both are responses to collectively experienced problems, usually involving deviant ways of achievement, found among rebellious working-class or disaffiliated middle-class youth. In this sense marginality is a feature in youth culture, as the Schwendingers (see Chapter 2) have suggested. The emphasis on masculinity usually reinforces sex roles in youth culture, but not always in a traditional manner. Youth culture has been male dominated and predominantly heterosexual, thus celebrating masculinity and excluding girls to the periphery. We shall examine some of these themes in detail in the following chapters.

Chapter 2

Street-wise. The delinquent subculture in sociological theory in the United States

Any consideration of the development of working-class delinquent subcultures must involve the surveillance and control of youth as a subsection of the labour force. The sixteenth and seventeenth centuries in Europe saw the old feudal agrarian economy replaced by a system which involved the consolidation of land and the development of a capitalist, market-oriented economy. Large numbers of displaced peasantry drifted to the towns, thus threatening the artisans resident in the city. The Poor Laws were passed to prevent this migration, and vagrancy laws were introduced to control homeless drifters and regulate city street life. As early as 1562 the Elizabethan Statute of Artificers restricted access to certain trades and confined youth in England to the country. As urban migration continued, concern grew over the vagrant bands of youth who begged, stole and prostituted themselves in the urban streets. In 1555, London's Bridewell was the first institution exclusively built and designed to control and contain destitute, handicapped, vagrant and orphaned youth. There has been always a concern with marginal members of the labour force, and a fear that the honest poor would be contaminated by criminalised elements. Street culture is a perennial danger; Mary Carpenter in 1859 classified working people into the labouring and the ragged classes. The ragged poor were an underclass containing two groups – the 'perishing' and the 'dangerous' classes. The former were worthy recipients of charity, struggling for respectability in the urban jungle, whilst the latter were a criminalised fraction. There was a constant fear, especially after the French Revolution among the urban bourgeoisie, that the perishing classes might be recruited into the dangerous classes of thieves, beggars and criminals and develop an insurrectionary force, disengaged from loyalty to the state by poverty and hardship.

A partial solution was offered by the New World to which cheap labour could be transported or persuaded to emigrate. For example, the settlement of Virginia in 1619 not only imported African slave youth, but also received orphaned and destitute children from the poor houses and Bridewells of England. Simultaneously, as in Virginia in 1609, it was perfectly legal to kidnap native American children and raise them as Christians. In early America, as in sixteenth-century England, the family was the centre of control rather than the state, and poor children were assigned to farming and domestic service. By the end of the eighteenth century the family ceased to be the central economic unit, being replaced by the factory process. Children had been apprenticed until then, a voluntary process for the wealthier groups, but wayward and destitute youth were compulsorily bound out to their masters. Industrialisation changed this, and during the early part of the nineteenth century children made up a large part of the labour force. Half of the New England factory workers were children and the under fifteen years old section increased right up until 1900. Immigration also expanded, so that unattached urban youth became a socially visible problem. There was public concern with white youth, usually immigrant, involved in casual labour, begging or destitute, or after 1910 with black youth migrating from the rural South. These changing social and economic circumstances paved the way for increased state supervision. Two main themes of care and control are visible throughout the history of state provision, which had its roots in such moral entrepreneurs as the Society for the Prevention of Pauperism (1817), which set up houses of refuge, the first in New York City in 1825. One concern was to prevent the further corruption of youth by providing separate justice systems, prisons and workhouses. The city was seen as corrupting young people, and the solution was to transport them to the country, no matter how inadequate this was in preparing them for urban life. Immigrant parents in particular were seen as maladjusted and, by 1875, the American Social Science Association demanded that the state act *in loco parentis* due to this inadequacy. Up to 1930 half of juvenile delinquency cases involved immigrant children (Haskell and Yablonsky, 1971), perhaps because they were the easiest to survey. Delinquents, orphans and the destitute tended to be housed together, although houses of refuge housed blacks separately (starting in Philadelphia in 1849) and kept girls apart also.

By the second half of the nineteenth century the Child Saving movement was under way (Platt, 1968). Basically, the urban poor were seen as struggling against the corruption of city life, without the supportive surveillance of the small community. Concern grew over street children, beggars and vagrants, and over exploitative working conditions. The rehabilitative model was the rural family and several measures occurred in the reformatory movements. Charles Loring Brace set up the Children's Aid Society in New York in 1853, and Judge Benjamin Lindsey set up his juvenile court in Denver in 1901, noting realistically that a hungry boy will steal. Lindsey was influenced by Chicago's juvenile court, America's first, set up in 1899 which led to William Healy's Juvenile Psychopathic Clinic (Chicago, 1909) which focused on the case study.

Misbehaviour in juveniles was seen as pathology or maladjustment and individual rehabilitation rather than social change were seen as the pathway to reform. From this came the medical model still used by child guidance clinics and juvenile correction and protection agencies. School social work also expanded with the visiting teacher schemes (Levine and Levine, 1970; Krisberg and Austin, 1978). This era, sometimes called the progressive era, from 1880 to 1920 occurred during a period of increasing immigration, condensed urbanisation, struggles between organised labour and industrialists, racism and technological development which itself threatened labour. Out of this grew the criminal justice system and a form of welfare state. In the 1930s one predominant influence was the University of Chicago. The Chicago Area Project was to become a model for large-scale, community focused work with youth. It developed at a time when thousands of people in Chicago were unemployed, especially blacks and immigrants. The project's analysis of social strain and social disorganisation led to a focus on work in the ghetto and the slum. Its use of detached workers became an accepted strategy, although its use of indigenous workers became neglected in the struggle for professionalisation. Its takeover by the Illinois State Division of Youth Services unfortunately turned it into a rather orthodox, bureaucratic organisation working on behalf of other agencies, rather than for the local community.

The war boom faded by the late 1950s, and substantial numbers of black and Hispanic people became unemployed. The ghettos became places of poverty, disease and crime. Riots occurred, and social scientists again began to suggest a social disorganisation thesis. The ghettos contained cultures of poverty and violence, and this was cited as evidence that they lacked a process of adaptation to urban life, completely ignoring the role of white investment and development in creating slum conditions. This view was later to be called by Ryan (1976) 'blaming the victim'. The serious nature of delinquency led to the development of detached worker programmes with gangs which remained in a psychoanalytic mode rather than directing attention to structural problems in the local community. Street workers were encouraged to redirect gangs into socially acceptable activities and if this failed to manipulate situations to disrupt them. Working closely with law enforcement officers, they shared information with them. During the late 1950s, the Ford Foundation became influential in developing more enlightened and liberal projects through its Grey Area programmes. One of the most significant was the Mobilisation for Youth which, with the Harlem Youth Project, will be discussed later. The consequent political difficulties with local authority structures led to their disbandment. Other programmes which developed were the Youth Service Bureaux which attempted to promote cooperation between local communities and their justice and welfare agencies, acting to divert youth from becoming involved in the criminal justice system.

There have also been attempts to rationalise juvenile justice systems, such as the California Youth Authority, and to move in the direction of reform in juvenile legislation and institutions. Community-based correction systems have been implemented which try to reduce institutionalisation by the use of group homes, partial release programmes and halfway houses. The present situation reflects the law and order debates. On the one hand, there is a concern with alleged increases in violence and a lobby for incarceration and punishment; on the other hand, the liberal lobby which keeps children in the home is often supported because it is less expensive to return children to the community. Unfortunately, children sent to institutions are now seen as the most dangerous and are therefore kept longer, often in conditions which are extremely poor, and then returned to impoverished social conditions with poor prospects to survive as best they can. Only too often young people have been seen as a social problem separated from broader structural issues such as education, employment, housing and poverty.

This concentration on youth as a social problem dislocated from the wider structural context of class, ethnicity, geographical location and culture has individualised the problem. By the 1920s considerable interest in the young was shown by psychologists, educationalists and psychiatrists. The British psychologist, Cyril Burt (1925) took a Durkheimian view that delinquency was normal, but determined by multi-causal factors such as interaction between genetic and environmental factors. Poverty of a moral rather than a material nature was influential, and the delinquent did poorly at school due not to lack of intelligence, but to simple underachievement. Margaret Mead (1928) introduced, as befitted an anthropologist, cultural relativism to theories of adolescence, indicating that the traditional storm and stress was a Western phenomenon. These approaches were highly influential, drawing a relationship between a social problem and a social situation of cultural and psychological poverty. Adolescence became seen as a distinctly social phenomenon.

The Chicago school and the social ecology of the city

The Depression years meant that youth became perceived, as a result of unemployment, as an area of social concern, in particular youth in working-class neighbourhoods, especially ghettos and slums. Chicago was particularly important, as we have noted, firstly for the juvenile court, then the Juvenile Psychopathic Clinic, which became the Institute for Juvenile Research and the Chicago Youth Project. The university became a centre of research into urban youth and working-class life styles. Under the influence of C.H. Cooley, G.H. Mead and W.I. Thomas, methodology was a mixture of urban documentation, crusading reformism and detailed empiricism based on the interview. Oral history was strong (Bennett, 1981), reflecting Robert Park's early training in journalism, which he gave up for philosophy. The first in a series of studies on social worlds and life styles was Andersen's *The Hobo* (1923), a study of the transient worker, 'the bohemian in the ranks of labor', and hobohemia's street society. Shaw (1930) did a similar ethnographic study of 'jack rollers' who robbed fellow tramps whilst they slept. The hobo is portrayed as a denizen of an urban ethnography, although there is a recognition of wider structural aspects, as in the interesting relationship between the hobo and Industrial Workers of the World's attempt to organise them as a conscious form of the lumpenproletariat. The Chicago model was based on plant ecology adapted to city life. Human beings, rather like plants, lived together in a state of symbiosis, with different species living in the same habitat. The social scientist's task was to seek out the well-ordered, mutually advantageous equilibrium known in plant life as the biotic balance, which was postulated to be present in urban life. As Matza suggests (1969a), the Chicago school was aware of social diversity, but as it was committed to a model of society in equilibrium, it was faced with the problem of resolving disequilibrium, without an appeal to the psychologistic notion of individual pathology. This was resolved by introducing the concept of social pathology – social disorganisation. In certain urban neighbourhoods the balance between competition and cooperation has upset the biotic balance, so that the values and cultural patterns of these neighbourhoods seemed socially disorganised. Causal features could be, for example, unchecked migration into the neighbourhood. The social system of the neighbourhood is thrown out of balance by urban growth, so that social solidarity and social control break down.

What has been recognised is that slums and ghettos had their own social structures with specific norms and patterns of behaviour, although these were analysed in the context of middle-class values. Distinct life styles were uncovered and given validity. Urban expansion had an effect on city areas, so that the poor became ghettoised, and the respectable artisans joined the lower middle class in the suburban areas of large cities. Park *et al.* (1925) attempted to isolate those features of urban life which ecologically encouraged delinquency. Park used the concept 'natural area' to attempt to trace relationships between specific geographical areas, and the physical structure and social organisation of those areas. The 'natural area' was a small residential area with recognised boundaries, inhabited by distinct cultural groups. A city was a collection of these natural areas, which became divisible into zones, extending concentrically from the centre to the periphery, reflecting industrialisation and urban sprawl. Morris (1957, p. 51) writes

> Originally the population of the city lived around the business central district, but this area was the most obvious choice for the location of the new commercial and industrial enterprises. As the industry moved in, the wealthier inhabitants moved out, and as the area declined in terms of desirability of residence, this depressed rentals so it became the obvious choice for newcomers to the city, usually poor immigrants in search of housing at lowest possible cost. The respectable artisans were as a result encouraged to move out, and they in turn began to displace the well to do who moved further out still.

Where an area was in the throes of transition from one phase to another, these were 'interstitial areas'. The social ecology model was adopted by scholars interested in gangs and delinquency (Thrasher, 1927; Shaw and McKay, 1927) or those interested in the social organisation of street corner groups, such as Whyte (1943) whose classic study of a slum carried on the post-war Chicago tradition, stressing the non-delinquent aspects of the street corner boy.

Thrasher focused on the urban gang, found in the changing urban areas as a result of social disorganisation. In his study of a particular area of downtown Chicago, the Loop district, he describes it thus:

> The central tripartite area of the gang occupies what is often called the 'Poverty Belt' - a region characterised by deteriorating neighbourhoods, shifting populations and the

35

> mobility and disorganisation of the slum. .... As better
> residential districts recede before encroachments of business
> and industry, the gang develops as one manifestation of the
> economic, moral and cultural frontier, which marks the
> interstice. (Thrasher, 1927, p. 20)

Methodologically, Thrasher felt it necessary to enter the world of
the delinquent, using his definition of the situation to understand
two things. Firstly, the delinquent's serious endeavour to make
sense of his life, and secondly, to distinguish the fantasy life of the
gang from reality. Territoriality was a central feature, coinciding
with Burgess's zones of transition, called interstitial areas by
Thrasher, and this was related to ethnic defence of 'turf'. Sixty per
cent of the gangs for which he had a record of ethnicity were
exclusively or predominately ethnic. The gangs reflected neighbourhood composition, rather than strict ethnic polarities: where
the neighbourhood was ethnic, the gang was ethnic; as the neighbourhood became mixed, so did the gang. Antagonism occurred
between gangs from different income groups. Thrasher saw the
gang as originating in the small, informal play group, which led to
the development of an internal structure and shared traditions.
Opposition and adult disapproval led to the formation of the gang,
and conflict was only one of several activities. Gangs were also
athletic clubs, secret societies, with both instrumental and expressive
roles. Later on they had relations with local politics and organised
crime, a point also noted by Whyte. Thrasher (1927, p. 32) notes
that 'Gangs represent the spontaneous effort of boys to create a
society for themselves where none exists for their needs'. For
Thrasher the adventure and play activities of delinquency were
important, often motivated by nothing more complex than hedonism, a factor often overlooked in favour of more complex causes.
In slum life, the street is a crowded, exciting and dangerous place
where children daily perceive illegal activities. It is of great cultural
importance, like the market and the tavern. Informal interaction
offers a social life to the old or the lonely; gossip and rumour
provide information and drama. The street is the playground of
working-class youth, and where there is little else to take pride in,
it becomes a defensible territory. It offers escape from adult surveillance and an apprenticeship in peer group deviancy and anti-
school norms. Brown (1967) paints a vivid picture in his Harlem
autobiography of desperate attempts by mothers to keep children
in front of the house to control the corrupting influence of street
life. Thrasher, like Shaw and McKay (1927), saw the street as an
adventurous free area, which was in contrast to the antithetical
constraining agencies of social control, seen by kids as weak, dull

and unattractive. Delinquency rates were seen as constant in these areas, despite substantial alterations in the composition of their populations. This Durkheimian perspective was explained by the view that delinquency was not determined by the actual location of an area, but inherent in a community with a competing system of contradictory values and weak family and community controls. Shaw and McKay (1927, p. 26) argue that 'The common element (among social factors highly correlated with juvenile delinquency) is social disorganisation, or the lack of organised community effort to deal with these conditions.' Important seminal elements are found in the Chicago school. There are the beginnings of an understanding of working-class youth culture. Links are hinted at but never developed between neighbourhood, class, ethnicity and culture.

> To what extent in any given racial group – for example the Italians in New York, or the Poles in Chicago – do parents and children live in the same world, speak the same language, share the same ideas and how far do conditions found account for juvenile delinquency in that particular group? (Park *et al.*, 1925, p. 25).

The problematics of generation are recognised as a uniquely American form of generation gap – there is a relationship between neighbourhood and ethnicity. However, as Matza (1964) indicates, whilst there may be a delinquent tradition in an area, this tradition is also found in more respectable cultures. There is a hint of differential association in Shaw and McKay: where there are opportunities to learn deviant actions over respectable ones, there will be a variable delinquency rate.

Criticisms of the social ecology model. The problems of pluralism – class, conflict and power

Several criticisms have been made of the social ecology model. Downes (1966, p. 71) points out the tautology of the social disorganisation thesis: 'The rate of delinquency in an area [is seen as] being the chief criterion for its "social disorganisation", which in turn was held to account for the delinquency rate.' The emphasis on diversity runs into a problem because of the suggestion that the socially disorganised neighbourhood lacks a coherent set of cultural norms. This was resolved by developing a theory according to Taylor *et al.* (1973, p. 115) where 'each specific area could be seen to represent the territorial base of a differing tradition. Social disorganisation became translated into differential social disorganisation'.

A thesis that a particular neighbourhood forms the territorial base of a type of differential social organisation is found in A.K. Cohen's (1958) typology of semi-professional thief, drug addict and conflict-oriented subcultures, and Cloward and Ohlin's (1960) similar typology. These pluralistic elements are present in differential social organisation, but absent in the social disorganisation model with its structural-functionalist stance. This pluralism opens up the possibility of conflict within a neighbourhood over scarce resources in the local economy, such as housing, education, health and employment, and cultural interpretations and ideological solutions to structural contradictions which are expressed in local subculture, but never materially resolved there.

This interpretation of the differential organisation model means we need to consider the material basis of this in a pluralistic society. Bourgeois theories of pluralism confuse the empirical presence of several cultures and subcultures based on class and ethnicity with political pluralism. Because there is a culturally rich and varied differentiation of social life in a complex, industrial society, this does not mean that the various communities have any basic influence, or access to equal power, concerning major political and economic decisions. The formation of interest and pressure groups is always cited as evidence of a democratic process, but the material wealth of Britain and America remains in the hands of a few. In America this is mainly a small number of corporations (Edwards *et al.*, 1972; Christoffel *et al.*, 1970), and in Britain among wealthy elites (Atkinson, 1975; Reid, 1977; Urry and Wakeford, 1973, and Westergaard and Resler, 1975). In Britain something like 2 per cent of the population owns 55 per cent of the national wealth, and in America 1 per cent owns 40 per cent. This minority is linked nationally by wealth, corporate interests, and often kinship. It shares a common background which reflects a ruling class rather than just one interest group amongst others. The political, economic and ideological control of the influential elites, or ruling class fractions extend, admittedly in a diffuse and mediated way, into the local urban structure. The ecological model of 'natural areas' must be seen against this context, and the exercise of social control through local police and judiciary. A stable order is in the interests of the ruling class, and this needs a docile and contented work force.

Criminal law is important because it can be seen as making an appeal above the interests of specific groups to the neutrality of justice. Delinquency can be separated off as dysfunctional to law and order and used to deal symptomatically with a problem which may exist structurally. In Armstrong and Wilson's (1973) Glasgow study a relationship was suggested between local city politics and delinquent neighbourhoods. The district of Easterhouse's built en-

vironment combined with local demography to structure the relationships of youth, who have a long history of their own in Glasgow, a notoriously tough city. Factors such as policing the area
from outside, the official designation and consequent stigmatisation
of Easterhouse as a 'problem area', and the social visibility of local
street corner groups escalated problems between them and the police. Violence and vandalism became a local party political issue
with vast media involvement. A situation of deviancy amplification
occurred as the media fed back to local youth an image of their
neighbourhood and their part in it. The situation was kept alive by
local political controversy over delinquency. This is in direct contrast to Shaw and McKay's view that delinquent behaviour is not
the result of local social control, and also shows how a particular
neighbourhood develops a 'tough' culture. The attitudes of police
in a local area are important; neighbourhoods and communities
have a definite reputation among law enforcement and educational
personnel, and this is related to their class and ethnic composition.
Local administration decisions, subject to middle-class pressure
groups, directly reflect these. High rates of delinquency and criminality in run-down areas contain an interplay between respectable
and deviant values. Whyte (1943) found in his Chicago slum that
street corner boy subcultures were more than simply delinquent.
The street corner was a social milieu for local boys to organise
their social life while unemployed. Infractions of the law occurred
but these were situations where the law was seen as irrelevant.
Delinquency in these areas is a normal form of behaviour supported by a mixed set of values. This gives rise to a differential
learning situation framed in a normative context differing from
respectable middle-class values, and allowing for apprenticeships
into deviant careers as well as respectable ones.

Youth culture and class

Youth and adolescence were central areas of study in the 1930s in
America as is illustrated by the American Sociological Association's conference in 1934 at Yale, which was given over to youth.
Reuter (1936; 1937) drew the attention of sociology in America to
the idea that adolescents lived in a different world from adults,
creating 'an inclusive social order' separated from adult society.
The anthropologist Ralph Linton (1942) also touched on the idea
that young people had their own distinctive culture patterns. The
idea of a separate adolescent culture was born, but it was Parsons
who coined the term 'youth culture' and articulated this (Parsons,
1942; 1950) for the combination of age and sex roles. For him,

youth culture develops inverse values to the adult world of productive work and conformity to routine and responsibility. Youth develops its own values concerning consumption, hedonistic leisure activities and irresponsibility. Parsons' view is ahistorical and dislocated from any class analysis. However, the characteristics he describes suggest high school teenage culture, concern with glamour, looking attractive, having fun, all located in the educational system. It is a world peopled with conforming figures, athletes, football jocks, prom queens and cheer leaders. At the time, through the media, this aspect of American youth culture was influential not only in the United States, but in Britain, Canada and Europe. For Parsons, youth culture is related to the bridge between the dependency of childhood and the independence of adulthood. It is a sort of adolescent 'rite de passage', and essentially a middle-class one; working-class youth exists only on the periphery. Parsons (1964) argues for a shift of emphasis in middle-class youth culture in the 1950s, where he saw a greater acceptance of scholastic achievement, replacing 'rebelliousness or sullen withdrawal'. Youth was given more independence and had developed a fierce group loyalty. A romanticism developed which was related to 'going steady' with the opposite sex, and to popular cult figures and folk heroes. There was an emphasis on masculine physical prowess, a reaction for Parsons to the emphasis on educational success. Middle-class youth had become more integrated into general culture which, he argued, was illustrated by its responsible use of alcohol and sex, two primary indicators of independence from adult supervision. Working-class youth remained outside this middle-class picture of success, reacting against school with delinquency and truancy. By 1962 Parsons has moved from his view of youth culture as 'a compulsive independence of, and antagonism to, adult expectations and authority' combined with 'a compulsive conformity' to the peer group. Peer group loyalty remains strong, but youth has become more responsible to conservative adult control, and hence more integrated into adult mainstream culture. Politically, youth favours justice and social change, is interested in activism, but is frustrated because of being deprived of power and influence. Parsons' conclusion is that youth is quite ready to work within, rather than in opposition to, the system, despite its anomic element. The radicalism of middle-class youth during the 1960s must have come as a shock.

Parsons' amiable 'glamour girls', 'swell guys' and 'good companions' are seen differently by Murdock and McCron (1976). For them Parsons' view is part of the Cold War ideological struggle, centred on the image of American society as a pluralist democracy involving individual choice and an open competition for power.

This view presents America in contrast to Soviet society – a total-
itarian state with a self-recruiting party elite manipulating a passive
and conforming population. Class was allowed to fade into the
background as a unit of analysis, and they compare Parsons with
Hollingshead's (1949) study of 'Elmtown' youth. Elmtown's youth
is analysed as having its social behaviour shaped by class. Hollingshead's empirical evidence does not bear Parsons out. Adolescent behaviour was diverse rather than common, and it was shaped
by the family and neighbourhood subcultures, but especially by the
particular clique the adolescent was in. Because the Cold War dis-
couraged class as an analysis, committed pluralism, such as in the
work of James Coleman (1961), became central. His investigation
of ten Illinois high schools argued that political pluralism grew
from cultural diversity. His aim was, firstly, to demonstrate the
essential pluralism of high schools through showing the diversity of
different status systems present in the school. Secondly, it was to
investigate the extent to which informal status systems among students supported, or were antagonistic to, the goals of the school.
However, Coleman's findings placed him in a dilemma because at
least four schools indicated that a student's status was determined
by his social class. This was resolved by emphasising, as Parsons
did, the separatedness of adolescent youth culture which was composed of:

> separate subcultures [which] exist right under the very noses of
> adults – with languages all their own, with special symbols
> and, most importantly with value systems ... that lead away
> from those goals established by the larger society. (Coleman,
> 1961, p. 9)

Coleman thus focused on youth culture, his second theme, rather
than on his findings that informal status systems were not open to
all, and a student's position in them dependent not on individual
achievement but class. Instead, for him, school students were cut
off from adult society, a feature further segregating them from the
growing youth market. Youth culture, then, was some separate
homogeneous culture dissolving traditional divisions. Youth was
linked to adult society only tentatively, and to the market economy
by consumerism. No attempt was made to link youth to wider
political and social issues. Popular music was a central feature of
youth culture, in particular the consumption of discs aimed as
specific age groups. However, Murdock and McCron point out
that an empirical study by Coleman's research assistant indicates
that there were distinct differences of taste. Presley had been publicised as the archetypal, anti-authority, sexual rebel, but only a
fifth nominated him as their favourite performer. The rest selected

Pat Boone, an adult-approved, mainstream artiste. The Presley fans were almost exclusively working class. We see here a selection difference which keeps recurring in popular music tastes: that they are class-shaped, and follow mainstream more than was originally imagined. The emerging concept of youth culture was to ignore class and ethnicity variables until much later, particularly regarding the relation these variables had to the composition of, and recruitment into, subcultures.

Another way of examining the city is to consider the social meaning that territory has in the local, working-class neighbourhood. Physical space is not a simple territorial imperative but symbolic of a whole life style. The status of the neighbourhood is central to this, but there is also the wider context of the struggle for decent housing. The inner city is inhabited by impoverished, stigmatised groups, often ethnic minorities and immigrants. As early as 1844 Engels writes of Manchester:

> all Manchester proper, all Salford and Hulme ... are all
> unmixed working people's quarters, stretching like a girdle,
> averaging a mile and a half around the commercial district.
> Outside, beyond the girdle, lives the upper and middle
> bourgeoisie in remoter villages with gardens ... in free,
> wholesome country air, in fine comfortable homes, passed
> every half hour or quarter hour by omnibuses going into the
> city. And the finest part of the arrangement is that members of
> the money aristocracy can take the shortest road through the
> middle of all the labouring districts without ever seeing that they
> are in the midst of the grimy misery that lurks to the right and
> left ... they suffice to conceal from the eyes of the wealthy men
> and women of strong stomachs and weak nerves the misery and
> grime which form the complement of their wealth. (1962 edn)

As the wealthy passed into the suburbs (and in the metropolis often back to the inner city displacing the poor), the migrant and immigrant groups took over older neighbourhoods. These areas often take on an ethnic character. However, as the housing stock is allowed to deteriorate by absentee landlords, the new arrivals become blamed for the deterioration of the district. As Downes (1968, p. 217) says of London's East End

> Virtually barred from council flats, the 'blacks' inevitably
> resort to this deteriorating property. Local white residents link
> the onset of the deterioration with the arrival of the blacks,
> and blame the newcomers for the deterioration.

In fact British studies (Rex and Moore, 1967) suggest a class struggle for housing, rather than the social ecology model. In their study

Rex and Moore found that the immigrants had no access to political power through traditional interest groups to housing, and were relegated by the market to slums, for which they were then held responsible. An extension of this is found in youth subcultures which defend their territory against other groups and newcomers.

The statistical presence of delinquency in the working-class neighbourhood

One main argument favouring the social disorganisation model was the high level of delinquency in the working-class neighbourhood. Official arrest rates are low before the age of ten, peak between fifteen and nineteen for the working-class male, then drop again after twenty-five. Fifty-seven per cent of all those arrested are under twenty-five (FBI figures, 1976), and there are more children arrested between eleven and fourteen than adults between thirty and thirty-nine. These offences are mainly theft, breaking and entering and stealing motorcycles. The figures for juveniles are complicated by vandalism and status offences, the latter being particularly high for girl offenders. Whilst juvenile crime has certainly risen, with a tendency to violence, this has to be seen in the context of an increase in the youth population, and a general rise in crime throughout the population. Wolfgang *et al.* (1972) looking at an entire cohort of Philadelphia males born in 1945, found that race was related to arrest rates. Blacks are indeed over-represented in criminal statistics, and class and delinquency also correlate. The complex situation in the United States is that class and race overlap, so that the arrest rate is highest among non-white working-class boys. This double jeopardy of race and class is confounded because they have the greatest number of residential moves and school changes with a consequential drop in grades at school. This group also showed more recidivism and more violence. Working-class youth, then, has a much higher arrest rate, and the lower income groups of the working class (who also happen to be black) show the highest rates of all. Self reports (Gold, 1970; Illinois Institute for Juvenile Research, 1972; Williams and Gold, 1972) indicate that racial differences are reduced, although black boys report more serious offences including violence (Gold and Reimer, 1974). Both black and white girls are less seriously involved according to their self reports.

There has been considerable controversy over the issue of class. Tittle *et al.* (1978) argued strongly against a relationship between class and crime, rigorously challenged by Braithwaite (1981) and Clelland and Carter (1980). Braithwaite's careful study of international figures finds a relationship between class and delinquency in the official statistics. He also looked at forty-seven self report studies, of which eighteen found that adolescents reported significantly higher levels of delinquency in the working class, seven found some support for the theory and twenty-two showed no difference. Rural and small town samples showed less class differences. There are, however, methodological problems with the confusion of misbehaviour and illegal actions in the items tested, using small samples with disproportionate middle-class groups, and setting the working-class cut-off points too high. Official statistics are an amplification of delinquent behaviour, but they may distort the picture. Thornberry (1973) also uses Wolfgang *et al.*'s data, and looks at processing juvenile crime. Holding recidivism and seriousness of offence constant, he finds black and working-class delinquents received more serious dispositions. Williams and Gold (1972), using the 1967 National Survey of Youth, found that it was not the seriousness of the offence which led to a court referral, but the background and perhaps the demeanour of the youngster. Their white, middle-class boys reported more serious delinquency than the white, working-class boys, but this difference (small but significant) disappeared by the time police records were reached. Self reports found little difference between race and class. Statistics, of course, reflect arrests, which in turn reflect perceptions of delinquency. Piliavin and Briar's (1964) classic study found that black boys are more likely to be stopped and interrogated, and their attitude is more likely to lead to procedure, rather than dismissal, by the police. Certainly Chambliss (1973) shows his middle-class group of 'Saints' were able to commit quite serious offences, because they could travel away from their neighbourhood by car to commit offences. His working-class 'Roughnecks' were perceived and labelled by the police, community and school as troublemakers and became the focus of police control tactics.

A deviancy amplification spiral occurs in working-class neighbourhoods. Their close policing has a self-fulfilling effect on police sensitivity to likely suspects. This in turn leads to a hostility to the police by local youth, especially in black areas where racism is blamed, with the results that increasing arrest rates are used to justify discriminatory police practices. Victimisation figures also show interesting evidence concerning working-class life. Despite the evidence of rising crime rates, the chances that the average person will be victimised in any given year are still not great, particularly for violent crime (Empey, 1978). Figures from the National Criminal Justice and Information Statistics suggest that victims are not members of the middle class, or the elderly, but young, poor, black males, young, poor, white males and young, poor, black females in that order. The setting is usually the ghetto, and victimisation figures reflect arrest figures.

Schwendinger and Schwendinger (1976a; 1976b; 1982) argue that youth has been marginalised from the main labour force, and that historically advanced capitalism has prolonged youth's dependent status, and thus its marginality. Their theory of delinquency (shortly to be published) poses suggestions both for theories of delinquency and for youth culture. Historically, they link differing forms of delinquency at different historical 'moments', traceable to the changes in the mode of production. The long-term decline in the accumulation of profit and the use of mechanisation made youth redundant in the work force after the nineteenth century. This exclusion from the market, and its long period of dependency, combined with the growth of institutions like the school, all contributed to marginality. Nowadays marginalisation affects not only the young and the old, but also the poorest in the work force. The allocation of scarce educational resources favours youth who are already the recipients of other advantages because of their class and ethnic location. The position of the least favoured deteriorates, and they become marginalised within the context of the school and the family in a process analogous to marginalisation in the economy. The results are 'anarchic behaviour patterns, created by students not motivated to achieve' (Schwendinger and Schwendinger, 1976a, p. 185); 'a youthful population of prototypic marginals, whose status is not actually determined by economic institutions' is generated. There are present, they argue, collective varieties of youth, 'relatively autonomous, highly variable, stratified formations' in fact 'stratified domains of adolescent groups' (also called 'stradom formations') which affect modal patterns among adolescents. Thus, delinquent relationships are not produced directly by socio-economic conditions but by changes in the life cycles of these stradom formations. This allows us to consider that most impoverished and working-class (including black) youth is not involved in delinquency, opening up the presence of what I would call youth subcultures. The hard core of marginalised youth is found in the working class, but marginalisation may also be found among middle-class and even upper-class youth who become involved in delinquency. Peer groups have their own stratification systems, either in high school cultures or neighbourhood street cultures. High rates of unofficial delinquency are found among adolescent social types known as 'socialite', 'colleeges' or 'frats' and found in college fraternities and sororities. These middle-class groups are protected by public opinion and social status, but even middle-class communities may have formations in the neighbourhood where enough delinquents live to form a street corner group of 'hodads', 'ese vatos' or 'greasers' which will then attract marginal middle-class youth into the group. The Schwendingers develop a typology of stradom and non-stradom formations. The latter group consists among others of 'prototypic intellectuals' who invest their time in academic achievement, and are outside the stradom formations because of their relationship to formal, ideological relations. The stradom formations consist of prototypic street corner groups who are usually the most delinquent in working-class neighbourhoods, such as 'greasers'. These are intermediate, perhaps with distinctive life styles such as 'surfies', but the 'socialite' is the prototypic bourgeois who, because delinquency cuts across class lines, is involved also in delinquency. Their delinquency differs in that it lacks the violence or types of theft of the greaser. Theft, such as vehicle theft, is for excitement as opposed to the burglary of the greaser. If there is a lack of street corner groups in a middle-class district, then the socialites may be the most delinquent group. Thus, the social relations of production produce marginality, family and school reflects this, the local neighbourhoods class composition influences types of stradom formations. The modality of delinquency is also a variable, both in incidence and form, and these all combine in different patterns to make up different collective varieties of youth. The locus of analysis for the Schwendingers is marginalisation which they use to develop a complex theoretical position to consider different types of behaviour and youth culture. From this they are able to offer explanations of why the self reports of delinquency produce less distinct relations with class. Self reports reflect the generalised delinquency modality, which is found in all classes, and is composed of less serious acts. They argue that unless one controls for types of adolescent stradom formation, one can expect, at best, low negative correlations between class and delinquency. This is because stradom formations mediate the relationship between socio economic-factors and delinquent modalities.

Differential identity in the deprived neighbourhood

If, as suggested above, cultural pluralism occurs in deprived neighbourhoods, it is important to consider the effects of this on the actor. In subcultural theory, Sutherland and Cressey (1966) postulate a learning theory model based on operant conditioning developed in psychology, and extended to a wider sociological base. Briefly, they argue that where there exists an excess of association with deviant actors, especially in conjunction with intimate, positive reference groups, motives are learned which rationalise anti-social behaviour. This mixture of social learning theory and symbolic interaction may explain how an ideology is brought into consciousness and even learned, but it fails to explain legitimacy of motives. Matza (1969b) has criticised it for its lack of humanistic purpose and meaning. Actors, he argues (1969b, p. 107), 'intentionally move in search of meaning as well as nourishment', and what Sutherland has failed to appreciate is 'the interpenetration of cultural worlds – the symbolic availability of various ways of life everywhere' (Matza, *op*, *cit*., p. 107).

Glaser has taken a more humanistic approach in his extension of differential association, as Sutherland called his theory, to incorporate symbolic interaction with cultural pluralism (Glaser, 1966). This indicates the use of imagery and role-taking in the construction of identity. Glaser suggests that, during their lifetimes, most actors identify with both criminal and non-criminal persons, and that this can be used to construct a theory of differential identification which Glaser (1966, p. 434), suggests is:

> In essence ... that a person pursues criminal behaviour to the
> extent that he identifies with real or imaginary persons from
> whose perspectives his criminal behaviour seems acceptable.
> Such a theory focuses attention on the interaction in which
> choice models occur, including the individual's interaction with
> himself in rationalising his conduct.

Glaser has taken note of Shibutani's (1955) point that reference groups are not only real, but also mythical or imaginary. It is less what subcultures are that attracts adolescents, but what they fantasise them to be. This can introduce what Giddens (1976) calls 'slippage' into subcultures. Slippage occurs when (Giddens, 1976, p. 162) concepts are 'appropriated by those whose conduct they were originally coined to analyse, and hence to become integral features of that conduct'.

The purpose and meaning of subcultures are important in the construction of an identity which is to evade the ascribed identity components in adolescence. Glaser (1966, p. 435) notes that:

> The image of behaviour as role-playing, borrowed from the
> theatre presents people as directing their actions on the basis
> of their conceptions of how others see them. The choice of
> another from whose perspective we view our own behaviour is
> the process of identification. It may be with immediate others,
> or with distant and perhaps abstractly generalised others of
> our reference groups.

Possible roles within the subculture, 'careers' on which to base the roles, and the meaning of the subculture are essential elements in constructing an identity. For example, the official school role of the pupil may be rejected by an adolescent who has a semi-conscious recognition of a structural problem: the failure of school to meet his or her needs due to contradictions in the actual purpose of education. The adolescent experiences this by perceiving school as meaningless. The deviant subculture appears as a positive reference group (just as the pupil subculture appears as a negative reference group) which offers symbolic and social support, with a counterideology to the official school culture. An achieved, alternative identity can be constructed from subcultural elements which are an alternative to the ascribed pupil role.

Plummer (1975) has noted important links between the construction of identity and subcultures. In the case of the homosexual subculture, there is a sensitisation towards a future identity, heightened in the homosexual case of feeling different. This feeling develops a heightened self-awareness about subcultures which appears to offer a compromise between one's desired identity and the present situation. Stabilisation of identity follows, supported by the normative system of the subculture. Stabilisation is obviously more temporary in youth subcultures, but the model is useful. The contribution that subcultural theory makes to symbolic interaction theory has developed beyond role and reference group theory to consider the complicated links in the development of identity and the important part various subcultures play in the construction of social reality.

Anomie theory and its influence on subcultural studies

Anomie is predominantly a Durkheimian concept that argues for a condition of normlessness which arises when a disruption of the social order occurs (Durkheim, 1951). People's aspirations rise in this situation so that they are no longer controlled by the collective social order and hence become aspirations beyond the possibility of fulfilment. The source of anomie is to be found in the strain arising between the collective moral authority ('collective conscience') and individual interests. Anomie arises where the 'collective conscience' fails to control individual aspirations. Horton (1964) suggests that this is a form of radical conservatism. Durkheim argues that an equitable division of labour, which permits meritocracy efficiently, would create social altruism and disinterest, reducing institutionalised, individual self-interest. Merton (1957) subtly changes Durkheim's meaning, implying a consensual notion of success. This is never defined beyond the crudely material; Merton sees anomie as endemic in American society, but moves away from Durkheim's radicalism about inequality and self-disinterest. Horton argues (1964, p. 284) that

Merton's anomie differs from that of Durkheim in one crucial respect – in its identification with the very groups and values which Durkheim saw as the prime source of anomie in industrial societies. Morality means to Durkheim . . . social goals obeyed out of disinterest and altruism, not self-interest and egoism. To maximise opportunities for achieving success would in no way end anomie . . .

The roots of Merton's anomie lie in a structural strain, generated by differential access to opportunity structures. Such a strain is dangerous to society (Merton, 1938, p. 678): 'The consequences of such structural inconsistency are psychopathology of personality, and/or anti social conduct and/or revolutionary activities.' A major social danger is to posit the ideology of egalitarianism concerning internalised success goals where there are no matching opportunity structures. Merton posits a model of adaptations (predominantly dysfunctional) as a response to the failure in society of both goals and means being acceptable to its inhabitants. This overlooks the complex diversity of values and actions in the modern industrial state and is naive about the relations between the state and the political economy. For Merton anomie is a facet of the built-in dissatisfactions due to the fostering of the need to consume, which entails ever-rising expectations that cannot be met. Merton's view that all members of a society have accepted material gain as a dominant value can be challenged. They may understand that money is essential to the maintenance of their life style, but that is not to argue that they have the same cultural goals.

Merton's influence on subcultural theory is, however, considerable. One notable response was the work of a major subcultural theorist, A.K. Cohen (1955). Whilst critical of Merton, Cohen remained outside the social ecology approach of the Chicago school. Cohen argues (1955) that Mertonian modes of adaptation to structural strain fail to account for 'non-utilitarian, malicious and negativistic' behaviour in working-class, delinquent subcultures. Delinquents steal, thus appreciating money, yet throw away what they steal, or concentrate on things of little value. Motivation of a delinquent nature is found not in anomie, but in adolescent status problems. Status occurs in a middle-class normative context. The paths to upward mobility are guarded by the educational system, which is apparently objective, but is dominated by the 'middle-class measuring rod'. The paradox for working-class youth is that, despite an adherence to working-class culture, they face 'middle-class criteria of status' which ensure that they internalise middle-class values. Because they are excluded by limited opportunity structures from obtaining middle-class success, the delinquent subculture

49

evolves as a 'collective solution'. This is particularly true for young working-class males because their success depends more on achievement. For some working-class boys there is the 'college boy' adaptation, the pursuit of middle-class education and life style. There is also the 'corner boy' adaptation which allows a minimally criminal adaptation to working-class values but is not divorced from middle-class approval. The subculture for the young working-class male is 'a way of looking at the world'; it is a 'way of life that has become traditional', with the delinquent subculture developing behaviour which is 'negativistic, malicious and non-utilitarian', committed to 'short run hedonism'. By a process of 'reaction formation' the delinquent subculture inverts the middle-class value system and offers a 'collective solution' in which Cohen (1955, p. 28) considers that, 'the delinquent's conduct is right by the standards of his subculture, precisely because it is wrong by the norms of the larger culture'.

A social psychological process ('reaction formation') is used in response to a structural problem which offers security 'against an inner threat to his defences'. The impossibility of avoiding the 'middle-class measuring rod', with its consequent threat to status and implied threats to working-class culture, causes delinquents to participate in a commonly experienced problem and so evolve a collective solution.

Cohen was considerably criticised. Kitsuse and Dietrich (1959) argued that Cohen failed to demonstrate that working-class boys cared about evaluation, and that their delinquent instrumentality was underestimated. Bordua (1961) felt that Cohen overestimated the non-utilitarian aspects, and underemphasised the family dynamics. Miller (1958) argued that delinquent subcultures reflected less a reaction to loss of status than an extension of working-class 'focal concerns' which differed culturally from those of the middle class. For Miller, delinquency was a product of lower-class culture, and it was lower-class culture that had an effect on delinquent subcultures rather than a reaction to middle-class culture. Miller suggested that 'focal concerns' were identifiable in working-class culture which he (1958, p. 7) defines as 'areas or issues which command widespread and persistent attention and a high degree of emotional involvement'. He identifies as focal concerns, trouble, toughness, smartness, excitement, fate, autonomy, and the acting out of these automatically violated dominant norms. He implies, then, that there is a close integration into the parent culture (working-class culture) of the delinquent subculture, with a focus on certain concerns, although Valentine (1968) suggests that his focal concerns can also be found in the middle class.

Cohen (Cohen and Short, 1958) replied to his critics by agreeing that there is more than one working-class, delinquent, subcultural type. A subcultural group of working-class delinquents ('parent male subculture') generates, especially in schools, three types of subculture;

1 The conflict-oriented subculture, whose primary interest was violence.
2 The drug addict subculture, developed as a utilitarian means of obtaining access to drugs.
3 The semi-professional thief subculture which, in mid-adolescence, provided a pathway into organised crime.

The emphasis remained on the parent male subculture defined as (Cohen and Short, 1958, p. 22) 'probably the most common variety in this country – it might be called the "garden variety" or delinquent subculture'.

Cohen's arguments are debatable. If working-class boys have internalised middle-class values (and the extent of this is an empirical question) they must also have internalised working-class values. It would seem that a delinquent subculture would not negate middle-class norms but adapt them in some form, together with working-class norms. What does emerge is a central concern with masculinity, the ability to 'handle yourself', which has a different meaning in working-class subcultures. It tends to emphasise fighting, whilst in middle-class cultures it emphasises articulation; yet both can be central to masculine ways of relating to the world. It is true that Cohen is seminal to much subcultural theory, and he makes the connection between the neighbourhood and the subculture as a solution. His influence is distinct in later subcultural theory. He emphasises (1965) that Merton's error was to conceptualise the solution to anomie as individual, whilst he, and also Cloward and Ohlin, were to emphasise the collective solution.

Cloward and Ohlin are concerned with the problems of economic justice, rather than middle-class status, for working-class boys:

> It is our view that many discontented, lower-class youths do not wish to adopt a middle-class way of life, or to disrupt their present associations and negotiate a passage into middle-class groups. The solution they seek entails the acquisition of high position in terms of lower-class rather than middle-class criteria. (Cloward and Ohlin, 1960, p. 62)

They combine elements of Mertonian anomie and Sutherland's differential association. Working-class males are committed to success in mainly material terms but also in terms of working-class criteria. They have little access to institutionalised means in terms of what they want and what they realise they will get. Their response is not reaction formation, but a turning to illegitimate means, which includes both learning and opportunity structures. Conventional goals are internalised, but legitimate means are perceived as blocked, so that strain occurs with consequent withdrawal of support for legitimate norms. Working-class neighbourhoods, however, possess access to illegitimate means, although these are admittedly differentially accessible. There is, then, a local neighbourhood opportunity system which gives rise to:

1 The criminal subculture, which offers an apprenticeship into adult crime.
2 The conflict subculture, which offers other adolescents rather than adults as peer models. This generates conflict gangs.
3 The retreatist subculture which offers a drug-using subculture for those who have failed both legitimate and illegitimate means. They are 'double failures'.

This typology is similar to Cohen and Short, and makes similar points about the social organisation of a neighbourhood and the local opportunity system. A stable, working-class district generates a criminal subculture; a disorganised district generates a conflict subculture, and a retreatist subculture develops where both legitimate and illegitimate opportunity structures are absent. Their solution, like Merton's, seems technocratic improve the opportunity structures and you eradicate inefficiency which causes strain in the system. They stress instrumental goals (concerned with deferred gratification, logic, planning and the seeking of status and income) rather than expressive goals (concerned with immediate gratification, hedonism, creativity and spontaneity) such as are found in bohemian subcultures. In his later work with Fox Piven Cloward takes a radical stance and abandons the notion of countering anomie merely because it is inefficient, stressing instead social justice, and criticising the use of welfare for labour control reasons, and finally launching into an insightful attack upon Reaganomics as a class war against poor people on welfare (Cloward and Fox Piven, 1974; Fox Piven and Cloward, 1982).

Young (1971) extends the concept of anomie as a result of a disjunction of instrumental means and ends to develop a theory of 'expressive anomie'. Once a culture becomes inadequate for solving a particular group's problems, the new cultural means are constructed. For him, cultures are transmitted inter-generationally, and hence class culture is important. These cultures become transformed to meet the exigencies of a new social situation in which the members find themselves. Young (1971, p. 92) argues that 'The old culture is the moral springboard for the emergence of the new.' For example, middle-class students, perceiving that the rewards of higher education are less fulfilling than they were led to believe, become disillusioned and drop out. They construct a bohemian subculture, related to their middle-class background, but structured to deal with their collective problem. Young (1971, p. 93), suggests that

> It will be like the culture of the working-class delinquent in
> that it extols expressivity, hedonism and spontaneity, but will
> have a middle rather than a lower working-class orientation.
> Thus it will value expressivity through non-violent aesthetic
> pursuits and hedonism, through a cool (i.e. controlled) mode
> of enjoyment, rather than a frenzied pursuit of pleasure.

The availability of soft drugs in student bohemia means that these are used to express culturally defined properties of the drug, aesthetic appreciation and bodily enjoyment. A new culture emerges, structuring and selecting the effects and use of a specific drug, which assists in solving the new problems. This can be contrasted, for example, with the selection and use of alcohol in Irish, immigrant, bachelor subcultures which is used to solve the problems of homesickness, the absence of marriageable women and the alienation of the itinerant worker.

The influence of American naturalism. Matza and the drift into and from delinquency

Matza, through the study of the delinquent subculture and deviancy, has not only raised the level of debate in these fields to a high level but has contributed considerably to phenomenological perspectives in sociology. Matza's framework is that of naturalism, that of being true to the phenomenon under study, and indeed his principal contribution to subcultural theory is his emphasis that it usually distorts what deviants themselves would recognise in the subculture – the essence of their reality. In his earlier work (Matza and Sykes, 1957) he rejects the traditional model of subcultural theory because of its claim that delinquents invert conventional values. Why then do delinquents defend their acts by a claim that they were morally correct, and why do they show guilt? They are committed to wider values which do not reject conventional morality, but which seek to neutralise its moral bind. Delinquents use 'techniques of neutralisation', linguistic constructs which make an appeal to special, mitigating circumstances. These act to neutralise pre-existing normative constraints, and five major types of neutralisation are seen as operative. These are denial of responsibility ('I didn't mean it'), denial of injury ('I didn't really hurt him'), denial

53

of the victim ('He was only some queer'), condemning the condemners ('Everyone picks on us') and appeals to higher loyalties ('You've got to help your mates'). These techniques reflect the forces of social control. What Matza suggests is that delinquents are not really different from other youths, and he also introduces the ambiguous element of human will. However, one can accuse Matza of naivety. Accounts, especially by delinquents, are skewed to what the interrogated suppose the interrogator wants to hear. McIntyre (1967) has argued the fallacy of assuming that the way actors define situations gives more than a part of the picture. Matza also ignores rationalisation as a defence to self-esteem.

Matza argues that the subculture is a setting for the commission of delinquent acts commonly known to the group. It in no sense provides a frontal assault on conventional norms but on the contrary indicates a moral bind to them. A 'comedy of errors' occurs with each group member mistakenly supposing the others to have a higher commitment to deviance than him. During periods of boredom, feelings of frustration lead adolescents to 'drift' in and out of delinquency. These are episodic moral holidays. Delinquents are ambivalent 'neither compelled nor committed to deeds, nor freely choosing them'. Hence they drift, as Matza (1964, p. 49) explains:

> Drift stands midway between freedom and control. Its basis is an area in the social structure in which control has been loosened, coupled with the abortiveness of adolescent endeavour to organise an autonomous subculture, and thus an important source of control, around illegal action. The delinquent transiently exists in a limbo between convention and crime, responding in turn to the demands of each, flirting now with one, now the other, but postponing commitment, evading decision.

The law is respondent to, not as unjust, but as unevenly distributed. Matza argues against determinism, and attempts to restore humanism to subcultural theory. Delinquents feel themselves to be objects, pushed about by forces in society outside their control. Their sense of desperation makes them 'attempt to restore the mood of humanism which the self makes things happen' (Matza, 1964, p. 49). This can easily be an infraction of the law, as fatalism has neutralised its moral bind.

Matza's case is subject to criticism concerning his empirical evidence based on delinquents' accounts of their misdoings. Working-class adolescents are the least articulate about their relationship to the world, and whether they are committed to some form of central value system is an empirical question. They are unlikely to advocate counterarguments to the dominant system, especially in court. Even if they understand the processes of the courtroom, they are too shrewd to address the bench on adolescent hedonism or the nature of class-based law. Most youths perceive the law as an external, unchanging force. Matza's evidence has been subject to much criticism. His data consist of a record of the attitudes of one hundred incarcerated adolescents about their reactions to a series of pictures of delinquent offences. Their responses led him to the conclusion that 'the adherents of the subculture of delinquency seem little committed to the misdeeds inherent in it' (Matza, 1964, p. 49).

He does make a distinction, however, between the 'radical justification' of those convinced of the righteousness of their behaviour (for example, politically motivated criminals) and the 'apologetic justification' seen as typical of the delinquent. Hindelang (1970) criticised Matza's lack of a control group, and his underestimation of how he would be perceived in the institution's staff hierarchy. He found in a similar study he carried out that delinquents approved more than non-delinquents of delinquency. Spector (1971) argues that Hindelang's middle-class sample and relatively innocuous acts of delinquency limit his findings. Ball (1977) argues that Matza sees serious delinquents as the only unconventionally committed ones, but asks why they then hold beliefs concerning neutralisation. Austin (1977) found that Matza underestimated delinquents who are unconventionally committed to their misdeeds. Moral restraint, Austin argues, is neutralised, not just by techniques of neutralisation, but by commitment to unconventional beliefs.

In another paper (Matza and Sykes, 1961) Matza suggests that delinquent values, the seeking of excitement, toughness, disdain for work are in fact not so much deviant as typical of swashbuckling leisure values held by us all. We indulge in them during competition in games, drunken orgies, gambling and 'concealed deviance'. These are not countervalues, but values shared with the dominant culture which in fact binds the delinquent to it. They are also of course male values, celebrating masculinity. The delinquent accentuates the 'subterranean values' of society, hedonism, disdain for work, aggression, violence, masculinity, excluding more official values, assisted in this by mythical heroes in the mass media. Such values can be contrasted with the Protestant ethic (Weber, 1970) summarised as ambition, individual responsibility, the cultivation of skills, worldly asceticism, rationality, manners, courtesy and personality, the control of aggression, 'wholesome' recreation and the respect for property (Downes, 1966). Young (1971) feels these have been replaced by goal-oriented values necessary in modern industry.

Unlike the Protestant ethic, which argued that man realised his true nature through hard work and duty, establishing his position in the world, the formal values of production emphasise that work is instrumental to gain money to 'spend in the pursuit of leisure, and it is in his "free" time that a man really develops his sense of identity and purpose'. (Young, 1971, p. 127). Work no longer expresses satisfaction in itself, in contemporary industrial society:

> It is during leisure and through the expression of subterranean values that modern man seeks his identity, whether it is in a 'home centred' family or an adolescent peer group. For leisure is at least purportedly non-alienated activity. (Young, 1971, p. 127)

Masculinity is an important element of identity, organising these values and we shall return to this in Chapter 7.

Matza develops a much more mature and comprehensive theory of deviance involving will (Matza, 1969b). He argues that deviants are not objects propelled by social forces, but subjects in meaningful action with their world, Naturalism is a major theme in this work. Social circumstances permit 'affinity' – a deviant has a predisposition towards deviancy because it has an 'attractive force'. An actor is attracted and he chooses. This affinity, this choice to commit infractions, occurs in the context of 'affiliation' or a willingness to be converted which, according to Matza (1969b, p. 169), is 'the process by which the subject is converted to conduct, novel for him but already established for others'.

One is able to perceive oneself as someone who might commit a deviant act – one is predisposed, not yet committed, merely 'turned on'. One may be prevented by 'ban', socio-legal control creating secrecy. Because 'ban' makes a deviant act more secret than necessary, the deviant is sensitive to organised authority, especially the state. 'Ban compounds disaffiliation and thus contributes to the process of becoming deviant' (Matza, 1969b, p. 148). The secrecy of deviancy may make actors more deviant than they originally intended. Because any deviant act to be concealed makes an actor play at being ordinary, he glimpses himself playing, which compounds deviation. Matza's sophisticated phenomenology is in direct contrast to the positivistic roots of traditional criminology. However, as Pearce (1976) suggests, his subjectivistic emphasis means that he loses the sense of the state as a concrete entity which acts in specific ways at particular moments in history. Nevertheless, Matza opens up the question of how actors choose deviancy, and why others do not, even in the same social situation. This is a useful counterdevelopment to the danger of structural determinism.

Conclusion

We have seen that the concept of subculture in relation to American delinquency theory has in many ways reflected the importance the problem of working-class youth has had for American society. It was essential at first to control working-class youth as the urban population increased, and as vagrant unemployed youth became a problem for the state. At the same time, there was a genuine, liberal attempt to rescue youth from corruption and exploitation, which matched the state's attempt to guard youth from idleness. Youth became an urban social problem, as visible in the depression of the 1930s as it is during the recession of the 1980s. Consequently, urban working-class culture, partly due to its ethnic mix, developed distinct forms of youth culture which were responded to as indicators of delinquency and immorality. The growth of secondary and tertiary education was believed to be a solution to this. As it became clear that this was not going to happen, the oppositional elements in youth culture were seen as a problem in American society. At a popular level, these were expressed in the fear of violent gangs, mugging, drug usage, signifying a fear that the urban jungle would spread to suburbia. Ethnic groups in youth culture became clear signs that the melting pot was a myth. A fear of the youthful, dangerous classes is seen in these images. These anxieties were displacements and projections of a social anxiety about American society. There was concern over its failure to develop an egalitarian society, dismissing criticism of illiberality and racism in its educational and employment institutions as unpatriotic or anti-American. Its internal cohesion was perceived as being threatened by, amongst others, youthful folk devils. With the recession America, like many other countries, has had to come to terms with controlling an impoverished and indignant working class, whose youth is beginning to feel desperation. Consequently, we can expect an increase of resistant subcultures, and of delinquency.

Chapter 3

Just another brick in the wall. British studies of working-class youth cultures

American subcultural theory has been viewed as inappropriate to Britain by many British subcultural theorists. Downes (1966) argues that American theory is intrinsic to its own culture, whilst the British working classes have their own highly developed historical traditions. The British social structure is more historically class-conscious, and most British people can tell another's class origins and length of education by accent alone. Britain lacks the neo-colonial immigrant past of the United States. Its non-white groups are recent immigrants, and it does not have a long history of nationally born, impoverished, ethnic minorities who contribute to the myth that the poor are non-white. Youth cultural studies have focused on school, the working-class neighbourhood and local peer groups. Gangs have been less closely studied, and usually in the context of activities other than delinquency alone. While gangs tend to be informally structured 'near groups', composed of a closely linked core with a looser network of peripheral members, subcultures have been seen as wider than this. They are the constellations of actions, values, style, imagery and even life styles which, through media reportage, extend beyond a neighbourhood to form a complex relationship with other larger cultures, to form a symbolic pseudo-community.

Subcultural theory has developed considerably since the post-war period. There are four approaches: firstly, the early social ecology of the late 1950s and early 1960s; secondly, the development of studies related to the sociology of education. This examines the relationship between youth, leisure and youth culture as an alternative to academic achievement. Thirdly, there are contemporary neighbourhood studies looking at local youth groups in the context of social reaction and labelling. Lastly there is the work of the Centre for Contemporary Cultural Studies, first at Birmingham University (known sometimes as the Birmingham School) and then

58

at the Open University. This work was influenced by the new criminology of the National Deviancy Conferences, and uses a combination of theories of culture, structuralism, Marxist theory and
theories of ideology, in particular Gramsci's view of hegemony.
Analyses vary from looking at contemporary theories of popular
culture, to relations between the economy and youth, to broader
aspects of the development of post-war politics in Britain.

The social ecology of the British working-class neighbourhood

The notion of the delinquent neighbourhood in Britain can be
traced back as far as the Select Committee Report on Criminal and
Destitute Juveniles in 1852. There are several accounts of youth
cultures during the late nineteenth century and the pre-war periods
but the 'major concern with youth came after the Second World
War? Ecological studies of various areas in Britain abound. Briefly
these studies emphasised poverty as being at the roots of delinquency, especially when combined with the absence of a father
figure. In the 1950s, under the influence of Bowlby, the absent or
working mother came in for criticism. Child-rearing practices were
compared, and working-class life was seen as divided into the
'rough' and the 'respectable'. Delinquency was found to have local
traditions and values. Mays' (1954) study of Liverpool found an
overtly delinquent tradition emphasising toughness, daring and defiance to authority, which also offered emotional solidarity. For
Mays (1954, p. 147) delinquency was 'not so much a symptom of
maladjustment as adjustment to a subculture which was in conflict
with the culture of the city as a whole'. Other studies in London as
well as Liverpool (Morris, 1957; Kerr, 1958) found that the local
community had a norm which acted against 'getting above yourself' so that educational scholarships, houses and jobs in other
districts were all refused. Theft from bosses, institutions or shops
was permitted, vandalism on property seen as not belonging to
anyone in particular and masculinity were all emphasised. School
was seen as useless, and the police and employers regarded cyni-
cally: 'No matter what you do, if you're making something on the
side, the governor's making more.' (Willmott, 1966, p. 143.) There
was a recognition that neighbourhoods generated their own values
which might run counter to those of middle-class society. These
had their own traditions; for example, the informal economy of the
working-class area allows workers to bring home from work things
they may need to do jobs about the house, or for moonlighting in
their spare time. This act of theft (known originally in law as
Larceny as a Servant) is condoned as a perk of the job, and there

59

is on record a suit by a medieval docker in the London docks against shipowners who forbade him taking home from the cargo a sack of goods. These were, he claimed, a traditional perk granted to his guild, and therefore a right. As in all working-class districts there were different values, but there was certainly no lack of values. They were based on different positions in the class structure with different traditions.

Education: anti-school culture and leisure

Downes (1966), in one of the best British discussions of subcultural theory, found little empirical evidence of American type subcultures in Britain. As regards delinquents,

> Their illegal behaviour seemed to be due not to 'alienation' or 'status frustration' but to a process of dissociation from middle-class dominated contexts of school, work and recreation. This disenchantment provoked an overemphasis on purely 'leisure' goals, sedulously fostered by commercial 'teenage' cultures – rather than on other non-work areas. (Downes, 1966, p. 257)

Class dominated the adolescent's access to school, work and leisure. Finding traditional forms of working-class culture no longer satisfactory in leisure areas, yet unable to achieve the glamorous elements of leisure consumption advertised in the media, he reacted against both middle-class and working-class culture. Disdain for the limited job opportunity market, consequent on educational failure, led to the adoption of a 'collective delinquent solution' in response to the newly emerging teenage culture. Downes argued that teenage culture was created for, rather than by, teenagers and is therefore synthetic. The view of the delinquent in the 1950s was that of a bored teenager with too much money, time and leisure. In fact the reality was that incomes were low, highly class-related and far from the teenage consumer pattern (Abrams, 1959) that was seen as part of embourgeoisified working class of the affluent Britain of the late 1950s. Young people were also conventional sexually, morally and socially (Eppels and Eppels, 1960; Schofield, 1965; Veness, 1962).

Downes drew attention not only to class inequality, but also to the meaninglessness of school for working-class youth. The child responds to the factory-like system of school, preparing him for the factory-like work life of his future, with fatalism, and what occurred was an opting out of the joint middle class and skilled working-class value system, whereby the adolescent of semi and unskilled origins is enjoined to 'better himself' or to 'accept his station in life'. To insulate themselves against the harsh implications of this creed, the adolescent in a 'dead end' job in a 'dead end' neighbourhood extricates himself from the belief in work, as of any importance beyond the simple provision of income, and deflects what aspirations he has into areas of what has been termed 'non work'. (Downes, 1966, p. 273)

Here we see the beginnings of the notion that youth culture was that area of leisure in which youth could invest itself because of the meaninglessness of school.

Education is the most central shared experience for all youth. Coleman (1961) argues for a distinct social system for adolescent society centred in secondary schools. Informal status determinants are constructed in opposition to the formal goals of school: athleticism for boys and appearance for girls. Sugarman (1967) also argues for a non-complex concept of youth culture, correlating those interested in dating, teenage fashions and smoking as also having unfavourable perceptions of school. He takes the patronising view that

It is no accident that the heroes of youth culture, pop singers, song writers, clothes designers and others have mostly achieved their position without long years of study, work or sacrifice ... youth culture is the new opium of the teenage masses. (Sugarman, 1967, p. 168)

Hargreaves (1967) takes this further, showing that youth culture is not homogeneous.[1] His study showed that during the last two years of secondary school two subcultures arise, reflecting streaming in the classroom. These are the higher educational streams of academically-oriented pupils identifying with the pupil role, and the lower streams dissociating from the school, forming a 'delinquescent' subculture, that is, one which is potentially rather than actually delinquent. This group comprises the youngsters about whom Holt (1969) writes in the United States:

these children see the school almost entirely in terms of the day-to-day and hour-to-hour tasks we impose upon them ... they were in school because they had to be ... it is a place where *they* tell you to do things and where *they* try to make life unpleasant if you do not do them or do not do them right.

One group is involved in hard work and conformity, and school has a meaningful relation to their future; for the others it is seen as useless, and is resented by 'mucking about in class', truancy and opposition. Class is influential in examining these subcultures. Murdock and McCron (1973) pursue this further by showing that youth cultural identification is mediated by class, then family and neighbourhood. Middle-class students were involved in school, and a minority took part in the 'underground' subculture, listening to progressive rock and reading the underground press, attracted to an anti-school middle-class culture, whilst working-class children favoured action, toughness, masculinity and physical rather than intellectual competence. They favoured dancing music with a heavy beat, group solidarity and aggressive working-class masculinity found in the skinhead subculture. As Murdock and McCron (1976, p. 18) argue, because young people reside in

> age specific institutions, it docs not follow that they are cut off from the wider system of class stratification. On the contrary through the insistent mediation of the family, the neighbourhood and the school, class inequalities penetrate deeply into their everyday lives, structuring both their social experience, and their response to it.

Working-class children dissociate from school, expecting nothing from it, as they expect nothing from work save wages. I have argued elsewhere (Brake, 1973b, p. 16) that

> Youth is not itself a problem, but there are problems created for example by the conscription of the majority of the young into the lower strata of a meritocratic educational system, and then allowing them only to take up occupations which are meaningless, poorly paid and uncreative. Working-class (youth) subcultures attempt to infuse into this bleak world excitement and colour, during the short respite between school and settling down into marriage and adulthood.

It is class which also generated divisions between British youth cultures after 1969, when hippies and skinheads clashed, then punks and skinheads, culminating in distinct class political struggles over race in the late 1970s. The classic distinction of two polarised intra-school subcultures is continued by Willis (1977) who looks at a group of anti-school young males, the 'lads' who oppose school authority, and reject the 'ear'oles', the conforming pupils, and the academically-oriented ones – the 'dummies'. What makes Willis, in the tradition of the Centre for Contemporary Cultural Studies (CCCS), different is his relating of this oppositional school culture as a preparation for the shop floor culture of general labouring work. Tough masculinity, having a 'laff', 'skiving' (not working), clothes, adult tastes are all preparation for coping with

62

work. School values are seen as effeminate; masculinity is cele-✗
brated through the tough manliness of hard, unskilled, manual
labour. The very values which help the 'lads' cope with school, are
the same ones which ensure their entrapment in manual labour,
just because they reject school.

We can now see that Willis's study is another aspect of the
relations between state institutions, an uneasy capitalism and the
problems of reproducing consenting social relations. For Willis
working-class kids take up working-class jobs because the 'real
functions of institutions work counter to their stated aims'. A
major problem would arise if kids absorbed the 'rubric of self-
development, satisfaction and interest in work' which schools try
to instil. Counter school cultures are located outside the immediate
institution, found instead in the very nature of capitalism, sexism
and general labour. The anti-school culture is paradoxically experienced by the pupils as true learning and resistance. There is a
relation between the counter school culture, regional working-class
culture and shop floor culture which 'provides powerful informal
criteria and binding experiential processes which lead working-class
lads to make the "voluntary" choice to enter the factory' (Willis,
1978), which then reproduces the class structure of employment
and shop floor culture. The culture allows them to enjoy a basically
alienating experience, already reflected in the anti-school culture,
its values refound in the actual physical work of heavy production.
The coarse humour, sexism, horseplay, badinage and vandalism
at work are developed at school, then used to develop solidarity
with workmates to resist the authority and meaningless of work,
as they did the authority and meaningless of school. 'When the lad ✗
reaches the factory there is no shock, only recognition' because he
is already familiar with defeating boredom by wasting time, having
a laugh, which he learned as real experiences of mediating alienation at school. The result is working-class fatalism ('Life's like that,
it's nobody's fault'). Ironically, this symbolic resistance never
develops into real power; on the contrary, it reinforces power relations. One negotiates the way between rejecting and mistrusting
official authority and making a living.

Societal reaction and labelling: moral panics, folk heroes and folk devils

In 1972 Stan Cohen published an important study, shifting away
from traditional delinquency research to develop issues in labelling
and transactionalist theory and applying them to youth culture,
mass media and public reaction. The establishment of the National

Deviancy Conferences in 1968 was as a critical reaction to the domination of criminology by Home Office establishment research. It had far-reaching effects leading to the new criminology, an analysis of culture and structuralism in conjunction with the CCCS, and theories of the state, and the political economy. Cohen's approach is definitional rather than behavioural, and shows how a particular set of phenomena, the emergence of two subcultural styles, 'mods' and 'rockers', became socially visible. The mass media treatment of them orchestrated a public reaction which designated them as 'folk devils' and created a 'moral panic'. Mass media coverage of a small amount of damage and violence on British seaside beaches on a rather dismal national holiday led to a situation of deviancy amplification. Once the deviant folk devils were identified and segregated, there was conscious embracing of the two deviant roles by large numbers of British teenagers. The identification of the larger extent of the problem led in turn to calls for stricter enforced punitive measures. The affrays between the mods and rockers were greatly exaggerated but societal reaction was definite. One seaside magistrate reported them as (Cohen, 1972, p. 109), 'These long-haired, mentally unstable, petty little hoodlums, these sawdust Caesars, who can only find courage like rats, in hunting in packs'. This indiscriminate prosecution, local overreaction and media stereotyping suggested a 'cabalism', that is, the solidifying of amorphous groups of teenagers into some sort of conspiratorial collectivity, which had no concrete existence.

No other studies were to relate the mass media and youth culture so well, but several studies were made of local areas and their relationship to local youth cultures.

Contemporary British ethnographic studies

We shall look at these studies as a local variation of Cohen's broader study. The most interesting study, methodologically, is by Willis, which has already been described. For Willis ethnography is the study of lived meanings, in this case the counter school culture of a specific small group, to make theoretical points about wider issues. An important aspect of working-class educational failure is understood through the collective volition of the students involved – a dynamic of self-exclusion from education occurs. For the students it is an act of resistance and opposition to the official school ideology, offering a separate and vigorous identity involving traditional working-class masculinity, work and values. It is an example of popular 'from below' culture in struggle with an official institution which also prepares the students for another cultural form, the site of which is the factory floor culture of adaptation to general labour and working-class life. Several other studies occur, but none of them have Willis's theoretical or methodological sophistication. Corrigan (1979) looks at kids in the industrial North East, discussing their relation to school in the wider context of the social relations of production. He focuses on the irritation that apparently 'doing nothing' has for adult authority. Patrick's (1973) study of violent Glasgow gangs, which seemingly have no counterpart in England, is set in the context of the West of Scotland 'hard man' cult. Toughness, clothes, sex, drink, drugs and 'patter' (fast, impertinent talk) all helped make up a status hierarchy related to the fighting of the gang. There was a fatalistic acceptance of educational, social and occupational low status. Parker's (1974) study of Liverpool looked at a street corner group in an inner city, deteriorating neighbourhood where, truanting from a meaningless school life and too young to work, the group became skilful car radio thieves. Plant's (1975) study of a small Southern town was in contrast to the harder Northern cultures of Sunderland, Glasgow and Liverpool in the previous studies. Plant compares two drug-using cultures: the 'heads' using hallucinogenics and living lower middle-class lives, and 'junkies', the poly-drug-using, working-class youths, homeless, drifting street people. All these studies examine the relationship of the local neighbourhood and culture in the wider context of class, to make sense of the meaning of various forms of behaviour.

The new wave of British subcultural theory

The studies looked at so far, except for Willis who is from the CCCS, have used subcultural theory to explore the local neighbourhood, and the more radical aspects of symbolic interactionism to look at deviant careers. Cohen's transactionalist analysis opened up the relationship of the mass media and youth culture, but two other major contributions, also influenced by the National Deviancy Conferences, were to come from Murdock's work on mass communications at the University of Leicester, and the collective under the guidance of Stuart Hall at the CCCS. These unlocked the complexities of aspects of popular culture, tending to pursue the relations between dominant and subordinate cultures. Murdock (Murdock and Phelps, 1972; Murdock, 1973; 1974; Murdock and McCron, 1973; 1976) follows the tradition of the relationship between school and youth culture, looking beyond the school to the role of commercial youth cultures.

Subcultures are the meaning systems and modes of expression developed by groups in particular parts of the social structure in the course of their collective attempts to come to terms with the contradictions of their shared social situation. More particularly subcultures represent the accumulated meanings and means of expression through which groups in subordinate structural positions have attempted to oppose or negotiate the dominant meaning system. They therefore provide a pool of available symbolic resources which particular individuals or groups can draw on in their attempt to make sense of their own specific situation and construct a viable identity.
(Murdock, 1974, p. 213)

There is certainly a hint of A.K. Cohen's original notion of a collective solution, and the constructing of a viable identity has been argued by myself elsewhere (1980), with the provision that it is an identity freed from the restrictions of class, school or occupation for a temporary period. Murdock (1973, p. 9) argues that

subcultures offer a collective solution to the problems posed by shared contradictions in the work situation, and provide a social and symbolic context for the development and reinforcement of collective identity and individual self-esteem.

This is a point I would agree with, seeing these contradictions as arising in the larger society (Brake, 1973b). We have seen that Murdock examined the tastes of different youth groups and in his study of ten widely different co-educational schools he found the standard pro- and anti-school subcultures, but with two major constellations attracting the counter school subculture. These are somewhat reminiscent of the Schwendingers' stradom formations. There is a 'street culture' of mainly working-class males involving soccer, cafes, pubs, dancing, hanging about with mates which all the subcultural studies reflect. There is also 'pop media culture', based on values, activities and roles sponsored by the mass media for adolescent consumption, involving music, fashion, magazines, television and movies. This is used by middle-class pupils who have no access to street culture. This group was involved with 'progressive' music, individualism (doing your own thing) found in the middle-class parent culture. Class membership is still the key determinant of social experience which has resisted any generational consciousness which the mass entertainment has emphasised. Where there is a vigorous street culture in a working-class district, the commercial aspects of youth culture have little influence.

The CCCS developed two aspects of analysis based on the differing weight given to structuralism and culturalism. Their studies of youth culture were in fact part of a broader approach to popular culture, especially in the British working class. Phil Cohen's seminal article of working-class life in East London (1972) was highly influential. It rests on the articulation of three structures; the neighbourhood, the family and the local economy. Traditionally, working-class families drew their strength from extended kinship networks set in close neighbourhood contact. This in turn was dependent on the local social ecology of the neighbourhood which gave working-class life its local culture, traditions and loyalties. The local economy tied the neighbourhood to the work place, but post-war development broke up the traditional neighbourhood through rehousing, speculative redevelopment and immigrant labour. An intense set of family relations replaced the extended family, reduced to a nuclear network 'isolated not only from outside, but undermined from within' (Cohen, p. 1972). The social space of pubs, corner shops and the street was replaced by dense, high-rise apartment blocks. As people left the area, those who remained were faced with material, cultural and economic deprivation. Youth has to resolve 'shifts' in material and economic forms which are also experienced in the 'parent culture' (the dominant working-class culture in the neighbourhood). Differentiated working-class subcultures arise to attempt to 'magically' resolve these contradictions. The solution is magical because, like Althusser's 'imaginary' aspects of ideology (they do not represent what is really happening in social relations), so subcultures can never resolve structural problems, only appear to do so or to divert from their 'true' nature. Subcultures try to retrieve the lost, socially cohesive elements in the parent culture; they attempt to relocate 'in an imaginary relation' the real relations which those in subcultures cannot transcend.

The CCCS has developed a sophisticated analysis using hegemony as a central concept which has been considered in Chapter 1. Classes are the largest social groups, and as such are defined as dominant and subordinate classes. It has drawn upon Parkin's use of the relationship between class and working consciousness which suggests that subordinate classes may be oppositional in terms of the dominant value systems, or aspirational (accept the world, but not one's place in it) or deferential (accept the world and one's place in it). The dominant value system is a normative order best considered as a series of competing meaning systems. Culture for Hall is lived practices which characterise a particular society, class or group, and its practical ideologies enable these to make sense of their conditions of existence at a particular moment in history. Using Gramsci's notion of the state as a set of social relations maintaining legitimation of a certain type of social order, Hall sees the state as actively drawing class and cultural relations into a particular set of configurations, but the consent of the subordinate classes rests always on a 'shifting equilibrium'.

Productive relations between classes are unequally ranked in terms of wealth and power, but cultures are also ranked along a scale of cultural domination and subordination. Consent has to be struggled for; ruling class hegemony is never total – it has to accommodate, oppose and negotiate but it is never homogeneous or total. Working-class culture wins for itself, or for local variations of it, 'space'. It is not that there is a lack of choices, but that the choices are shaped by a hegemony which makes alternatives and opportunities appear in a situation where the authority of ruling groups seems spontaneous, normal and natural. Proceeding from this analysis, the CCCS has followed different aspects of youth culture. Clarke (1976a) uses Lévi Strauss's concept of 'bricolage' to argue that objects and symbols become reordered and recontextualised to communicate fresh meanings. There is a transformation and rearrangement of what already exists into a new context. Youth cultural style is a text which can be read at a level beyond the verbal through the pattern of styles, argot and appearances. During the contest for hegemony, youth cultures contest for 'space' over various 'focal concerns', often in the area of what Althusser calls 'ideological state apparatuses' – social, cultural, educational and legal institutions. Subcultures, because they remain in the area of leisure, are negotiated rather than oppositional forms. They do offer a symbolic critique of the social order through a symbolic representation of social contradictions. Willis (1978) concerns himself with the relations of a homology, or fit between certain types of style, artefacts and group identity. Style indicates the subculture's boundaries to other youth, as well as projecting an image indicating a very different cultural solution to its peers. Willis indicates a homology between loose group affiliation, subjectivism, immediacy and West Coast rock, drug use and the hippy life style for hippies. Clarke (1976b, p. 179) suggests that

> the eventually produced style is more than the simple amalgam of all the separate elements – it derives its specific quality from the arrangement of all the elements together in one whole ensemble, embodying and expressing the groups self-consciousness.

There are two approaches in the CCCS analysis: one to uncover the relations of subcultures and class, the other to unravel the meanings of style and fashion; one looks at signs, the other at signifiers. Hebdige (1979) uses both bricolage and homology to

examine Rastafarian and punk subcultures. Clarke (1976b) informs
us that an object and its meaning together constitute a sign, and
these are assembled in a culture but can be put into a different
context (bricolage) and so convey a different message. Teddy boys
expropriated the elegant Savile Row, Edwardian suit of the 1950s
stockbroker, and gave it a new meaning, teenage working-class
dandyism and menace. For Hall and Jefferson (1976) homology
showed how appropriated objects were related to focal concerns,
group structure, collective self-image; these appropriated objects
were now where subcultural members could see their central values
held and reflected. This could be the intense activism, physicality,
taboo on introspection, externalisation, violence, dancing and early
rock music which Willis found in his bikers.

Hall *et al.* (1978) have also developed their approach, analysing
it in the context of the crisis in hegemony in post-war Britain.
During the 1970s there was a moral panic over black street crime
which they used to show how, when a country is beset with anxiety
about changing social conditions, this anxiety becomes displaced
and projected onto a specific target.

> A 'generalised' moral anxiety about the 'state of things'
> becomes first precipitated with respect to 'youth' which came
> to provide, for a time, a metaphor for social change and an
> index for social anxiety (Hall *et al.*, 1978, p. 235).

The central youth figure in the late 1970s was the black teenager.
This situation arose from the moral panic over mugging and street
crime which in Britain became synonymous with black youth. The
mugger, according to the media was part of 'unBritish' youth, a
product of black immigration, part of the menacing, 'dangerous
classes' gathering in the gloom of the collapse of the British Empire. The mugger occupied a central position in a generalised law
and order debate which was part of a longer crisis in legitimation
and ideology. The very real material base of this crisis can be traced
to the deteriorating economic conditions, inflation and unemployment, which occurred as capitalism in Britain began to fail after
1960. The consent given by subordinate classes to the ruling groups
came to be seriously threatened. New economic exigencies gave
way to a period of wage restraint. By the mid-1960s the state had
replaced its liberalism with a 'control culture' fanned by panics
about the student left, militant trade unions and aspects of the
'permissive society' (including gays and feminists). This gave
impetus to law and order campaigns which, combined with a right-
wing populism, particularly the racism generated by British neo-
Nazi groups, gave credence to the Thatcher government elected in
1979. A similar, but somewhat more complex, series of reasons,

combined with the divided opposition to Thatcher, returned her with a massive majority in 1983.

This broad cultural approach by the CCCS is complemented by Willis's (1978) focus on production, its relationship to youth culture, masculinity and the material and ideological production of the male workers' world. Hebdige's elliptical study, coming from a more structuralist tradition, focuses on consumption. It examines the paradoxical relationship between black and white youth culture, a feature which Bane (1982) does for America, showing the interpenetration of musical form between the races. Hebdige fuses Dada, the surreal and Genet to develop a semiotic analysis. He uses this to explore the common-sense categories of youth subcultures in order to consider style as a signifying practice, to uncover the struggle for the sign. He develops a methodology which goes beyond the obvious and indicates that style can be read as a text. Not all subcultural studies in this genre concentrated on culture. Mungham and Pearson (1976) presented a collection which drew on the National Deviancy Conference, as well as the CCCS, to explore working-class youth culture, including studies of the working-class dance hall, Paki-bashing and machine-breaking, compared historically, and the emergence of different subcultural groups. The CCCS has been subject to criticisms of romanticism (Woods, 1977); of overlooking the negative elements of working-class youth subcultures so that personal responsibility is removed in place of economic and ideological abstractions; and of too dense theoreticism (Clarke, D., 1980) with too little empirical data. Cohen has been sceptical of the resistance found, firstly methodologically:

> The conceptual tools of Marxism, structuralism and semiotics, a Left Bank pantheon of Genet, Lévi Strauss, Barthes and Althusser have all been wheeled in to aid this hunt for the hidden code. (Cohen, S., 1980, p. ix)

When uncovered this is then utilised so that:

> historical evidence is cited to prove that mass proletarian resistance to the imposition of bourgeois control did not after all die out. It lives on in certain forms of delinquency which – though more symbolic and individualistic than their progenitors – must still be read as rudimentary forms of political action.

This is presented as the

> proof that something like Paki-bashing is a 'primitive form of political and economic struggle' lies not in the kids'

understanding of what it is they are resisting ... but in the fact that the machine smashers of 1826 would *also* not have been aware of the real significance of their action.

In all fairness it must be pointed out that the CCCS, as opposed to Mungham and Pearson, in fact argue that it is in popular culture, that is working-class culture of which delinquency is a behavioural aspect sometimes, that resistance is located. Dorn and South (1982) make the point that too often, too little attention was paid to how juvenile actors themselves accounted for the phenomena. This has importance concerning the form and direction of oppositional cultures. There are highly reactionary elements in working-class life, and these may express themselves in youth culture (Brake, 1974), as with skinheads who take up racist stances to defend 'the British way of life' against immigrants.

Frith (1978; 1983) has examined the relationship between the manufactured synthetic culture of the commercial teenage market and young people as consumers. Abrams (1959) first emphasised the teenager, from all classes, as a major consumer, relative to income. However, he overlooked important age and regional differences, both in earning and spending (Jephcott, 1967; Smith, 1966). The myth of teenage affluence persisted as an extension of the general myth of working-class affluence. The youth market is, or at least was until the present recession and unemployment, a large one. Over four million dollars is spent on musical products in America, and Britain produces 160 million records, of which 90 per cent are popular music. In fact, the twelve to twenty year old age group accounts for three-quarters of popular music sales. Frith argues that rather than seeing rock music as a romanticised revolutionary symbol, we need to consider, as Murdock did, patterns of consumption and monitor how adolescents see their cultures themselves. His own research indicated sharp class differences. Middle-class children tended to be interested in the alternative values expressed in the lyrics, but working-class children selected records for the beat and to dance to. Age, he argues, is a major factor in music consumption, far more than class. For most young people music is a background, not a focus for their lives, and we cannot freeze the adolescent world into subcultures dislocated somehow from everything else. As Frith reminds us, music is a massive industry; the audience response is carefully researched and monitored by the market. Its direction can never be predicted and whilst it may project visions which could become critiques of reality, the mass media industry and ideology can control this, using the material ambitions of performers. Frith suggests that the industry has to respond to the emotions, hope and anger of its

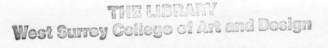

71

audience, so that there is a battle between artistic control over material and market production, with the kids' dreams, hopes and desires in the middle. It is this which gives rock its disturbing, joyous and intoxicating force. Laing (1969) makes a similar point arguing that capitalist cultural forms contain both liberating and oppressive elements. Rock music results from the music industry's attempts to develop new markets, and its youthful audience's attempts to find a medium expressing its own experience. Musicians can exploit this tension to find a creative space in which to develop their art. Marketing influences are never total, so that there is a cultural struggle in the commercial arena involving both musicians and audience, creating problems for progressive artistic form. Another problem is Hebdige's (1979) point that subcultures create new and innovatory symbols which become translated into commodities and made generally available. They become ideologically and commercially incorporated into a commodity form, and seen as less than authentic by the subcultures, which move on to relocate old symbols and signs, or invent new ones. 'Youth cultural styles may begin by issuing symbolic challenges, but they must inevitably end by establishing new sets of conventions.' (Hebdige, 1979, p. 96.) Punk clothing, for example, began by using the most rejected and contemptible clothing basis – garbage bags. But punk attire moved up market as Zandra Rhodes used it as a fashion theme, and it then became mass mail order marketing. Subcultures create styles which become living art homologous with musical form and which creates its own intoxication. Audience and interpretive artist become caught up in a dialogue of experience that must speak and make sense between them. It is thrilling and sensuous, musically, or perhaps as Mick Jagger puts it 'I know it's only rock and roll – but I like it.'

No future – a brief history of British working-class subcultures and their styles

It is important to see how British subcultures developed in the post-war period, creating a mini history of culture of their own. Most youth was not involved in these, feeling it had an investment in the system as it stood, responding deferentially or aspirationally. Membership is a difficult problem because there are always righteous, full-time members and part-time adherents, and outrageous styles reduce marginal membership. There are then varying degrees of style, from the most outré to a slight indication. Bricolage may be constructed from previous styles. But the death knell of a style is its gradual adoption by younger and younger age groups for whom it has less meaning. The author has seen pre-school Fonz lookalikes, with no conception of nostalgia for the mythical 1950s. At this age it is specific folk heroes, of course, and not styles which are appropriated.

Teddy boys – 'gonna rock it up – gonna rip it up'

The teds were the first post-war, working-class dandys in the late 1950s, a drab and dreary period in Britain after the war. They were the first rebellious folk devils, mainly from unskilled backgrounds (Fyvel, 1963), left out of the upward mobility of post-war British affluence, lacking grammar school education and unable to gain entrance into white-collar work, or apprenticeships into skilled trades. They confirmed the myth of the affluent worker to the affronted genteel middle class, appropriating as they did the Edwardian suiting of the prosperous upper classes, which they combined with a Mississippi gambler image, drape jackets, velvet collars, pipe trousers, crêpe-soled shoes and bootlace ties. Hall and Jefferson (1976, p. 48) saw them in this way;

> Thus the 'Teddy boy' expropriation of an upper-class style of dress 'covers' the gap between largely manual, unskilled near-lumpen real careers and life-chances, and the 'all-dressed-up-and-nowhere-to-go' experience of Saturday evening.

The cult heroes were Brando's menacing biker hipster, Dean the sensitive mixed-up kid, but the prime masculinity model was Memphis's Elvis Presley. The working-class Southern boy from the wrong side of town with sexy, black movements and voice spoke beyond the United States to working-class youth everywhere. The butch image of the ted set off his dandyism to protect his masculinity – elegance was no longer ladylike. Societal reaction was outrage, as shown in this article 'by a family doctor' (*Evening News*, 12.5.54):

> Teddy boys are ... all of unsound mind in the sense they are all suffering from a form of psychosis. Apart from the birch or the rope, depending on the gravity of their crimes, what they need is rehabilitation in a psychopathic institution ... because they have not the mental stamina to be individualistic they had to huddle together in gangs. Not only have these rampageous youngsters developed a degree of paranoia with an inferiority complex, but they are also inferior apart from their disease.... It is the desire to do evil, not lack of comprehension which forces them into crime.

Teds became responsible for everything, and off-duty soldiers were forbidden to wear the teddy boy suits. Melly (1972, p. 38) reminds us of the atmosphere at the time;

> The fights and cinema riots, the gang bangs and haphazard vandalism were produced by a claustrophobic situation. They were the result of a society which still held that the middle classes were entitled not only to impose moral standards on a class whose way of life was totally outside its experience; of an older generation who used the accident of war as their excuse to lay down the law on every front; of a system of education which denied any creative potential and led to dead-end jobs and obligatory conscription; of a grey, colourless, shabby world where good boys played ping-pong.

The importation of rock and roll from America, 'a contemporary incitement to mindless fucking and arbitrary vandalism: screw and smash music' (Melly, 1972, p. 36) led to riots in cinemas and dance halls. In fact popular music was transformed internationally by Bill Haley in 1953, then by Presley, Little Richard, Muddy Waters and Chuck Berry. By 1957 record sales reached a peak not seen again until the Beatles in 1963.

Mods – 'the kids are all right'

Two attitudes to working-class life prevail among youth, the heavy machismo celebration of often conservative working-class values, and the cool distance of sophistication. As the teds had done, mods developed in East London, but with an attempt to abstract themselves from their ascribed class location with a neat, hip image. Originally called 'modernists' (a bebop phrase) they reflected the elegant dandyism found among young blacks in America. Tough, but reflecting the lower white-collar, upwardly mobile groups, their appearance was a polar opposite to their enemies, the class-bound, butch rockers. Both groups appeared in the early 1960s. The two images, as Nuttall (1969, p. 333) states, are that ' "Mod" meant effeminate, stuck up, emulating the middle classes, aspiring to be competitive, snobbish, phony, "Rocker" meant hopelessly naive, loutish, scruffy.'

The mods were suspect because they were too elegant, their dances too elaborate, their drug use – pills – too laid back. They were the pioneers of consumerism, inspiring Mary Quant and Carnaby Street. Their music was ska, West Indian popular music, although commercial spin-offs were the Who, and Rod (then the Mod) Stewart and the Faces. They were stratified into the art school, high camp version who reappeared in glamrock and new wave, wearing make-up and carrying purses; mainstream mods with suits, neat, narrow trousers and pointed shoes, accompanied by short-haired, dead-pan elegant girls; and scooter boys with their Italian motor scooters (a working-class sports car) covered in accessories and anoraks and wide jeans. Finally, there were the hard mods, aggressively working-class in dress – jeans, industrial work boots – who developed into skinheads. Speed was a theme, as a drug, as a life style, and Jamaica too, with ska, dark shades and stingy brim hats found among the West Indian 'rude boys'. Clubs were a glamorous dream world (eventually becoming discos) where elegance transcended the dull neatness prescribed by family, school and work. Interestingly in this subculture, girls moved around in their own right, either in pairs or groups.

Rockers – 'leader of the pack'

Completely opposite to their cultural enemies, rockers are bikers or greasers. With their black leather jackets, studs, boots and jeans, they were violent, studiedly working class, butch – 'wild ones' – anti-domestic and anti-authority. Barker and Little (1964) found rockers to be low paid, unskilled manual labourers, whilst mods were semi-skilled, white collar workers. The rockers were either free spirited 'easy riders' or 'greasers' less involved with the cult of the motor bike. They reappeared at different times, and Willis (1978) found a homology between rockers' masculinism, rejection of the deferred gratification of middle-class life, dancing, the music of Elvis, Gene Vincent and Eddie Cochran seen as having a nostalgic unchaining violence and sexuality, and the motor bike, itself a symbol of freedom, mastery and intimidation. They were a kind of motorised cowboy outlaw (as with the Hells Angels), loners and outsiders linked by the camaraderie of the bike. Their sexism showed in a contempt for the mods (effeminate) or women, the traditional ties of responsibility and respectability.

Skinheads – 'violence on the terraces'

Aggressively working-class puritans in big industrial boots, jeans rolled up high to reveal them, hair cut to the skull, braces and a violence and racism earned for them the title 'bovver boys', 'boot-boys' on the look out for 'aggro' (aggravation). Stylistically they have roots in the hard mods, forming local gangs called after a local leader or an area. Ardent football fans, they were involved in

75

violence on the terraces against rival supporters. They espoused traditional conservative values, hard work, patriotism, defence of local territory, which led to attacks on hippies, gays and minorities. They became a metaphor for racism, admittedly expressed by them, but which was endemic in British immigration policy and politics (see Brake, 1974). 'Puritans in boots', they opposed hippy liberalism, subjectivity and disdain for work, attempting to 'magically recover the traditional working-class community' (Clarke, 1976a). By the end of the 1960s, they were, due to their high social visibility, a major folk devil. Their music was West Indian, ska and bluebeat followed by reggae until it became too involved with black pride. Rastafarianism excluded them from reggae, as black pride kept them out of West Indian clubs. They were to reappear again in the later 1970s and 1980s. Their aggressive racism made them targets for neo-Nazi recruitment by the National Front and the British Movement. Their apolitical attitudes prevented them from being a real threat. By the 1980s they were followers of 'oi' music, with bands such as the '4 skins' and, with other groups, became involved in some of the 1981 riots.

so they are no threat to society?

↳ such as southall riots!

Glamrock and glitter

As the old dance halls were replaced by the new provincial city leisure centres and discotheques, these combined with the commercialisation of football to signal the embourgeoisement of leisure (Taylor and Wall, 1976), from which emerged glamrock. Hippy sartorial elegance and skinhead hardness were combined. The musical forms were Lou Reed, Bowie (Iggy Pop phase), Bolan from an earlier period, and Gary Glitter who appealed to the younger age groups. Reminiscent of mods in their extravagant clothes, high heels and make up (often offset with tattoos), hard-working lads masculinised their decadent image composed of a collage of Berlin Thirties and New York gay. It was a butch version of camp rock offerings. 'Bowie's meta-message was escape – from class, from sex, from personality, from obvious commitment – into a fantasy past ... or a science fiction future.' (Hebdige, 1979, p. 61.)

Punks – 'white riot'

Glamrock gave way swiftly to punk, which became popular in Britain in 1976, after somewhat unsuccessful promotion by the musical trade papers several months earlier. It has been defined (*Melody Maker*, 28.5.77) as the sound of less musically competent but more rebellious bands, whilst New Wave was seen as its more sophisticated version, the same bands later on in their careers as it were. Punk bands were amateurs, using verve and rawness common to British rock, whilst the only similar category in the United States were the garage bands of California, most American musicians being more technically competent and musically educated than their British counterparts. Musical form can be traced to John Cage, New York Dolls and Lou Reed, the latter also providing the style. Their imagery, camp and outrageous appearance was drawn from Warhol's factory, performance and conceptual art forms. Lurex, old school uniforms, plastic garbage bags, safety pins, bondage and sexual fetishism were developed into a self-mocking, shocking image. Hair was shaved close to the head, dyed outrageous colours, then later, spiked up into cockatoo plumes of startling design, individual to each person. Bands developed characters as stage personae, as Bowie had with Iggy Pop, offering escape from one's ascribed personality, status and role. In the early days of punk, integrity to the movement was measured by an ability to create one's own costume and therefore persona. This resisted commercial influence, and divided the righteous and the leisure punks. Anti-romanticism showed in the musicians' names – Poly Styrene, Johnny Rotten, Sid Vicious, and in such songs as 'Belsen was a gas', and 'If you don't want to fuck me – fuck off'.

Marsh (1977) saw the punk movement as 'dole queue rock', drawn from the ranks of unemployed youth who despised superstars, complex electronic music, musical technical virtuosity and high prices for concerts, all of which emphasised the gaps between commercial musicians and unemployed fans. There was also a reaction to hippy romanticism, lack of structure and middle-class status. Frith (1983) argues for the first post-war, working-class bohemianism. Punk, however, like the mods, contained several strata. There was a distinction between middle-class, art-school influenced punks, and working-class, hard punks. At one end the art school students, with their Mohican haircuts, indicated their separation from non-bohemian careers, aligning themselves with cultural rebels and the new outré consumerism, whilst working-class punks underlined their refusal to conform, to follow ill-paid, dead-end jobs by making sure they would not be employed. At first they despised work of a routine nature, but as the recession increased, they could not find even general labouring work. In different ways both sought to shock the bourgeoisie: the middle class by creating a fantasy world which excluded outsiders; the working class by celebrating their unemployability. Gradually, punks tended to align themselves with the Rock against Racism movement, and the Anti-Nazi League. As such they became the enemies of the skinheads, following traditional class lines found in the differing strata of education.

Punk celebrated chaos, linked to the surreal and to situationism, making public the perverse elements of sexuality such as bondage or fetishism, and emphasising yet mocking it. Dances were the robot, the pogo and the pose, presenting collages of frozen automata, which re-emerged in break dancing. Fanzines were deliberately anti-professional, rejecting the expensive glossy magazines, roneod and scruffily produced. Hebdige finds a distinct homology (1979, p. 114)

> between trashy, cut-up clothes and spiky hair, the pogo and amphetamines, the spitting, the vomiting, the format of the fanzines, the insurrectionary poses and the 'soulless' frantically driven music. The punks wore clothes which were the sartorial equivalent of swear words, and they swore as they dressed – with calculated effect, lacing obscenities into record notes and publicity releases, interviews and love songs. Clothed in chaos, they produced Noise in the calmly orchestrated Crisis of everyday life in the late 1970s.

Punk rock originated in New York, connecting with the underground cinema, the cult of the street, the literary avant garde with artistes such as Patti Smith and Richard Hell. It took off in Britain in 1977 after Malcolm McLaren (once manager of the New York Dolls) put together the Sex Pistols. They became notorious after swearing during a live television interview, their songs were banned and, interestingly, their hit 'God save the Queen' went to the top of charts having never been played on the British airwaves. They denied any political context for their work, but took a nihilistic stance (popular among punks before their anti-racist stance), describing themselves as being anti-social and 'into chaos'. Punks managed to upset everyone, rebuked by left-wing intellectuals for an insufficient political stance, and abused by right-wing groups disappointed by their sporting of the swastika without espousing its Nazism. The swastika was another piece of bricolage, used to enrage those who would encompass them, a symbol of contempt worn cosmetically, denuded of meaning. It has also been worn by bikers and surfers (Irwin, 1973), and for punks it was removed from its Nazi setting and replaced as shock-provoking jewellery.

In some ways the political disappointment in punk is puzzling. A cultural rebellion by professional artists and their followers is not political, and artists are always rebellious – anarchic rather than committed, disciplined politicos. They are libertarian not Leninist, often far out, seldom right on. Punk did occur during a period

of increasing youth unemployment, and did attack the capital intensive form of music production, reintroducing social comment
and political criticism into music. The affiliation with the Rock
against Racism concerts attracted thousands to the free concerts
(usually for the music, but politics should entertain). Songs were
written about being out of work, the West Indian Carnival in
London, racism, the monarchy and general anarchy. Protest returned, not just in punk, but in white reggae as with UB 40. These
statements may have some contact with what young people experience, but it is easy to be cynical about lyrics in rock music –
skinheads would join Tom Robinson in 'Glad to be gay' for example. Certainly, public dissent in a subcultural setting must not
be confused with political change, but as Frith (1981) reminds us,
the Pink Floyd's 'We don't need no education' gave kids a powerful anti-school chant. A simple slogan wedded to music can speak
of common anger and shared despair. Punk has both committed
and uncommitted music, and quite often there are progressive and
reactionary elements in the same song. Laing (1978) correctly
showed that the important aspect of punk is what Walter Benjamin
called 'shock effect', as were the hippies. Punk offered a parody,
a taunting portrayal of popular culture, an attack on uncritical
consumption of mass-produced artefacts and style. It was
healthily cynical about social democracy and its benefits during a
recession.

The tight lines and long tradition of the British class system
means that youth cultures are more closely linked to them. In the
United States, youth culture has focused on delinquency, and on
the hippy culture. Matza's traditions of delinquency, radicalism
and bohemianism probably fit better, although a close analysis
does reveal class connections, especially with black and Latin cultures. The situation is complicated by the wide geographical spread,
immigrant history and ethnic minorities. Violence and delinquency
have been examined separately from class and neighbourhood.
There are a vast set of youth cultural forms; surfers, greasers, frats,
hitters, Latin low riders with their special low-seated cars driving
slowly through town, punks and dupers. The campus culture was
expressed through clubs and institutions of the universities and
colleges until the 1960s. This was extended in a mini form in the
junior and senior high schools. Only in the 1960s when civil rights,
the draft, the university involvement in state research all became
an issue which students had to relate to did they look outside
of the campus. Cultures vary from the 'aggies' (agricultural college educated) found in rural 'redneck' groups to the self-conscious, quasi-manufactured 'valley girls' themselves stratified with
punks, mainstream and so forth. We need now to pass from the

delinquent informed subcultures to ethnic and campus and bohemian subcultures.

The 'youth riots' of 1981

The summer of 1981 saw a series of youth riots which has been well documented (Brake, 1984; Cowell *et al.*, 1983; Kettle and Hodges, 1982; Taylor, 1982; Scarman, 1981). Non-white communities saw these riots as insurrections against a state which had severely curtailed non-white immigration, practised institutionalised racism in its legislation and who encouraged harassment by an unsympathetic police force, all exacerbated by increasing unemployment. Relations between Afro-Caribbean and Asian communities had broken down into mutual hostility and mistrust over the years. Racist attacks had become common on housing estates and in the streets, and the visible presence of racist neo-Nazis during the 1978 general elections had caused considerable anxiety and fear.

The uprisings involved both black and white youth, and some of them occurred in all-white neighbourhoods. The forerunner occurred in Bristol, a seaport with a large West Indian population, containing St Pauls, a multi-racial ghetto with shebeens (illegal drinking clubs), gambling, prostitution, drugs and a teeming social life typical of such an area (Pryce, 1979). The increasing unemployment, which affected black youth in particular, led to a strain on the West Indian family; young people rejected the dead-end work open to them and, with that, they rejected their parents' sense of respectability. Zealous implementation of local health regulations closed social centres for black youth, such as local cafes, leaving only one open in St Pauls. This was raided in 1980, leading to a situation where the police were barricaded in the cafe by black youth. Reinforcements were paraded in a show of strength, and the ensuing riot forced them to retreat, leaving the district a no-go area for several hours. In the spring of the following year, London's Brixton exploded after 'Swamp 81', a high density search operation, was carried out without consulting local community leaders. This was seen as a police attack on a black area. The London police have a long history of confrontations with young black people. Several cafes and youth clubs, gathering places for young blacks, had been raided in 1971, 1972, 1974 and 1979 and became *causes célèbres*. Nevertheless, the accused were eventually cleared. The annual Notting Hill Carnival, a major West Indian street celebration in London had been the scene of several confrontations between the police and black youth. The killing of a young white anti-racist teacher, during a demonstration against racism, was believed popularly to be the responsibility of the Special Patrol Group, an elite police corps notorious for its public order confrontation tactics. In the January prior to the riots, a house had been burned down in South-East London and thirteen teenagers had been killed during a birthday party. Despite evidence that it may have been a racist attack, and that a fire bomb may have been thrown, the case was never solved. The black and brown communities were of the opinion that the authorities were little concerned with assaults on black people, and Asians found themselves questioned about their passports when they called the police. The July of 1981 saw an uprising in the Asian district of Southall (it should be noted that Britain has no non-white areas; the highest density black population is 52 per cent). The area had been leafleted by a Nazi group, and when young skinheads (some of them plainly young neo-Nazi members) attended a concert organised in the Asian area, there was a fight and a riot. Two evenings later, young black and white people barricaded parts of Liverpool against the police, resulting in the use of CS gas and rubber bullets for the first time outside Northern Ireland. A young crippled man was killed by a police jeep during this riot, which was followed by others throughout Britain.

The background to these uprisings is the racist implications of legislation by both Labour and Conservative governments concerning immigration and racial integration, the impact of race in housing, work and education, poor police community relations and the development of a politically aware youth culture among non-whites. The protection of the basic right of free speech of the neo-Nazis meant that black people saw their avowed enemies protected in a way they had never been themselves. The visible appearance of black youth in unemployment, and hence on the streets, makes it especially subject to police surveillance. Black youth has been successfully criminalised in the eyes of the public, a feature assisted by the racist propaganda of the National Front and British Movement groups. Street crime is of course carried out by both black and white youth, but black muggers are highly publicised. White youth sees black youth as causal in its own unemployment, especially in racially mixed areas. Struggles occur over public space between the authorities and youth; public order becomes an important symbol, and maintaining surveillance over youth is a metaphor for maintaining surveillance over the unemployed. The British state plainly sees black youth as its most potentially explosive population. Unemployment now means that the problem for British working-class youth is growing up working class without work. The situation has worsened, for in Britain the state has on

81

the one hand decided to offer all unemployed school leavers a year's 'work experience' whilst at the same time looking for reasons to reduce welfare benefits to youth living at home. This increases the financial burden of whole families who are living on unemployment and welfare benefits, and increases the dependency of young people unemployed through no reason of their own.

Chapter 4

The trippers and the trashers – bohemian and radical traditions of youth

The cultural rebels – bohemian and middle-class delinquency

> They were ... well Beautiful People ... not 'students', 'clerks',
> 'salesgirls', 'executive trainees' – Christ, don't give me your
> occupation-game labels! We are the Beautiful People,
> ascendant from your robot junk-yard ...
> (T. Wolfe, The Electric Cool-Aid Acid Test)

The concept of 'youth culture' has been applied popularly to bohemian subcultures. Although they have been conceptualised as being outside class, they can be linked to middle-class intelligentsia in origin. Middle-class subcultures can be differentiated from working-class ones both in their formation and their organisation. Working-class youth subcultures are clearly part-time, temporary episodes of short duration, neighbourhood-based with local peer group affiliations. As we have seen, the neighbourhood is an important element in the transmission and interpretation of working-class youth cultures. Working-class youth tends to be involved in leisure activities which mediate the control of adult authority. Middle-class subcultures tend to be more diffuse, more self-conscious, particularly of international aspects. Obviously they are nationally shaped, but there is a wider sphere of influence as, for example, student cultures, which may reflect political and cultural ideas articulated into a more distinct style and form. They have a longer influence over their members' life styles, and have a distinct relation to the values of dominant classes, although these may be 'stretched'. (For example, 'doing your own thing' could be seen as a hippy 'stretched value' of the middle-class evaluation of individualism and self-growth.) Explorations may also be made of alternative adaptations of middle-class forms of dominant institutions, for example, 'alternative' life styles, communal child care, 'free' schools, fringe medicine, self-awareness groups and so forth. Often these involve a fusion of the distinctions between work and leisure – 'work and play' – and a relationship to material production involving a connection to surplus where welfare provision, or the use of rejected consumer goods, provides a modest minimal standard of living. A central economic element had been the provision of higher education grants and loans; indeed, the very notion of 'dropping out' presupposes a location in the class structure from which to drop (and to return), as opposed to the harsh reality of working-class life, which is instead a flight from the 'never had'. The discipline of industrial life acts as a great socialiser. After a weekend of 'Saturday Night Fever' the young worker has to face Monday morning at work. Leisure and work remain firmly separated, work providing the means to enjoy leisure, and play, which is involving enough to detract from the boredom of work, being a luxurious element too expensive for young industrial workers.

The diffuseness and articulation of middle-class cultures means that when they are oppositional they tend to be more overtly political and ideological in their critique of work. They have been assisted in this by the development of the underground press which, during the 1960s, presented a political and cultural criticism of the establishment and which also spread the notion of an organised and coherent counterculture.

One problem which arises in distinguishing working-class and middle-class youth cultures is membership. The marginality of membership is a problem, and whilst youth subcultures tend to follow class traditions, individual members may be exceptions. Buff (1970) found that in Chicago his working-class boys tended to become 'greasers', but some took up hippy subcultures. This means that there may be a considerable working-class element in apparently middle-class subcultures, such as student or 'freak' subcultures, usually known as 'street people' or young vagrants. They are subject to distinct stratification and prejudice, mainly because of their lack of income and predatory ways. Brake (1977) found a hard core of working-class 'drifters' in his hippy sample, rejected by the underground for many of the reasons for which wider society had rejected them: lack of skills, capital, education and prospects, combined with quasi-criminal interpretations about 'liberating' property and 'free love'. Punks also have both working-class and middle-class groups which sometimes overlap. Class is also complicated by age. Monod's (1967) Parisian working-class youths adopted a 'snob' style (based on Rolling Stones imagery) which marked them off from the local gay community (who had a similar image) and from the younger 'voyou' boys with their greaser style.

The emergence of youth counterculture in the United States

A complication in delinquency studies is the degree to which it can be found in the middle class. Its presence there has been attributed to several causes – unhappy, broken homes, lack of parental concern and discipline (Nye, 1956), academic failure and absent fathers (Greely and Casey, 1963), downward mobility (Pine, 1965), and family conflict (Herskovitz, Levene and Spivak, 1959). Most studies concentrate on minor offences (Vaz, 1967a) and favour psychological explanations. They tend to overlook subcultural attachment, although England (1967) does suggest that adolescents do see themselves as a collectivity with similar interests, and therefore 'youth culture' does have an effect on middle-class delinquency. Youth culture has been used uncritically in post-war American literature, as has been suggested earlier, favouring a generational rather than a class membership. The model used is the Parsonian one, seeing youth culture as a separate cultural system shared by the young. A 'more or less specifically irresponsible' youth culture exists in conflict with the adult world's sense of responsibility, conformity and productive work. It emphasises hedonism, and 'its recalcitrance to the presence of adult expectations and discipline'. Smith (1962) notes a generational conflict in America, but mainly over sexual matters, although he takes note of subcultural features such as dress, language, appearance, strong peer loyalty and youth's own forms of conformity. He, and also Hollingshead (1949), note class differences in youth culture. Barnard (1961), in a monograph produced as youth once again became enough of a social problem to come to academic attention, stresses class as pervading all parts of teenage culture, including its political views. She notes also its use to the adult economy due to its consumption, a point made also by Friedenberg (1966, p. 102):

> Only as a customer . . . are adolescents favourably received. Otherwise they are treated as a problem, and potentially as a threatening one. . . . Adults attribute to them a capacity for violence and lust, in this respect teenagers serve the rest of us as the occasion both for wish fulfilment and for self-fulfilling prophecy.

On the whole, however, youth culture was explained in terms of a generation gap, rather than conflicts and divisions due to class. This approach was reflected as we have noted, in Coleman's (1961) discovery of the student and high school cultures favouring sociability, glamour, social status and athleticism, rather than academic prowess. Polk and Halferty (1966) argued that where a lowering of the commitment to success was present, there was a move towards youth culture, with an emphasis on anti-achievement and delinquent behaviour, reflecting middle-class and working-class youth cultures respectively. Berger (1963b) notes that Coleman's youth culture closely reflects American values in the adult world. Youth culture, he reminds us, has often not much to do with youth; instead 'What we are in the habit of calling youth culture is a creature of some young and some not so young persons' (Berger, 1963b, p. 394). Instead the type of behaviour witnessed in youth culture is also found in bohemian cultures, certain working-class occupations, rather than in the younger *per se*. The youthful, rather than the young, create youth culture. Berger challenges the overgeneralisations of explanations of youth culture. Its roots are to be found outside either the delinquent subculture or the oppositional nature of some universalistic, general youth culture.

Youth culture was cited for what it was contrary to, rather than analysed as to what it was. Matza (1961) suggests that deviant patterns of adolescent behaviour are in fact unconventional versions of conventional traditions. Teenage culture may, in fact, prevent individual adolescents from adopting deviant behaviour patterns. There are three subterranean traditions of youth (Matza, 1962) springing from the mainstream of rebellion which has created a special appeal to youth, a rebelliousness which is frequently stigmatised as immaturity and irresponsibility. These traditions are:

1 Delinquency which, whilst not denouncing property
   arrangements, violates them. It rejects methodism and routine,
   especially within the school system.
2 Bohemianism, whilst actually indifferent to property, attacks
   puritanistic and mechanised bureaucratic society.
3 Radicalism which, by focusing on economic and political
   exploitation, has a less generalised cultural attack,
   concentrating on specific areas of economic exploitation.

These traditions remain true of youth cultural analysis today, and form much of the body of analysis in this book. The delinquent tradition has already been discussed, but the consideration of middle-class youth cultures can be subdivided into political and bohemian formations of rebellion. Both groups may overtly use deviancy as a weapon against the prevailing hegemony and dominant class formations. Certainly the late 1960s saw interesting fusions of the radical and bohemian traditions which used forms of collective anarchy and libertarianism to develop new dimensions of consciousness. There developed the understanding that for the left, there had to be a cultural revolution as well as a fundamental material redistribution of resources. Certainly the particular moment in history (the late 1960s) generated a spill-over into extra parliamentary and extra trade union struggle involving issues of housing, community politics, feminism (Brook and Finn, 1977; Mayo, 1977; Wilson, 1977) and gay rights.

The beat generation

> They danced down the streets like dingledoodies, and I
> shambled after as I've been doing all my life after people
> who interest me, because the only people for me are the
> mad ones ...
>
> (Kerouac, 1959, p.9)

In post-war Paris, there developed on the Left Bank, traditionally a student area, a youthful subculture of bohemian intelligentsia, of 'existentialists'. Existentialism has a long and honourable tradition in European philosophy, but the work of Sartre and de Beauvoir, whose followers congregated in student cafes, the Cafe aux Deux Magots, on the Boulevard St Michel, attracted a youthful subculture. As is common with bohemian subcultures, there was an intellectual-artistic nucleus which was the centre of a far larger expressive social movement. It generated followers of a life style where existential values of the futility of action, interspersed with a nihilism about social change, were used to excuse any action. Sartre's left-wing political activities were largely ignored by the subculture which focused on individual action, in a way reminiscent of upper-class youth in the novels of Turgenev and Dostoyevsky. Expatriates during the 1950s spread this life style, with its attendant uniform of blue jeans and plaid shirts, to other parts of Europe and North America (known in America as 'boheys'). The movement reflected the concern in the avant garde at the time with the subjective and the interpersonal, aided by the growth of an interest in psychoanalysis and surrealism. It was to reappear in libertarian movements such as the Situationists International with their roots in Dada and the Absurd. Hofstadter (1955) argues that during the 1920s 'bohemianism triumphed over radicalism' among young people, especially in the middle class, and the depression of the 1930s produced a 'lost generation', unemployed, drifting through a world where effort and reward had little relationship to each other (David, 1936). The 1940s were dominated by the Second World War, but the 1950s saw the growth of Riesman's 'found generation, polite, conforming, suburban, "other directed" people lost in the "lonely crowd"' (Riesman, 1951). Individualism was a major theme,

87

the solution to alienation sought in psychoanalysis. However, against this conventional background, existentialism attracted interests in a bohemia which took note of Eastern mysticism, jazz, poetry, drugs and literature. This area has been well documented (Powell, 1962; Krim, 1960; Kerouac, 1959; Feldman and Gartenburg, 1959) becoming known as the beat generation.

Beat, according to Holmes (1960), was a condition 'emptied out ... a state of mind from which all unessentials had been stripped, leaving it receptive to everything around it'. The beat life was a search for new visions and realities composed of a refusal to be committed, to be drifters and vagrants both symbolically and geographically. When accidentally thrown into contact with women, they treated them with a romanticised irresponsibility, highly sexist in its attitude. They possessed a romantic, anarchic vision, their politics anti-Establishment rather than focused on a new order. Their mysticism extended to experimenting with drugs, especially early hallucinogens, and to sexuality. Withdrawn from the straight world, dropped out of conventional society, they dressed as workers, intermingled with black people, using ghetto jive argot, and involved themselves in blues and folk music. They remained cool to the world, but took a definite stance against racism, as part of their hatred of conventional America. Homosexuality was tolerated; there were attempts to cross class lines, but the beat remained in the background of social movements. Poetry and jazz were fused. Ginsburg's famous beat poem, *Howl* (1956) comments,

> I saw the best minds of my generation destroyed by madness,
> Starving, hysterical, naked,
> Dragging themselves through the negro streets at dawn,
> Looking for an angry fix.

Beats replaced the artistic, left-wing, Greenwich Village bohemia with a disaffiliated, non-political protest movement. Bohemian values such as spontaneity, expressivity, creativity which were used in art, were used to develop life styles. The beat separated from the 'square' – the grey flannel mind in the grey flannel suit. The beat writers celebrated the hipster as folk hero. The hipster, working class, often black, was a cool cat, living on his wits. He was a violent extension of the beat, stripped state of mind, who dissociated from his feelings, and who felt (Powell, 1962, p. 367) that 'violence jolts to jar him out of his lethargy'. There were two models in beat life, the beatnik and the hipster. Both detested the straight world, yet each saw elements of the square in each other. Beats saw hipsters obsessed by expensive commodities, caught up in consumption and status, and hipsters saw beats as failed middle-class retreatists. Class separated them in the classic dilemma

Quote drug dealer

88

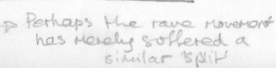
Perhaps the rave movement has merely suffered a similar split

of the middle-class intellectual trying to connect with the working-class hipster. The cultural ambience of the beat world differed empirically from its sociological elements. Polsky (1971), in his empirical study, suggests that beats successfully avoided interaction with squares. Two-thirds of his sample were middle class, but were highly antagonistic to middle-class life and careers. Like many bohemians, they were radical in their criticisms of society but naive concerning the role of the state in their analysis. They voluntarily espoused poverty, disaffiliation from family ties, careers and prospects in any conventional sense, withdrawing from a society they detested. Being basically present-oriented, as befits existentialists, they sought individual rather than collective solutions. They lived in a bohemian ghetto, were involved in religion, drugs and existential insecurity, and their subcultural focal concerns could be said to be:

withdrawal – from all but the barest minimum contact necessary for survival with the square;

disaffiliation – from traditional family, social and career structures; and

existential solutions – to what were conceptualised as basically existential problems

The beats replaced the suburban career and family with dope use, casual work and sex (including homosexuality), dropping out of conventional occupations into a *demi-monde* of blacks, working people and fellow outsiders. Ehrenreich (1983) sees the beat world as one of male bonding, where women only exist as the shackles of an unsought responsibility. Beats were attracted by the virility of working-class life, saw everything middle class as feminine, except money and power. Ehrenreich argues that working-class life for beats was 'an unwanted reminder of the invisible classes outside, and the repressed masculine self within'. She illustrates how beat life became accommodated by the Playboy philosophy and also by the anti-nuclear family and anti-responsibility in relationships. Hefner disclaimed the scruffy, bohemian image of the beats, renaming his philosophy the ethics of the 'up-beats'.

Despite this attempt at accommodation of and upmarketing of bohemia, the beats definitely presented a criticism of square life and mounted an attack on the Protestant ethic. They moved across America in the early 1960s from the centres in Venice West, California and Greenwich Village, New York, to North Beach, California and the Lower East Side of Manhattan. Finally driven away by the chic gentrification of bohemian districts, they retreated in California to the Haight Ashbury district of San Francisco, which in turn was to become the predominant hippy epicentre, the new cradle of bohemianism.

Hippies, freaks and heads – the counterculture

The term 'hippy' obviously covers a vast array of bohemian and student subcultures, and as with the beats there is a hard core of artistic-literary intelligentsia, also an aristocracy of rock musicians, and a vast following of life style rebels. Hippies have been conceptualised in the literature as educational drop outs, seeking an escape from the technocratic, materialist society of modern industrialism, seeking a romantic revival of a pastoral innocence. Their life style, especially their use of drugs and their sexual experimentation, has been discussed in great detail (Berger, 1967; Davis, 1967; Willis, 1978; Young 1973). In the American literature hippies have been explained as a generational unit, who produced a counterculture against technocracy, and challenged traditional concepts of career, education and morality. Because age cohorts are seen as starting their life courses at unique points in time, they share a historical base, which can influence generational consciousness. It is argued that because of important changes in the economic and social institutions of America, the vision and analysis of that society was distinctly different for middle-class youth by the 1960s from that of their parents. The analysis favoured is that of Mannheim (1952), who narrows age cohorts to generational units, that is, actively involved members of an age group who influence social change. Laufer and Bengston (1974, p. 186) delineate this further:

> We would argue that generational analysis, as distinct from cohort lineage, or maturational analysis, is concerned with age groups as agents of social change, with their intellectual and organizational alternatives to existing world views, values and life styles; with the sources of opposition within the existing society, and with the developing relationship between these agents of social change and others within their age strata.

A generationally based movement for social change occurs when the traditional criteria for social and economic patterns of leadership change. Changes in life style and values arise in response, occurring mainly in the upper-middle and middle-class groups, just because subordination is largely a feature of age in these groups. Laufer and Bengston (1974, p. 188) argue the hypothesis that, 'The more intense the experience of subordination (racism, sexism, class exploitation, ethnic discrimination), the greater the continuity of experience across age boundaries.'

∴ Clamp-down on youth through legislation could mean the final a complete amalgamation of youth as a whole.

The exclusion in the here and now of this age group from power, and its self-conscious development of the relation of self and society in higher education (Keniston, 1972) develops an oppositional consciousness. Their distrust of the political establishment and their critical awareness of inequality and affluence led to a generational identification as a process for social change. There is a concern for the quality of life, and a rejection of the 'system', although opposition was often oversimplified to the 'people' versus the 'pigs'. Analysis was replaced by slogans, which accepted the subjectivity of age consciousness, but overlooked the objective elements of class and its contradictions. The state was totally absent as a unit of analysis at any sophisticated level. Youth's response was to explore alternatives to the received traditions of career, life style and occupationally linked identity. This disaffiliation took different forms, for some militant and political, for others mystical and religious. Wieder and Zimmerman (1974) found in their research on hippy communities that generational units exist which showed intense hostility to, and alienation from conventional American values. Their freak sample showed distinctly oppositional values to the Protestant ethic, favouring immediacy, spontaneity, hedonism, rejecting property because it ascribed status, and having no qualms about welfare or 'pan handling'. They sought an identity outside occupational role or family, which I have suggested is a dominant feature of youth cultures. Youth in itself seemed to be a conscious political role for them (Abbie Hoffman warned them to trust no one over thirty). This self-consciousness of youth is found in Reich (1970) in *The Greening of America*. For him, the dominant contemporary social force is technology, and the corporate state usurps all values. He suggests that Consciousness I, the traditional values of rugged individualism and self-help found among the farmers, small businessmen and workers of the nineteenth century, were replaced by the values of organisational society or Consciousness II. The 'contradictions, failures and exigencies of the Corporate State' generated Consciousness III which, not unlike Marcuse's new sensibility, is non-violent, non-judgemental and honest, and which, according to Reich (1970, p. 1), 'has originated with the individual and with culture and if it succeeds it will change the political structure only as its final act'.

Political change, then, starts not with materialism but with idealism, with the world of values and ideas. Consciousness III is against uncontrolled technology, the destruction of the environment, the decline of liberty, pointlessness of work, absence of community and the loss of self, and it will counteract these negations. Roszak (1970), also influential at the time, examined youthful opposition to technocracy, which he sees as based on the work of Marcuse,

Norman O. Brown, Ginsberg, Watts, Leary and Goodman. Visionary experience has been subordinated in our culture, and the counterculture will present a new vision of how to live. Again the emphasis on idealism with its ignoring of political economy and the state are at variance with more Marxist explanations. Flacks (1971, p. 129) argues that:

> The culture that is needed to mesh with our state of technological development is one that is incompatible with capitalism. The culture that is struggling to be born stresses cooperation over competition, expression over success, communalism over individualism, being over doing, making art over making money and autonomy over obedience.

These values were made possible by a technology which eliminated much routinised work, allowing the development of a meaningful life, but which was blocked by corporate capitalism which reinforces the mode and social relations of production, in turn generating class exploitation and material inequality. Meaningful and creative work experience remain the privilege of the few, and the hippies mistakenly thought it the right of all, possible by changing attitudes. Hall (1969) argues that the hippies constituted a distinct grouping at a particular historical 'moment', providing a sketch of future possibilities in terms of post-revolutionary society.

Hippies have contributed style – they lived their disaffiliation; for them their culture was a lived process, adding new scripts to the dramaturgy of revolutionary movements. They developed a new set of countervalues; a new kind of subjectivity was prefigured. They gave shape to the non-economic aspect of political life, representing the expressivist rather than activist pole, stressing the personal, the private and psychological – that is, subjectivity in politics. This is their major contribution, and also the roots of their erosion. Even within the politics of the personal, they had neglected the role of women, seeing them rather as earth mothers than equal comrades. They were to be overpassed and depleted by their own contradictions. Their ignoring of the state and class was to destroy them economically as the recession increased, and their anarchic consciousness was to be supplanted by feminism which took note of their irresponsibility to women, again relegated to traditional nurturing and domestic roles. Those unable to develop and take note of feminist criticism were to be relegated to the cultural dustbins of history.

The structure of the counterculture

Hippies gave bohemianism a new, immediate expressivity. They represented a counterculture, rather than a politically active movement (Westhues, 1972). Distler (1970) sees this as a flight from a patristic, instrumental culture to a matristic, expressive one, resulting in a cultural gap. Consequently, hippy values were rationally and emotionally outside the comprehension of most parents, which is a theme found in most commentaries on the hippy scene. A major variable which aroused great indignation was the use of drugs, especially hallucinogenics such as LSD. Davis (1967) argued that the lessening importance of academic qualifications in contemporary society developed a movement best conceptualised as a social experiment in life styles. He also saw (Davis and Munoz, 1968) drug use as a natural extension of middle-class values, such as individualism, symbolising an attack on normal forms of consciousness, and a disregard for normal society and its values. The argument is interestingly developed to differentiate the various meanings that drug use has. LSD is seen as a 'negotiated' version of the basic values of self-exploration and self-improvement found in middle-class life. Young (1971, p. 157) also stressed the social meaning of drug use:

> The bohemian seeks his identity through the pursuit of
> subterranean values. He is intent on creating a culture which is
> short term, hedonistic, spontaneous, expressive, exciting and
> unalienated. Hallucinogen drugs facilitate such aims admirably.

I have argued elsewhere (Brake, 1977), in an empirical study of the hippy culture in Britain, that it was a relatively well-organised subculture, peopled mainly by students and ex-students, who had suffered a dissociation from the goals of higher education. Membership was very important symbolically to its members. Student grants or welfare permitted them a period away from home where they could experiment with new life styles and identities. Their admittedly small incomes gave them, combined with their cultural capital, an independence which made a marked contrast with the part-time membership of working-class youth cultures. Working-class hippies were caught up in the contradictions, and had to make a severe adjustment if they were not to be rejected because they had failed to comprehend or reciprocate appropriately in the loose normative context of the counter culture. Hippies were relatively older, more educated and middle class (although they reported themselves as working class), with better work prospects than those in other youth cultures. They also saw themselves as continuing to be hippies always. Willis (1978), in his British hippy study, found

a homology between immediacy, drug use, an omniscient spiritual-
ity and a sense of identity in the hippy community, symbolised by
their style and appearance. Hippies' uncertain grip on their own
identity was experienced as a source of richness rather than a cause
for concern. Immediate subjective experience, preferably intense,
was important, and drugs assisted this in projecting them beyond
the coercion of the world. The world was seen as coercive, and this
knowledge was conceptualised as liberating, because the hippy felt
nothing could touch him again. Hippies were concerned with tran-
scendence and fuller states of awareness, but this awareness was by
its very nature unrealisable. The unending possibility of resolution
meant that the starkness of failure need never be faced. The East
was admired just because it was anti-technocratic. There was an
important interaction between progressive rock music and life style;
the music matched in complexity and rhythmical asymmetry the
hippy life style; setting the form through hallucinogenic drug use
could undercut the linearity of the straight world. The hippy culture
was experienced as cutting away at society's roots, a lived-out critique of the materialism and philistinism found in contemporary
industrial society.

In order to make sense of an often conflicting mass of material,
it is important to consider the contradictions within the hippy
subculture, its relation to the wider society and the massive societal
reaction it had to contend with. The counterculture, or underground as it was called in Britain, was a loose, expressive, social
movement, complicated by different researchers looking at disparate elements of it. It developed in a time of relative economic
prosperity, and indeed if the estimated one and a half million drop
outs in the United States during the 1960s had demanded jobs, the
situation might have been quite different. The economy was able,
in a prosperous boom more apparent than real, to carry substantial
numbers of voluntarily unemployed people living on subsistence
incomes, based on surplus. A production-oriented economy has
moved to a consumption-oriented one, accompanied by a shift in
values among middle-class consumers. The hippy subculture can
be seen as fitting in at an overlap of values emphasising leisure and
consumption, autonomy and individualism. The counterculture
was formed in an affluent society, with an advanced technology, and
as such was parasitic upon the surplus of the dominant society, yet
remained antagonistic. Hippies were unconcerned about materialism, but lived on a welfare system related to surplus value and
wage labour. They were disdainful of technology, yet listened to
complex, stereo systems and watched complicated light shows.
They disdained impure foods, but consumed street synthesised
drugs; they felt freedom was an individual element, but were con-

trolled by a powerful state. The hippy culture generated software, music, lyrics and design, yet the hardware and promotions remained in the possession of the media entrepreneurs. Small businesses run as collectives, such as craft shops, or restaurants are a traditional solution for the marginalised, petty bourgeoisie, yet they depend on wage labour. The contradictions soon showed, as when in 1969 Haight Ashbury found itself with 100,000 teenage runaways with no assistance from the Public Health Department. Rape, violence, disease and exploitation increased, 'freak outs' were common, and the Manson family showed itself as the evil joker in the pack – cruel and vicious exploitation in the Aquarian age (Brake, 1973a; Smith, 1970; Smith and Luce, 1971; Smith and Gay, 1972). The impoverished 'street people' began to 'rip off' their brothers and sisters by theft or sexual exploitation, and 'burned' them with bad dope deals. The more enterprising organised open air rock concerts with expensive seats and inadequate services, or sold the recording and visual rights for vast profits. There were also positive elements such as communes which genuinely attempted to explore alternative living and child care (Abrams and McCulloch, 1976; Houriet, 1973; Rigby, 1973; Teselle, 1972). Ecology became a genuine political concern, leading to the development of pure food-shops, preventative medicine, organic farming and pollution campaigns against large corporations. The necessity to develop new, alternative, legal, health and social services led to a new interest in community politics, legal aid centres, free clinics and holistic medicine. Consciousness raising 'rap groups' developed a recognition of oppressions outside traditional class lines, which became essential in the development of feminism and gay politics in their struggle against patriarchy and sexism.

The hippy movement provided for its members a moratorium of approximately five years in which to consider one's identity and relationship to the world. This luxury, common in student cultures, is noticeably lacking in working-class life and working-class youth cultures. It also contained a blurred yet definite social system. There was a top elite of 'aristopopcracy', a high status, wealthy section of rock musicians and media superstars, who were beyond the relationship to scarcity, as Young (1973) notes, and who possessed considerable, sometimes absolute, sexual power. Next was the 'alternative bourgeoisie' with specialist knowledge (such as electronics, production, communications and organising skills), or who else were elements of the bohemian avant garde symbiotic to the counterculture. The 'lower middle-class drop outs' lacked the skills of the above, but were employed in a minor capacity by them, often in exploitative wage relations. Finally there were the 'lumpenhippies' or 'street people', working-class, tough vagrants, who were 'street wise'. They had run away from a difficult home life and, whilst attracted to the hippy life, found they had no place in the alternative society. Usually this was for the same reasons that they had no place in straight society – they lacked skills, articulation and capital. Poor, often desperate, they became brutalised and lived on their wits by pan-handling, petty theft, prostitution and street dope dealing (the least rewarding and most dangerous form of this activity).

Societal reaction to the hippy culture was considerable, and they swiftly became threatening folk devils. Between 1965 and 1969 British newspapers reported the hippy as a wilfully idle, promiscuous, dirty and drug-using vagrant. A typical report (*People*, 30.7.67) shows a naked male longhair, dancing at the Alexandra Palace 'love-in' with the caption, 'If you disagree with this – then this paper gives you ten out of ten – the hippy cult is degrading, decadent and plain daft.' The alarm was international; reports came in from Germany, Holland, Canada and America as hippies took up residence in the new epicentres. In the United States they moved, with the beats, from Venice West to San Francisco, first North Beach, then Haight Ashbury, the famous 'Hashbury'. Both quiet, rural areas and large cities resisted the hippy invasion. The picturesque English village of St Ives, fearing for its tourist trade, refused to serve, house or tolerate hippies, as did the hamlets of Big Sur, California. 'No hippies' was a common sign outside restaurants. In England the London Street Commune occupied an elegant, empty Georgian mansion in the heart of London at 144 Piccadilly. A much quoted report (*News of the World*, 21.9.69) describes the squat as 'lit only by the dim light of their drugged cigarettes' emphasising:

> Hippies – Drugs – The Sordid Truth.
> Drug taking, couples making love while others look on, a
> heavy mob armed with iron bars, filth and stench, foul
> language, that is the scene inside the hippies' fortress in
> London's Piccadilly. These are not rumours but facts, sordid
> facts which will shock ordinary decent living people. Drug
> taking and squalor, sex – and they'll get no state aid ...

The conservative *Daily Telegraph* (19.6.69) noted that on evicting the hippies a hospital governor vomited, a policewoman became ill and a policeman refused to allow his dog into the premises 'because of the filth'. On the Spanish island of Formantera, hippies were expelled so as not to affect the tourist trade. In the same week the *Daily Mail* (2.8.69) quoted an 'ex Military Medallist':

> 'It makes me ashamed to be British, they have ruined the

island. They live around in filthy clothes mauling each other in the streets. No wonder our country has gone to the dogs'.

In the edition of 4.8.69 the complaints of an English tourist were added:

'One of the hippies came to my table, as my wife and I were having a drink. He was obviously drugged to the eyeballs and shouted "Life is beautiful, make love together".'

By this time billboards appeared in the United States proclaiming 'Beautify America – cut your hair'. One unique aspect of the underground was that it could develop and articulate genuine resistance and alternatives. The underground press argued a counterideology and analysis which gave coverage to political and social events not reported in the 'overground' media, so that a counter information service was developed (Glessing, 1970; Lewis, 1972). Its middle-class followers, with their education and skills of literacy and articulation, gave it an advantage over working-class youth culture. The confidence to argue an alternative came from a class familiarity with verbal and writing skills.

Reportage in the conventional media, with its consequent societal reaction, amplified the contradictions present in the hippy subculture. In the early days of the Summer of Love in 1966, spontaneous friendship and generosity were common, and the music and dance in hippy districts lent them a fairytale romanticism – a permanent sense of carnival prevailed. The hippy community faced the hazards of all urban communities – health hazards, disease and exploitation. There was insufficient input from conventional public health services to deal with the spread of ill health; police harassment and exploitation resulted in advice centres and free clinics (Brake, 1973a). Poverty and violence appeared, and Haight Ashbury became a teenage slum. During the Altamont rock festival the contradictions came to the fore. The Hell's Angels appointed as a security force by the sponsors became police, judge and executioners, and murdered a black student before 300,000 fans while the Rolling Stones performed 'Sympathy for the Devil'. Eisen (1970, p. 163) put it well:

There occurred a strange kind of self-glorification on the part of drop-out society ... so eventually there came about the idea that somehow an essential and fundamental break had been made as a result of the drugs, the new vocabulary, the music and the new life styles. An illusion of superiority had suffused itself though the hip world ... it was as though identification with the new culture, with long hair and serious differences with your parents, meant that somehow you possessed a

97

superior way of life and a superior insight into the nature of the universe. . . .

The hippy culture evaded rather than confronted the state. It overlooked that any political solution at a reformist or revolutionary level must involve a relationship to the political economy, and the problems of working-class people in general. Exploitation developed within the hippy culture, either at a material level or a sexual level as with the Manson family, or due to irresponsibility as at Altamont. Individualism and art were presented as solutions. Its politics (Lydon, 1971, p. 117) were:

> a sort of turned on liberalism, that thinks the Panthers are groovy, but does not come to terms with the nasty American reality. The politics of the much touted rock revolution – they add up to a hazy belief in the power of art to change the world, presuming that the place for the revolution to begin and end is inside individual heads.

Solutions were located in ideas, not material reality. As art and music became commercial possibilities, then they were transformed into a commodity for the larger society. The artistic transformation of musical form in popular music was financed by astute backers, whether it was San Francisco rock, the Rolling Stones or the Beatles. The Free Press was financially saved by pornographic film syndicates; head shops were taken over by mass production.

However, this is not to argue that this era produced nothing. Important advances were made in consciousness, experiments in alternatives carried out by committed people, and politics transformed from arid economic determinism to a wider exploration of the relationships of differing forms of exploitation and their effects on people's lives. By 1970 the hippy subculture had divided into mystics and politicos. The politicos had become involved in New Left politics, combining politics and life style, the personal and the political, combating Old Left puritanism and economism. Gradually they moved to the periphery of class politics, becoming involved with community politics, or raising the contentious issue of patriarchy, especially those feminists who had suffered from traditional and alternative sexism. Many retreated from anything political, and became part of what Tom Wolfe has called the 'me' generation, with encounter groups, bioenergetics, massage or diet. Others became involved with ecological politics, and it should be remembered that the importance of ecological devastation gave impetus to the peace movement of the 1980s, and the interest in organic and preventative medicine has led to an interest in holistic medicine. The mystics tended to a pastoral arcadism, retreating into the countryside, and became involved in agrarian communard-ism with a supportive mysticism. Much of the emphasis on liberal permissiveness was a response to the small town puritanism and Protestant ethic of the larger society. However, the permissive toler-ance degenerated, and consequently any music sounded good if you were stoned enough. The notion that everyone should do their own thing led to sexual exploitation for hippy women, and gener-ated a tyranny of structurelessness in morality and responsibility. Escape was sought from a genuinely oppressive and exploitative society, but the hippies refused to take the straights along with them. The genuine critical thrust became lost in the contradictions and oppositions which had been clouded over by rhetoric. The hippy culture never faced up to the internal divisions of its own social structure, in terms of the relationship to scarcity, and there was no comprehension of the reality of its dependence on, and relationship to, the larger socio-economic system. Gleason (1970, p. 219) shows this lack of analysis:

> We've all gone along with the illusion that Ginsberg and
> Dylan and Baez and the Beatles and the Stones were all part
> of the same thing. Well they are part of one thing, in the sense
> that we're all human beings, and we are all part of the world
> and each other. So is Lyndon Johnson, so is the Mafia head of
> Chicago, so are the Hell's Angels. We've tended to make the
> distinction between Us and Them. Now if we've got to
> recognise anything, there's not much difference between the
> Angels beating that kid over the head with a pool cue, and the
> Chicago cops beating you over the head because you've got
> long hair.

A full-time leisure, expressive subculture can only develop in an economy with sufficient surplus and full employment, but as this changed, then so did Flower Power. The Flower Children faded and died in the desert of unemployment, exploitation and economic crisis.

The focal concerns of the hippy subculture are difficult to assess because the term 'hippy' is used very loosely. Nevertheless, certain major concerns do show themselves.

1 Passive resistance The political stances of domestic and foreign policy in the 1960s, and in particular the Vietnam war, led to a disenchantment with politics. Instead there was a romanticism which argued that if love prevailed everything would be all right. This apolitical myopia concerning the functions of the state led the hippy subculture to take up expressive values and idealism as an alternative to rational analysis and activism. Power as a major variable in political struggle was ignored, and mysticism and ritual magic appealed to. In a very real sense the solution was seen as magical and 'imaginary'.

2 Movement There was a concern with movement, both in the geographical sense of travelling, and in an existential sense. There were movements across the United States, usually to the Shangri La of the West, or to the East, usually Asia, and sometimes to Latin America. The hippy trail was blazed in search of mysticism and drugs through Turkey to Afghanistan. It was also felt that one should move oneself – indeed psychodelic drugs were seen as mind expanding – and one moved with their usage, or with the use of mysticism, religion or self-exploration. Any journey was then both physical and existential.

3 Dissociation Dissatisfaction was felt with the formal education system, usually at the university level for hippies, and there was discontent, both with the curriculum seen as non-humanistic, and with post-college career structures. Hippies tended to come from materially comfortable families and wanted something more than a mere career. They sought creative work, or a vaguely expressed spiritual satisfaction. Poverty was voluntarily entered into, unlike working-class youth who were born into it.

4 Expressivity A creative, rather than affluent, work situation was sought. There was an attempt to break down the barriers between work and play, with a feeling work should be joyous and creative. Expressivity was against thrift and deferred gratification; it was a protest against materialism.

5 Subjectivity Subjectivity resisted the standards and intrusions of the objective world, which were seen as competitive. Subjectivity opened the self to experience, assisted by drugs and by religious and mystical, even magical, explanation. Tomorrow becomes unimportant. Pleasure, excitement and fear are increased. This explains the absence of standards in much of hippy life – if you are stoned enough, and in a good space – everything is fine. It also explains their hostility to 'put downs' or personal attacks. Subjectivity and expressivity also act against intellectualism, which is seen as too heavy. The danger is that idealism becomes a prime unit of analysis (if you think you are free, then you are free), with devastating effects on health, hygiene and exploitation.

6 Individualism This was a reaction to the facelessness of mass society. It meant 'doing your own thing' and also evading the contradictions of this argument. It meant believing that freedom was 'in your head', not part of some objectively oppressive social structure with its attendant institutions and social relations. Politically it meant romantic anarchy, or apoliticism. Eisen (1970, p. 163) notes this as,

> Straight equals bad, freak equals free, and therefore good. This in turn has led to a permissiveness, an encompassing tolerance that accepts everything that puts straight society and the pigs uptight. Doing one's own thing is the real byword for the culture. . . . But what has resulted has been a relativism that refuses to judge because it has abandoned moral standards. . . .

It was this lack of analysis and refusal to face the contradictions of the relationship between the state and the political economy which led to retreatism in the counterculture. This means that:

> The hippies have shown that it can be pleasant to drop out of the arduous job of attempting to steer a difficult, unrewarding society. But when that is done, you leave the driving to the Hell's Angels. (Winckle, 1971, p. 27)

The hippy world has developed its own social history, documented in its own media. It was highly socially visible, and unlike the beats who kept out of the limelight, it deliberately attacked the perceptions of the silent majority. Men were flowing-haired and bearded, and both sexes wore elaborate robes of a non-functional form. The beats had used marijuana and mild chemical hallucinogens up to the late 1950s and by 1958 mescalin was produced and added to peyote as a leisure drug. The cheap manufacture of LSD began in 1962, and the proselytising of Timothy Leary at Harvard and the illicit acid factories of the White Rabbit, Owsley, led to San Francisco becoming the acid centre of the world. Acid only became illegal after October 1966, in California. The use of acid by musicians contributed considerably to the progressive rock forms, as well as the influence on graphics. Ken Kesey's 'magic bus' journeys, and his 1966 Trips Festival in San Francisco spread the use of acid as a recreational drug. The Summer of Love, 1966, was the peaking of the acid experience. After this, despite peaks such as Woodstock, there was a confusion between politics and youth culture escalated by police persecution. The Chicago Convention saw the growth of the Yippies (Youth International Party) and the Diggers as prominent community political forces. The Democratic Convention of Chicago, which led to a police riot and the consequent trial of leading youth culture figures, did much to subdivide the counterculture into mystics and militants. In Britain the trial of the Rolling Stones for drug use in 1966 led to a resistance by young people, and a severe crisis in confidence in the state amongst youth. There grew up an amazing series of alternative projects and a strong supportive network which was critical of the wider society. Arts Labs, involving various forms of multi-media work, were launched; legal advice centres defending hippies against landlord and police harassment, information centres and crash pads were developed for the young homeless. The Diggers in San Francisco were the prototype (based on Winstanley's Diggers in the English Civil War who dug up the common land in a primitive form of anarcho-communism) who first ran free stores offering clothes and food. A network developed which protected youth, politicising it and offering refuge and friendship. Long hair was accepted as a cultural statement of affiliation. The drug laws, especially the marijuana laws, seriously alienated many young people, who because of their leisure consumption, appearance and life style found themselves stopped, searched and bullied by law enforcement agencies. Hallucinogenics caused a massive paradigm shift in thousands of young middle-class people. They were joined in this by large numbers of working-class youth who, despite the stratification of the hippy world, were able to explore a political criticism, which was fun. By the 1970s the hippy world had ceased to be a subculture for the young, and had become a subculture for, as Berger puts it, 'the youthful' – those who were sympathetic to youth rather than young. A series of communes, both rural and urban, grew up which explored ways of living, and alternative centres for health, legal and welfare assistance. Drug usage developed an interest in spiritualism and contemplation, and the general spirit in the early days was pacifist. Police raids and streets sweeps waged war on hippy neighbourhoods, and arrests and beatings were common. Street people came to prey on the more gullible of the young, and drug dealing and sexual exploitation spread. Eventually the spontaneity and generosity gave way to suspicion and hostility. Resistance became rip off. As Widgery (1973) points out, the hippy male treatment of women reduced women to earth mothers, sexual conquests or companiate appendages rather than true and equal partners. But the women were also thinking and organising. They demanded responsible relationships and more equality in domestic and non-domestic life. Communes had to face these contradictions and rethink domestic labour and child care or dissolve. Women and children were demanding their rights and an equal share of responsibilities. However, this was the beginning of innovative and imaginative community projects, the development of a sense of community politics, and the growth of new forms of sensibility.

Religious imperialism – the rise of the cults

The confusion of both conscious and unconscious drug usage left many young people open to domination by a strict authority figure, or a rigid controlling system. The trip, and its inner exploration, left many young people to search for guidance and meaning in life, to counteract the existential angst produced. The mystical aspect present in hippy life tended to encourage spiritual rather than materialist explanations, and many hippies were either anti-political or apolitical in the formal sense of politics. The spiritual explanations were usually based on elements of Eastern religions, or Western interpretations of Zen Buddhism, or sometimes extremely fundamentalist explanations of Christianity. The anti-materialist philosophy of the hippies attracted large numbers of young people who had difficulties in finding meaningful or interesting work, or acceptance in personal relationships. They were attracted by the counterculture's structurelessness and its disdain for work. By the early 1970s, it was calculated in the United States there were over one million young runaways, nearly all of them under age. Hippy information centres and cafes had their walls covered with advertisements from desperate parents asking their children to contact them. Religious cults became refuges for many of these lost children. Often actively recruiting and evangelising in the streets, the cults provided structure in an otherwise structureless life. Consciousness-raising techniques and communal life styles were used to build up organisations which subsumed the individual into the institution. Friendship, emotional support, a new life and a new identity, often symbolised in ecclesiastical tradition with a new name, were offered as membership of a collective group identity. By the mid-1970s something like three million young people, aged between eighteen and twenty-five years of age were involved in over 3,000 groups. Unfortunately, thousands of naive young people were left open to exploitation by charismatic, and often ruthless and exploitative, leadership. They raised funds for the cult by various forms of begging, obtaining 'donations' or recruiting through offers of friendship, sexual favours or a new life. The cults were often religious in nature, ranging from a fundamentalist and harsh interpretation of Christianity to a vague Eastern mysticism. At the head of the cult was often an individual or a small group who clearly gained financially from the free labour and begging of their young followers. The groups ranged in size from several thousands, internationally linked, to small groups such as Manson's family.

Not all cults were religious or youth-based. As well as the colourful, rather bizarre groups, such as the Krishna Consciousness group with their saffron robes, shaved heads and chanting of Hare

Krishna, there were also groups such as Jim Jones' People's Temple. This cult attracted poor families and the single elderly from the black community. The People's Temple acted as a form of anti-church, drawing on religion, so important in black life, and offering services and a support which its members could not find elsewhere. In some ways its collective community base 'acted as a substitute for a left that did not exist in the Bay area (or in the rest of the country)' (Easton *et al.*, 1979). Unfortunately, a hierarchical organisation dominated by a powerful personality can only be challenged where there is a tradition of genuinely democratic and libertarian organisational models. This is especially difficult in America where the stress on individualism, and anti-left-wing hostility inhibits this. Jones was able to offer something to disaffiliated black people, and gained an uncritical left-wing support, because any opposition was written off as racist. He exploited this situation, which led to the kidnapping of children, an exodus to Guyana, and the mass murder and suicide of his followers. Ironically this distortion of freedom and community activism is often presented by conservatives as an example to be used against socialism and collectives, although in fact it had nothing to do with either.

In youth culture, we see desperate young people seeking the security of a hierarchical organisation which then thinks and decides for them. Their drifting lives are held together by a subjugation which exploits and oppresses them, rather than preparing them for self-reliance. The more successful cults are based on anti-intellectual, non-rational, pseudo-religious, evangelical recruitment for a self-declared messiah. Atomised individuals, often rootless and homeless, isolated from family or support networks, join a cult which becomes a substitute family, and indeed often calls itself by a familial name. Isolation occurs within the cult because information is strictly controlled as the recruit becomes absorbed in cult-related activities. A formal declaration renouncing the recruit's previous life may be insisted upon. The recruit learns a new language, a new value system, and will often wear a new, distinct costume, all of which assists in the forging of a new identity. A different primary group combined with intense indoctrination literally programme the new recruit into the new life. A regressive dependence is encouraged, leading to an uncritical acceptance of the cult leader and his rules. One's previous life is used to illustrate one's previous lapses, and the symbolic universe of the cult member is systematically reorganised. The attention of the recruit is monopolised, pro-cult information systematically reinforced, and resistance to outside influence taught. Total acceptance is demanded, and this means total acceptance of material and sexual exploitation, in the sense that the male/female roles in cults are highly traditional, as is the division of domestic labour. Members then joyfully cooperate in their own exploitation. The concept of God is a highly traditional one, certainly not open to question, and often fearful. Personal responsibility becomes replaced by cult rules. Cults provide meaning, direction, security and a purpose in life for those who found such things lacking in the wider society. By force, both physical and psychological, members surrender ties and relationships outside the cult. The recruit's family often reacts to this by kidnapping and deprogramming members with the assistance of organisations whose purpose is to do just this. This, however, raises the same ethical issues as their original recruitment into the cult. At one level young people have a right to mess up their lives, and for those for whom there is little in the outside society, the cult often offers security and a meaning to life. However, enforced dependency upon the cult, material and sexual exploitation, an unloving and patriarchical view of God, all lead to an uncritical passivity which aids no one but the exploitative leaders of cults, who feed both economically and in terms of power on their followers.

The radical tradition – political militancy and protest movements

There is a symbiotic relationship between the culturally rebellious, and the tradition of militant radicalism found in the young intelligentsia. The culturally rebellious raised issues ignored in the traditional analyses of class politics found in the revolutionary left, predominantly the place of a cultural revolution in the transformation of society. They raised libertarian criticisms of bureaucracy, anarchistic issues about hierarchies, and raised the politics of personal life. They therefore went beyond class to look at other areas of exploitation, and playfully challenged the deadly seriousness of the Old Left. Radical issues, however, were certainly raised by the fear among youth of nuclear war and its consequent devastation. In Britain, the Campaign for Nuclear Disarmament (CND) organised massive marches from 1958, which escalated after the dangers of the Cuban missile crisis in the 1960s, and then underwent a renaissance in the 1980s. A survey in 1951 found that 41 per cent of its members were under twenty-one years of age. It was predominantly a form of pacifist, middle-class radicalism.

> Whereas working-class radicalism could be said to be geared largely to reforms of an economic or material kind, the radicalism of the middle class is directed mainly to social reforms which are basically moral in content. (Parkin, 1968, p. 2)

The difference between the two is that:

> Whereas the former holds out the promises of benefits to one
> particular section of society (the working class), from which its
> supporters are drawn, the latter envisages no rewards which
> will accrue to the middle class specifically but only to society
> at large, or to some underprivileged groups. .... It will be
> argued that in fact the main pay off for middle-class radicals is
> that of a psychological or emotional kind – in satisfactions
> derived from expressing personal values in action.

This tends to ignore the concerns of all members of society for
issues over which they feel they have little direct political control,
such as nuclear weapon build-up and testing. CND was, however,
a central focus for youth, and part of British youth culture, with
its beat associations, protest music, outlandish clothes, and its raf-
fish mixture of anarchy and bohemia. Its members were young,
mainly under twenty-one as stated earlier, mostly in full-time education, and from radical, middle-class homes. In this sense they
reflected the Berkeley radicals of the 1960s. It was important as a
movement because it was the first time that youth from privileged
backgrounds came into direct opposition with the police in such
large numbers. CND was a focus for protest outside organised,
parliamentary politics. It brought moral issues into the political
arena, and expressed the sense of alienation that millions of people
felt concerning the destruction of large parts of the globe by nuclear
war. It was to be a precursor for ecological politics.

In the United States the large single-issue campaigns were over
civil rights, the draft and the attendant campaign to stop the Vietnam war, and abortion. The Vietnam war, apartheid in South
Africa, racism and abortion were all important campaigns in Britain, but the original main critical focus was on Britain's nuclear
deterrents. CND was definitely not respectable, and quickly became
a sign of 'permissive' and disaffected youth. It provided a fertile
political education; it led to intellectual and theoretical bodies of
dissent in British left-wing politics – the Labour Party decision to
opt for unilateral disarmament is still a contentious issue – and it
laid the ground for anarchist and hippy movements. Its pro-life,
humanistic, active campaign against the cynical 'old men' of politics gave root to the youthful interest in pacifism and environmental
movements.

In Britain the Hungarian uprising, and the Suez crisis in 1956,
polarised disillusionment with the official party line of the Old Left,
in both the communist and Labour parties. CND provided a
springboard, unhampered by an authoritarian hierarchy, which
applied the principle of direct action and non-violence. This era

marked the beginnings of humanistic socialism in the young Marx, and gave rise to a New Left. The model of the Leninist centralised party gave way to progressive forms of Trotskyism, and interests in syndicalism and libertarianism. The New Left showed factional splintering along the lines of these criticisms during the 1960s and 1970s, but a major confrontation was to come during the 1970s from feminism, aided by gay liberation. After this all progressive parties and revolutionary organisations had to rethink their analysis to consider the feminist and gay issues. In CND the disparate elements separated in analysis and action after the 1963 Cuban missile crisis. The division was over extra-parliamentary pressure groups, or direct action by invading the missile bases. It was the Vietnam war movement which was to recapture an interest in the peace movement, and wed it to radical protest concerning militarism, neo-colonialism and racism. Passive resistance responded to state violence to take a more aggressive, liberating revolutionary action, which emerged in the campus battles of the 1960s. Not until the mass movements over ecological issues, and the rebirth of concern with nuclear war in the 1980s, was there such an upsurgence of middle-class radicalism, with its emphasis upon humanitarian rather than class issues, on moral rather than economic reform, although these issues were to become more intermingled during the mid-1970s.

In the United States, the first major radical cause involving youth in the post-war period was the Civil Rights Movement. American students began to question a system which stressed its justice and democracy, but did nothing about the legal rights of its own minority groups. In a country, which was one of the wealthiest in the world, much attention was paid to military and corporate interests but little was being done for its poor. The labour movement had been co-opted and integrated into the established political system. Anti-communist feeling was so successfully injected into mainstream ideology that the radical movement, with its support of specific causes rather than a general class struggle, had a more established history of popular resistance than class politics. Students adopted the populist, egalitarian views of the movement, and developed a generationally focused rhetoric and style. They were involved in the Civil Rights Movement, took an active part in resisting the Vietnam war, and saw action in the campus demonstrations, draft resistance and the Chicago Convention. Race had become a major issue with the lunch counter sit-ins in the South in 1960 (although there had been demonstrations in the late 1950s), and this had led to the Student Non-violent Co-ordinating Committee (SNCC). At the same time Berkeley students were protesting about the San Francisco Un-American Activities Committee. As with CND in Britain, non-violent, direct action was used, one high-light being the Washington Peace March in 1962. The Civil Rights Movement was a black and white coalition, focusing on the South and using the process of law as an ally. It was essentially middle class, non-violent and reformist using Martin Luther King and the National Association for the Advancement of Colored People. Violent Southern resistance, particularly by law enforcement personnel, increased student activist groups such as SNCC and Committee for Organising Racial Equality. The Civil Rights Movement, as the Solomon Report shows, organised large amounts of black youth to confront racist policies directly. Crime rates in those communities involved in civil rights dropped significantly. The move from passive resistance to militant action was notable after the murder of King in April 1968. Urban riots significantly increased in the ghettos, and white assistance was regarded with suspicion and hostility. The separatism of the Black Muslims gave a new pride to black identity. The anti-colonial political and cultural resurgence of black activism made race riots and civil insurrection a central issue. In 1966 the Black Panthers were the central focus of militant struggle and were systematically attacked by the police and the FBI. Threatened with destruction they focused on community action and local politics, but their analysis and their pride in blackness gave a dignity and inspiration to a militancy found in contemporary Britain, the West Indies and Southern Africa; they became the target of police racism and harassment (Skolnik, 1969) and many of their organisers were shot.

Focusing on the Civil Rights Movement, the Students for a Democratic Society attempted to organise students for social change in society, using universities as arenas for activity, analysis and discussion to radicalise grass roots movements. The desire to change the wider society was often expressed in campus issues as free political speech on campus, such as the Berkeley Free Speech issue 1964, which had wide publicity concerning direct action techniques and which was to become a model for future student strategies. This was a turning point in white student activism. As white involvement in civil rights for blacks began to fade owing to the increase of the demand for Black Power, white students were called upon to demonstrate their radicalism. Up to 1965 students criticised the failure of the political system to carry out its avowed objectives, but after this there was a distinct disillusionment with the authority of the state and a cynicism which demanded a revolutionary alternative which lasted until Watergate. University involvement with the war economy came under heavy criticism. Research involvement, police on campus, the censorship of criticism of the war or of the government meant that the university had ceased to be a bastion of liberal discussion. The draft, based on scholastic achievement, also became an issue, as did the pointlessness of most academic curricula to contemporary problems. By the mid-1960s, the Civil Rights Movement had entered a new militant phase; the federal government seemed to be a cooling-out agent rather than a facilitator of legally established rights. The War on Poverty, a response to civil insurrection, was seen as preserving rather than providing significant reforms; the university was seen as preventing criticism, and the war had escalated. Passive resistance and protest had no effect on the Johnson administration; the war was misrepresented by the establishment. Students placed in competition over the draft resisted it. There was a spill-over from these issues into a concern with poverty, urban decline and oppression, spreading from pollution to community control, such as the People's Park in Berkeley, to urban guerrillas. Police violence in the confrontation at Columbia University and at the Chicago Democratic National Convention in 1968 meant that violent overreaction on the part of the police radicalised countless, previously middle-of-the-road students. The politics of confrontation became a common political weapon in student militant protest.

Student protest was of course not confined to America. Students were involved in transitional changes in Latin America, in the Chinese cultural revolution, in Japan over the alliance with USA, with the Vietnam war and with the use of land for commercial purposes. In Europe there were struggles over an antiquated educational system in Italy; over democracy in Spain and Portugal; and over the heritage of authoritarianism and Nazism in Germany. The conformity of West German education was challenged on several fronts: by the SDS (the socialist German students' revolutionary organisation); by social experiments, such as Kommune I, and by a massive anti-Vietnam campaign. The main targets were police brutality, regulations preventing Marxists working in the public service and the Springer media campaign against the left. In 1968, in Holland, a series of demonstrations against the Vietnam War and the monarchy had led to violent police reaction. The Dutch anarchist group, the Provos, using a series of peaceful and imaginative tactics, gained considerable sympathy among the young. Out of the libertarian roots of this movement, aided by the Amsterdam youth culture, sprang the Kabouters, offering community politics and environmental protection. An alternative society was suggested, developed from the Provo 'white bicycles' and free transport for everyone. Alternative services were suggested for the elderly, the young, for food distribution and child care. A similarity can be noted with the San Francisco Diggers. The major student uprising was in May 1968 in Paris. The French student movement had been active against the Algerian war at a time when the organised Left had remained silent. In 1967 French students at Lyons had begun to organise against sexual surveillance in the halls of residence. Nanterre was demonstrating against poor cultural facilities, and the attempts to control this started the Nanterre student movement. Arrests of anti-Vietnam organisers led to an occupation. Nanterre was closed and student organisers were ordered to appear before the Sorbonne administration in May 1968. A protest by the student left led the Rector to ask the police to clear the buildings. The students put up barricades, the police attacked, and a mass confrontation with the state occurred. Workers joined in student demonstrations, factory occupations occurred and an interesting mixture of violent confrontation and imaginative street slogans, the latter inspired by the Situationist International, took place. We can see a link between the Situationist International and the 'enragés', who fused theory and practice in the immediate situation, arguing that praxis creates its own theory, and the libertarianism of the Kabouters and the American Yippies who also 'seize the time' to show up contradictions in society, and to create a political strategy. A general strike followed which turned into massive factory occupations involving nearly 10 million workers. De Gaulle called for support for his government and, playing on fears of a communist takeover, broke the strike. One contradiction was that the industrial workers wanted fuller participation in, rather than an overthrow of, social democracy.

One extreme polarity of the student unrest was the growth of the urban guerrilla movement. The Black Power movement threw up urban guerrilla defence groups such as the Black Liberation Front and the Black Panthers. However, the group which attracted most attention because of their contradictory position was the group composed of middle-class, white ex-students, the Weathermen, who had sprung from the youth culture and from the SDS after the Chicago Convention of 1968. The group was pledged to bring the war back home. American society is racist and violent; it has no real history of class struggle based on socialism as Europe has; it also has the wealthiest working class in the world, and as such class boundaries are far from clear-cut. Impatient with populist traditions in the movement, the Weathermen saw the American working class as bourgeoisified. Seeing a 'white honky-tonk pig racist Amerika' they decided to escalate the struggle, even against the people, envisaging an economy eventually ruled by a world proletariat. They wished to stand up with black militants against a white society, and to escalate a reaction which would reveal the oppression of the state (Walton, 1973). The logic of this was carried through so that support was offered even for Charles Manson. The

Weathermen saw all whites as counterrevolutionary unless involved in active struggle against capitalism. In 1969 they changed their name to Weatherpersons to combat the sexist implications, but by the end of the year they had become Weather Underground. A bomb-making factory in New York blew up, killing three of their members and forcing the survivors to flee underground. They were pursued by the FBI and became a convenient scapegoat by being blamed for some 4,000 bombings – an unlikely number for such a small group. Both men and women played leading roles in this organisation, and it says much for the radical left in America that they were able to remain underground until capture and surrender into the late 1970s and early 1980s. They were to emerge, having hidden in the Upper West Side of Manhattan, not far from their original bomb factory. Yippie leader Abbie Hoffman was also forced to flee, hiding in Europe, Mexico and Canada as well as the United States until 1980, where he emerged near the Canadian border, having obtained some local notoriety as an environmental protest organiser.

The same impatience with the process of conventional parliamentary procedure was shown by the Red Army Faction, organised by Baader and Meinhof, by similar Japanese groups, and to a lesser extent by the British Angry Brigade, although strategies differ on whether property or persons are the target. The full contradictions of this approach was shown in the 1974 activities of the Symbionese Liberation Army. Composed of black ex-convicts who had been politicised, and middle-class white radicals from the Venceremos group, this group killed Foster, the Oakland black school's superintendent, and kidnapped Patty Hearst. They show many of the contradictions of the New Left of the time. They emphasised the feelings of alienation and meaninglessness they experienced, rather than considering firstly a theoretical analysis which understood that social change for the dispossessed can only be obtained by working-class support, and which has to be worked at for decades. The working class cannot be expected to give up what little they have because of the fervour of a group they are suspicious of, and who may belong to a different class and culture from them. Basing their guerrilla activities on Debray and Fanon, they failed to realise that they were working not in an agrarian Third World setting, but in a Western, industrial, urban society which had little history of class-consciousness, and an economy which rewarded different strands in the same class. The romanticised violence and the brutalised aggression of the ex-cons presumably escalated the fervour of white middle-class radicals in the group who feared to look squeamish or fearful. Unlike the Panthers they were not offering armed defence to the ghetto, and the killing of Foster meant that they could not hide in black 'safe houses'. Violence followed the worst sort of masculinist protest which believes that relieving one's personal pain may be useful to a whole class. It was a misapplication of the new sensitivity. Such adventurism is dangerous because it gives the forces of oppression new reasons for increased legislation, and the romanticised violence can turn dangerously against the class it is supposed to help (Bryan, 1975; Belcher and West, 1975; Carney, 1975).

In Britain, the CND campaigns were replaced by anti-Vietnam war demonstrations. In 1967 there were student occupations at the LSE, and then at Essex University and Hornsey College of Art in 1968. The authorities feared that LSE would be made the base for the Grosvenor Square anti-Vietnam war demonstrations, and indeed it was used for planning strategies, once it was occupied, and as a hospital for the demonstration. This militancy was occurring at a time when Flower Power was coming to the attention of the British public, so that often the militants and the hippies were confused in the public mind. In 1970 the sit-in at Warwick University led to the discovery of secret political files kept on staff and students, as well as a record of the influence that various industrial enterprises had on academic courses and research. Occupations spread over the country, and the invasion of the Garden House Hotel at Cambridge led to a pitched battle with the police. This was the year that Germaine Greer published *The Female Eunuch*, feminists disrupted the 'Miss World' contest, and *IT* was charged with obscenity. The mid-1970s (although one cannot generalise about decades) began to show a change away from student power. The Vietnam war drew to a close, and Ireland became an important political issue for the English New Left. Neo-colonial warfare moved nearer home. In 1971 the trials of *Oz* for obscenity and the Angry Brigade were the result of charges of conspiracy, to corrupt public morals for the former and to cause explosions for the latter. These cases shared an interesting point, that the life style of the defendants was citable as evidence for the prosecution, and that this has become common in charges of conspiracy where life style is considered deviant (Bunyan, 1977; Chibnall, 1977; Griffiths, 1978; Robertson, 1974; Palmer, 1971). The Angry Brigade were libertarian situationists in a Marxist framework. They presented a particular bogey for the general public. On the one hand, the underground was seen as publishing morally-corrupt obscenity, as in *Oz*, and on the other, it was seen as escalating the struggle beyond mere street demonstrations, and this by middle-class educated men and women. They were placed by a puzzled mass media into the conspiratorial lunacy thesis. They sparked off moral indignation which supported the increase of legal and police powers which were being more and more commonly used in 'political' and ideological matters. By the mid-1970s, Ireland had come to the fore amongst radicals, the first demonstrator had been killed in modern times in Red Lion Square (1974), and feminism had become a serious issue, as had gay liberation. The activities of the Red Army Faction in Germany caused a reactionary backlash there, with strong support for law and order. In America the Vietnam war had ended, the black militants had rethought their strategy and, for survival, had proceeded with community action and formal politics, the Symbionese Liberation Army being the last major shoot-out. Watergate had revealed the corruption of the President and the United States could no longer believe the integrity of even the highest in office. The counterculture had given way to an interest in ecology, alternative psychology, especially sensitivity groups, and various types of therapy. Individual rather than collective action concerned young adults.

Looking back over the 1960s and mid-1970s certain issues show themselves. In America, because of the lack of a hard class-consciousness, class-based politics were not a heritage and did not fit a collective solution as easily as in Europe. People began to explore their oppression outside of class lines. For blacks they had an economic oppression, but even for the middle-class black there was a clearly visible, cultural oppression and because it was linked to an unalterable visible stigma – colour – there was some inter-class basis for solidarity. There was a development of black pride, a rewriting of black history, a call for black power and an appreciation of black beauty and identity. These were the beginnings of the politics of the personal. Values, culture and identity have a political force, not just a psychological dimension. The counterculture, composed of middle-class radicals and bohemians, protested not out of poverty, but against an affluence which had no moral content. Admittedly, voluntary stigmata, such as long hair, can be removed, but the embracing of such visible symbols was a statement of protest. Poverty and oppression were redefined in the counterculture. As capitalism developed into a fusion of production and consumption, it was necessary to develop an awareness which would assist this. Middle-class radicals come from a highly educated group, educated not just for increasingly complex skills of selling for consumption, as Mitchell (1971) suggests, but also to consume and indeed understand what was being sold. Mitchell suggests that ideologies are cultivated in order to develop choice over a consumer market but that this can boomerang (Mitchell, 1971, p. 31).

The cult of 'being true to your own feelings' becomes dangerous when those feelings are no longer ones that the

113

society would like you to feel. Testing the quality of your
world on your own pulse can bring about some pretty strange
heart-beats.

Contradictions arise, then, with the development of any kind of
consciousness. Those educated to a critical awareness of society
become aware of contradictions both within it, and in their relationship to it. When this occurs questions are asked about the
institutions which produce values and emotions, and this involves
a critical stance concerning the quality of life of the questioner.
Middle-class women, for example, may well accept a social and
economic place in the world, yet question the emptiness of their
lives as women. This will provoke a reaction which may lead them
to reconsider their relation to the world, and which may (but not
necessarily, of course) open their horizons to make links across
institutions to other elements of their personal oppression and the
oppression of other groups. Middle-class groups may well morally
question cultural institutions, but it must be remembered that cultural institutions are predominantly middle class. A crisis in
middle-class educated youth means a critique of the structure and
ideology of the apparatuses which produced it. This is especially
true for the women of this class, and it is not an accident that
initially the women's liberation movement was a middle-class
movement spread through the universities. As a result many things
have been questioned: the nature and value of domestic labour,
sexuality, the privacy of the family, the ideal of domesticity and
sexual property and in fact the very nature of heterosexuality, not
only in its institutionalised form, but also in its construction.

The mode of production in contemporary capitalism requires
expendable goods, style and debt, not thrift and sobriety and deferred gratification. New forms of escape from the old values were
necessary, usually contained within Marcuse's (1964) 'repressive
desublimation'. The contradictions within predominant values,
which were a necessary response to a changing mode of production,
were responded to by reactionaries as a collapse of, or a conspiracy
against, dominant values. Social changes in the family, for example,
were seen in the early 1960s, as the breakdown of the family; in
fact, changes such as easier divorce and 'latchkey' children indicated the arrival of serial monogamy and a necessity for wives to
work. At present the educated middle class, who have no wish to
alter the mode of production, but who have become sensitive, for
example, to the psychological strain, contradictions and alienation
of mass society (there are at present an exceptional number of
single young adults), have prompted the growth of encounter
groups in California.

There is a recognition that affluence is not a solution to unhappiness, isolation and competition, and group dynamics offer a way of exploring these problems in the supportive structure of other like-minded individuals. Consciousness may be raised on a number of issues, but the direction it takes, and the critique it makes, are eventually collective political struggles. We can see that middle-class subcultures, whether political, bohemian or militant, are also the result of contradictions in the social structure. They are, because they are experienced in the middle class, more indicative of changes in the mode of production, and they reflect changes in the values necessary to support these changes. As such, as Hall and Jefferson (1976, p. 69) suggest, 'they also prefigure, anticipate, foreshadow – though in truncated diagrammatic and "Utopian" forms – emergent social forms. These new forms are rooted in the productive base of the system itself . . .'.

Middle-class radicalism among the young has been seen since the late 1950s as subversive, especially when it publicised and criticised the contradictions in society such as racism. Working-class youthful protest was always enmeshed in socially disapproved acts such as hooliganism, vandalism and theft. It was easy to respond just to the disapproved behaviour indices. Middle-class youth, with its pursuit of hedonism and its criticism of puritanism and hypocrisy, was responded to with a mixture of disapproval and envy. Again, transgressions of the criminal law were publicised, for example arrests of leading underground figures for drug possession, and pornography charges against critical underground magazines. When more political action was taken, legal control was increased, particular use being made of conspiracy charges allowing evidence of life style to be brought into court. The conspiracy thesis and the writing-off of militant action as 'mindless' came to a new level with the fear of urban guerrillas or 'terrorists'. With black youth, the policing of the ghettos and the poor relations between the police and the immigrant community were dealt with by conspiracy and the suspected persons legislation. Campaigns for law and order are an important issue in present electoral campaigns. The fear of society is that it has lost the confidence of its young and hence social control. This is expressed (often ambivalently) instead as fears about sex and drugs and rock and roll. It becomes extended to fears about the results of youth unemployment. What evolves are moral panics about urban decay, mugging and youth riots. This contributes to, and indeed escalates, fears which become part of the crisis in hegemony.

Chapter 5

Hustling, breaking and rapping – black and brown youth

Black people, culture and the economy

Any consideration of black youth and their subcultures in the United States has to be seen in the broader context of Afro-American people in contemporary America. Black culture itself takes place against the scenario of poverty and racism. The high unemployment of black youth and its position in the official delinquency figures has to be seen in the context of social class relations in general, and race in particular. Social class relations for black people are distorted by the presence of race. The situation of black people in Britain and America is historically different of course. Both groups have their roots in slavery, but in Britain most black people arrived as immigrant labour only a generation ago. Nevertheless, they have similar positions in the political economy. According to classical Marxist economic theory, industry, in order to maintain the accumulation of profit, has called upon techniques and work processes which have created a section of the work force which is disposable. This 'reserve army of labour', as it is known, is part of the marginal surplus population which responds to the laws of supply and demand that operate upon the required work force. This peripheral or marginal group can be used or discarded as mechanisation and smaller work forces replace the high, labour-intensive market economies. Black people have been a major part of this reserve army, both in Britain and North America, whether they are indigenous people or imported from the West Indies, Latin America, Mexico, Puerto Rico or the African and Indian subcontinents. Women have always featured highly in the reserve army, and youth increasingly so. Slaves, brought to the Caribbean and the United States as part of the colonial economy of imperialism, were essential to the large plantations. Attempts were made to obliterate African culture. African names and lan-

116

guages were forbidden, but the subversive element of African music remained, combining the West African rhythms of work songs with religious and folk music of the New World. African singing was forbidden, so the context was American, but the roots African. Even the rhythm and syntax of Southern black accents can be traced to West African dialects. The involvement of singer and chorus, of performer and audience, is African; the varying pitches in black speech are found in the same tones of instruments and vocals in the blues. What arose and was reproduced in black American music was the personal experience of Afro-American people.

The emancipation in 1865 freed the slaves, often to become no more than impoverished share croppers living at a subsistence level little better than slavery. The expansion of industrialisation resulted in the migration North where black people joined immigrant workers from Europe and Central America. After 1914 immigration was curtailed, and between 1910 and 1920 60,000 black people had come North through the larger Southern towns from the country. By 1920 14 per cent of people in the North were black, bringing with them central elements of their culture, mainly religion and music. During the decade after the depression and throughout the Second World War black people continued to migrate to the larger cities of the North and West, replacing the earlier European immigrants and being joined by Mexicans and Puerto Ricans. With them came the blues, jazz, gospel, all musical forms which were to become recognised as the central force in popular music. The music was never respectable, played as it was in bars, brothels and honky tonks, but it spoke of love, the battle of the sexes, gambling and the raw poverty of the big city. The two world wars gave black people an international sense, and a sense of racism as peculiar to America, and not an inevitable consequence of different races living together. Black civil rights movements started, Marcus Garvey stressed the Africanism of black people, but the depression severely affected black people. Gradually, in the city, the old light skin/dark skin differences gave way to a status based on acquisition. In this sense consumption among black people reflected the wider aspects of American society. Consumption was conspicuous. In a society where black people were kept out of desirable suburban residences and decent schools and their civil rights were resisted, symbols of affluence were important. Clothes, cars and other goods were deliberately and openly flaunted. Whether it was the zoot suit, the conked hair, the city clothes of the hep cat or Superfly, or the big car and the expensively dressed woman, these were all signs of money, often where no visible income was present.

During the decade after 1940, the non-white population had doubled in thirty metropolitan cities (Finestone, 1976) and the line of demarcation which separated the unskilled working class from the rest of society had become a colour line. Nowadays, most people residing in the ghetto were born there, their parents having followed the common migration pattern from the rural South to small town to metropolitan city. Family links with the South are strong, but migration is now a mere trickle. Less than 5 per cent in Harlem, for example, are newcomers (Ryan, 1976). In this sense migration follows immigration patterns in Britain.

The urban reserve army, then, is composed of non-white people (this includes Hispanics, Asians and orientals in America and Asians and orientals in Britain), although not exclusively. A large proportion are women or young people. Non-white people in North America and Britain have been disproportionately unemployed when compared with whites. This has increasingly affected the young. During the 1950s Marris and Rein (1967) showed that, during this period, slow economic growth, rising unemployment and automation combined with racism, poverty and poor educational prospects to keep youth dammed up in the ghetto. One-third of black youth leaving school were unemployed. During the 1960s, even during the war-induced boom, black unemployment was twice that of whites, and in 1967 26.5 per cent of non-white teenagers were unemployed against 10.6 per cent of white youth. In 1966 a US Department of Labor analysis found a subemployment rate of 32.7 per cent in the ghettos, nine times the national average (Kushnik, 1982). The position of Hispanic workers is cruelly ironic. Many of them are illegal immigrants, and as such not permitted to work. Yet, in California, agrarian economy has depended at different times on this labour for harvesting its crops. A pattern arises of illegal entry, exploited labour conditions, deportation and illegal re-entry.

Sadly, black people are also disproportionately represented in the prison population, the twenty to twenty-four age group being the most prevalent. Attempts have been made to reduce this. The Chicago Area Project, as mentioned previously, was set up at a time of urban labour unrest which had led to an expansion in relief projects. Concern was shown over ghetto life as Southern agriculture collapsed and migration increased. Indeed, the ghetto dweller was seen as a rural migrant who found adaptation to city life difficult in a violent criminal area, rather than a subproletariat involved in a class struggle over housing, income and health. Social agencies were staffed by white people living outside ghetto life. Another significant programme was the Mobilisation for Youth (MBY), which began in New York on the Lower East Side in 1962. The intention was to organise local people to realise community resources so that welfare recipients could define their own problems and goals and negotiate them. However, as soon as the programme became involved in political struggles over power and resources, New York officials made accusations that it was 'riot producing, communist-oriented, left-wing and corrupt' (Weissman, 1969). Funds were halted until after the 1964 presidential election, and the MBY then took a more traditional approach. Similar struggles went on with Harlem Youth Opportunities Unlimited (HARYOU), which also tried to organise the local community. The report of HARYOU, which indicated that ghetto children were seen by their teachers as ineducable 'because of their background', and that they were consequently rewarded for poorer performances (Youth in the Ghetto, 1964), led to accusations of the project being communist infiltrated. Models for delinquency prevention, as suggested in Johnson's Crime Commission, were based on the MBY project. The difficulty was delivering remedial services for education, work and welfare without developing political conflicts over community control. Black power had developed ethnic pride; leaders such as Malcolm X, Cesar Chavez, Huey Newton and Bobby Seal had had considerable influence. Riots in Watts, Harlem and other ghettos led to the development of projects trying to reach those involved in the disturbances. An interesting development was the involvement of ethnic gangs, such as Black P. Stone Nation and the Vice Lords in Chicago. Federal funding helped them develop as self-help groups. The Young Lords Organisation, first in Chicago and then in New York, focused on the barrio. Based on the Black Panther Party, the Young Lords used a mixture of ethnicity, revolutionary consciousness and a sense of injustice to organise community projects involving services for the elderly, the sick and children. Wrangles arose over the use of funds and political conflicts and splits in the local community all led to the taking over of these programmes by the Youth Services Bureaux. Helmreich's (1973) study of the Black Crusaders shows a similar pattern. A politicised street gang, they were viewed with suspicion by moneyed segments of the influential black community. Arrested after a project to paint a wall with portraits of black militants, they used the situation to move against police harassment. They developed a black guard against the police, who represented a concrete symbol of that vague abstraction 'the system'. They also promoted an anti-drugs programme, resisted recruitment into the armed forces and raised the consciousness of the elderly. However, the media promoted a negative image of the group, the local city hall opposed them and this, combined with a failure to make clear their aims before opposing local political administrators and the apathy and lack of unity in the community, led to their disbandment. Unfortunately, the more conventional agencies replacing the militant gangs were seldom attuned to community needs, and often worked too closely with the authorities. Their operational philosophy was justified as a realistic way of obtaining funding, and as a result of the increased violence—reasons that were similar to those offered in the 1930s for moving away from the Chicago Area Projects. Community control of local resources is a contentious political issue, but an essential one for ethnic minorities. The state's attitude to militant ethnic groups was tragically revealed in the recent admissions concerning their infiltration and destruction (Perkus, 1974). The killing of several leaders by police officers was regarded by the black community as deliberate. The Kerner Commission (Report of the National Advisory Commission, 1968; Center for Research on Criminal Justice, 1975), quoted as one of the most liberal federal commissions, nevertheless recommends better control capabilities in ghetto areas, better discipline and command structure in the police, more non-lethal weaponry (CS gas) and better criminal information filing. As the Center for Research on Criminal Justice (1975, p. 32) correctly point out, this is an attempt to regain confidence in the authority of the state, and 'an overall thrust toward reorganizing the police as an effective combat organization'. There is no doubt that the American state mounted a massive programme against militants (COINTELPRO), against black militants, anti-war and left-wing groups. Activists were arrested on dubious charges, and high bail and long pre-trial delays kept them off the streets. Shoot-outs occurred and as the danger of civil rioting increased it was essential to develop projects which would accommodate and buy off militant groups, or escalate local conflicts to legitimate the system and defuse any opposition. Funds were put into neighbourhoods to prevent local community insurrection, and threatening groups were either criminalised or accommodated into the system. Youth in particular is part of the reserve army, and was seen as a threatening presence in the ghetto. In Britain and America youth employment has reached 40 per cent, and this is often disguised by the proportion of middle-class youth in full-time education. Women are also casually employed in the ghetto. Something like 29 per cent of the American working class is part of the reserve army (Quinney, 1977) and 15 million poor people are never recruited into the work force at all (Balkan *et al.*, 1980). This is the context in which young ghetto dwellers grow up.

In the ghetto – formal and informal economies

Ghetto dwellers are employed at the bottom of the wage scale. The formal economy of the ghetto is the secondary labour market of temporary, deskilled and often part-time work. This is the world of the service workers, migrant farm hands, sweat shops and quasi-legal employment, which ignores health and safety regulations such as illegal truck or cab driving. Income from this work cannot maintain adequate living conditions, and a cruel element in ghetto life is that food and housing are relatively more expensive. The big supermarkets do not offer cheap deals and housing is scarce and inadequate. The reserve army has to be maintained during unemployment by public funding which makes its survival at subsistence level possible. Lack of material support, permanent employment or opportunity means that investment in the system is tenuous. The line between the perishing and the dangerous classes is thin indeed. It is hard to persuade those elements of the respectable poor, with little investment in society, from rebelling against it, or living by crime. The marginalised labour force is no longer a small group. Its expansion makes it potentially disruptive, especially when the situation is compounded by race, making it conscious of its subordinate position. This can disrupt into violence, as in Miami in 1980.

The formal aspects of the ghetto economy are welfare and hustling. The economy is in a state of fiscal crisis. The monetarist economic policies of Reagan and Thatcher pose a problem because they are based on low wages and unemployment to reduce inflation. In order to reduce the actual purchasing power of wages, inflation has been allowed to continue, rather than have governments face the political conflicts of actually cutting welfare and wages. Investment has been reduced in the public sector, and welfare state policies have been decentralised. This means that for many, permanent unemployment is a grim reality, especially for the black school leaver, and that the other element of the informal ghetto economy – hustling – has to be practised. Hustling differs from organised crime: basically, it is supplementing your income by living on your wits through knowing how to raise money without working formally. It 'exists on the blind side of the law' (Hall *et al.*, 1978, p. 352) and ranges from working the numbers (an illegal lottery) to selling stolen goods, prostitution and drug dealing. One can also hustle welfare, by lying about the presence of adult males, the rent, working on the side, and so forth. It is a clear survival strategy in poor neighbourhoods, and as Betty Lou Valentine (1978) reminds us, it is extremely hard work, taking up a lot of time and energy.

These features are also found in white, working-class life, but the salient feature about ghetto living is that it is set in the context of racism. Racial consciousness of injustice is a dangerous, explosive element with a long historical memory. Black people exist as an ethnically demarcated class fraction, and as such are usually

⮕ Minimum wage.

alienated from the white working class. Being black has a distinct caste attribute to it, and black people therefore exist as an exploited underclass in the wider, white working class. They have been seen as living in a form of internalised colonialism (Blauner, 1969; Harris, 1972) which is different, as we shall see, from the West Indian colonisation of the British, working-class neighbourhood. In the metropolitan enclaves of America, this internally colonised group is powerless, dependent and unevenly developed so that it has only a peripheral status in the national economy. This subjugation and political dependence gives rise to a form of super-exploitation (Tabb, 1970; 1974). Despite theoretical criticism (Blauner, 1969; Harris, 1972; White, 1981), this does indicate that black politics focuses consequently on black consciousness and is located in the local community.

Being black and poor is thus a profoundly different experience from being white and poor. The hustler who is successful is a distinct symbol for black youth. Smartly dressed, making a living with no obvious source of income, he is a positive model for black youth in Kingston's Trenchtown, London's Brixton and New York's Harlem because he is 'one of the few not cowed by oppression, not tied to the daily grind of low wage poverty' (Hall *et al.*, 1978, p. 378). Racism reproduces its social relations through the mainstream institutions of education, law enforcement, housing, work and poverty. Black people relate to white people through experiences mediated by racism. Racism also guarantees a subordinate position for Hispanic people from a culture of Indian-Spanish descent, and for native Americans and native Canadians. Black youth experiences similar structural problems generationally to white youth, but race remains the primary mode through which these problems are experienced. As such, race also gives them a comprehension and consciousness that permits them to deal with their exploitation. This may take the form of political consciousness, but it may have to revert to primitive rebellion, refusing dead-end work, dropping out of school, hustling and crime.

Black families in the ghetto are beset by poverty. Alcohol and drugs are ever present as highly destructive forces, yet most people are hard working and decent. They are not in trouble with the police, and have no wish for their children to be delinquent. They are not permanently involved in hustling or on welfare. Life is exceptionally hard, so that even when in work they have to moonlight to subsidise their wages. Black culture is resistant, and grew up in a resistant tradition. Despite racism, ill health, poverty and unemployment, there are frequent street parties with joyful, lavish entertainment; money is spent on cars, clothes and expensive items. This deliberate, conscious spending is often held up by the respectable as an example of the fecklessness of the poor, but it is part of ghetto life, of working-class culture. Sudden spending sprees make no structural difference to the position of ghetto dwellers with their inadequate social services. The black family in the black ghetto mediates the mainstream culture of American life to its youth. The black family has been subjected to stereotyping since Moynihan's matri-focal model, with its unstable form and absent males. The legal requirements of welfare mean that males are reported 'absent' whether they are present in the family or not. Payments are made only to single mothers. Most families are intact, although they may not always state this. Families fluctuate between welfare and wages, and although a line is drawn between the respectable and the unrespectable (i.e. those on and off welfare), in reality welfare touches most people, albeit temporarily. Black people, then, live in two cultures, the mainstream American culture mediated through education, the mass media and work, and the culture of the ghetto. The ghetto takes note of the expressive life of black people, with its rural, Southern antecedents, social events, churches, neighbourhood networks, entertainers, organisations and street life. Black culture is resistant, avoiding white authority and stating black authenticity, and it is also celebratory. Black music means something to the ordinary black person. It is performance music; it speaks of risk and danger (traditionally blues were played in risky settings – bars and brothels). It is rhythmical, and as such, sensual – dance music. White objection to Presley was his sensual 'black' movements. Black music celebrated the authenticity of black life, this is what having soul means. This can be seen in beautiful complex murals in the black and Hispanic ghettos, and on every street corner as kids perform complicated dances, leaping, flipping, doing handstands as they strut and break. Teenagers can also be seen on the street rapping, that is, putting voice-overs across record tracks (dubbing as West Indians have called it for decades), using a portable microphone and cassette player. The ability to create dances and sounds spontaneously from very little (for example, the dustbins of the West Indian steel band) reflect ghetto life. It is the ability to resist, to remake a subordinate position into something the ruling groups cannot touch. Newton (1961, quoted in Jones, 1963) argued that even when separated by success, black musicians' behaviour is determined by their origins in the ghetto. Black musicians for him are bohemians, but not the bohemians of reversed bourgeois morality, but of a bohemia based on

the pattern of the unskilled labourer magnified. . . . For the star was what every slum child or drudge might become; the king or queen of the poor, because they are poor people writ large.

We can see this in the turn of the century music hall, or again in country music stars. There is a relationship between performer and audience, a recognisable similarity of background. Implicit in black popular culture is a belief in the superiority of black people's musicality, the meaning of their emotions and lack of inhibition. In the same way, there is a belief in the superiority of their dancing and rhythm, which is a metaphor for the superiority of their sexuality, a fear in most white people that explains some of the irrational features of racism.

Black on blues – black culture and youth

We have seen that racist social relations have different cultural consequences from class relations, and that the material construction of black people's lives is consolidated by the racial element. Afro-American people have given to the world that section of American culture that is seen internationally as uniquely American: 'American' popular music, which means black music, mainly blues and jazz. It is the expression of black American life – soul. From the early sorrow of being black in a white racist society, found in rural blues with its memory of slavery, one follows urban blues with its perplexed lament of urban life. The blues celebrates the basic stuff of life – sex, love, jealousy, violence and poverty – the good times and the bad times. Keill (1966) suggests that Afro-Americans have three major traditions: sacred music or gospel; the profane tradition composed of urban and rural blues, with pre-war jazz, and that synthesis of jazz, blues and gospel which has emerged since 1945. The history of black America is present as an oral tradition, from slavery, emancipation, the migration North, to the everyday events of funerals, picnics, singing for rent, travelling and the ever present religion. It is a music keenly aware of struggle, politically and domestically. For Keill, the urban bluesman is a key figure in black culture, to be ranked with the hustler. Bluesmen, like preachers, have their hustle; they are the exponents of soul, reflecting back to their audience their experience of being black in America.

> The bluesman is in a sense every man; the country bluesman is an archetype of the migrant labourer; the city bluesman is a stereotype of the stud, the hustler ... the credentials for being a bluesman or a soul singer are listed by Al Hibbler as having been hurt by a woman, being 'brought up in that old time religion', and knowing what that slavery shit is all about. (Keill, 1966, p. 152)

The blues singer is a travelling man, exhibiting a particular type of masculine behaviour, a singer whose work is also his life. Whilst the preacher offers spiritual comfort and a respectable example of militancy, the bluesman sings of sex, prison, gambling, whisky fighting and love, 'the common coin of ghetto life', yet both tell it like it is. Both give an explanation and a consciousness of black experience, and both offer a sense of collective identity through these commonly experienced problems. The preacher and the blues-man are polarised aspects of black manhood and of soul. For the poor, the preacher is the epitome of respectability and responsi-bility, whilst the blues singer is a 'no good man'; one celebrates the integration of the sexes, the other the traditional battle between them. The devil's opponent and the devil's music.

Jones (1963) argues that the growth of cool music, as in hard bop and progressive jazz, reflects the disaffection black people showed to white America. This cool is reflected in the style of certain types of hustlers, who have withdrawn from the intense struggle of ghetto life. However, as jazz became more esoteric and complex, soul became the predominant form of popular and dance-able music. The non-participation of cool was replaced by the black pride of soul which, despite the enormous popular success of the Beatles, remained black people's dance music. However, the most important music seminally was probably rhythm and blues, taking the gospel beat and the blues sexuality to become a major dance music. It was disc jockey Alan Freed, who on his Cleveland 'Moon-dog Show' radio show in 1953, first called the new music 'rock and roll'. However, black singers such as Muddy Waters, Chuck Berry and Little Richard were popular among black audiences, but not until Presley took up the black sound and the black movement did rock and roll really become popular. White audiences had to have a white culture hero for a real commercial success. Rock and roll developed both blues and country elements to symbolise the uneasy relation between black and white music. From then on most white music was a response to black music in many ways, although Bane (1982) argues differently. Rock for him is not a mutated form of black music, 'white boy singing the blues', but a fusion of blues, country, and gospel where 'we find the continuous battering of black against white, forcing the music to change again and again' (Bane, 1982, p. 17).

By the 1970s Superfly was in, and cool was back. Disco became the dance music par excellence. Erotic body music, it swept out of black discos using complicated movements and steps. It passed into the gay clubs, where its sexuality and ecstasy made its performance a stylised orgy to the rest of the dance world through *Saturday Night Fever*. Affluence, elegance and control were back in fashion in a way that would have delighted the mods, and black dance was again expropriated.

Black culture, of course, does not remain uninfluenced by the wider white culture, particularly its more commercial aspects. Liebow (1967, p. 22) puts this well:

> The street corner man does not appear as a carrier of an independent cultural tradition. His behaviour appears not so much a way of realizing the distinctive goals of his own subculture, or of conforming to its models, but rather as his way of trying to achieve many of the goals and values of the larger society, and of failing to do this, and concealing his failure from others and from himself as best he can.

Unemployment in the ghetto is a collective experience. The street corner subculture offers support for the unemployed man, who finds others like himself, and therefore no better than he is. Liebow does not see the determinism of a simple cultural transmission as an explanation but similarities between black fathers and their sons, which

> do not result from 'cultural transmission' but from the fact that the son goes out and independently experiences the same failures, in the same areas, and for the same reasons as his father. (Liebow, 1967)

Generationally, young blacks face the same structural problems as their parents, modified or amplified by the immediate economic conditions they have to live in. However, they have survived in a different youth culture to that of the adults, shaped to their specific difficulties, and their response is different. The ghetto offers a supportive culture which makes a dent in hegemony. Black popular culture, music, dance and style articulates this specifically for youth, creating a 'space' which enables them to resist. As such, culture is a lived practice enabling the young black person to make sense of particular conditions of existence. Dance has taken on primary significance; breaking or break dancing where breaks in the music signify a break into another dance style and hip hop where a contest takes place between dance crews. Starting in the Bronx, and spread by DJs such as Afrika Bambaata, who had been around the gangs, it replaced fighting as a male contest. Hip hop incorporates rapping, where a sung version of the 'dirty dozens' means rivals try to outdo each other using an elaborate rhyming sing song of insults over a musical base. This is often done to 'scratching', music created by spinning discs on turntables to make a rhythmical counterpoint to the music on the track. Hip hop has been given a commercial boost by Michael Jackson, and his 'moonwalk', a dance which is performed by gliding backwards. Breaking, rapping, hip hop, wearing distinct clothing, painting murals, spraying graffiti on subway cars or 'bombing', are all visible symbols of resistance. Firstly, they are things white kids cannot do or do as well; secondly, they make the culture socially visible; and thirdly, they generate a reaction, usually hostile or fearful, sometimes admiring among white adult authority. Because circumstances and reactions are complex, so the culture changes and adapts itself to new circumstances. For today's youth the South is a distant past, militancy ebbs and flows, but danger in the streets is much higher, as is crime. Other features remain, such as the ghetto culture which teaches children from an early age to avoid the questions of landlords, police, social workers and debt collectors. These are all symbols of white authority. Accommodation always occurs, but is never total. Graffiti art finds its way into coffee table books or exhibitions; black cultural resistance may become accommodated into the lives of radical chic. The black cultural response, then, is to move elsewhere to rebel, taking full advantage where possible of any financial advantage of inclusion in middle-class hip culture.

The world of the ghetto generates a bimodality of cultural forms reaching back into the mainstream and into black slum life. The culture of poverty no longer seems so singly deterministic when compared with this. Ryan (1976) has indicated that the black family is doing quite well. Three-quarters of black families are male headed, seven in ten children are with both parents, and most births are legitimate. Even within the single parent family there is a wide variation of child rearing practices, so that the myth of a single, homogeneous culture is dubious even within the terms of the argument. Black adolescents grow up in the ghetto with a system of police surveillance which acts against them. Carter and Lohmann (1968) show that police surveillance in their two middle-class towns was significantly different from the national average concerning informal release. Cicourel (1968) showed how middle-class families can mobilise resources to avoid criminalisation, but even when crime and recidivism are held constant, race and class show a relationship concerning more serious dispositions. Using Wolfgang *et al.*'s (1972) figures, Thornberry (1978) found that black and working-class delinquents received more serious dispositions at the level of the intake hearing, the police and juvenile court, especially the last two. Williams and Gold (1972) found that black youth was treated more harshly by the court intake rather than the police. Piliavin and Briar (1964) found that one-third of black juveniles apprehended were basically arrested for uncooperative attitudes as compared to only one-sixth of whites. Because arrest figures are high in the ghetto, this becomes a justification for racist attitudes to black people, even though, according to Ryan (1976), black arrests have reduced from 58 per cent to 46 per cent of the arrest rate. The police in Britain and America face similar problems with working class people, hated for harassment but also for failing to protect their neighbourhoods from crime. The Kerner Report, like the Scarman Report, speaks of aggressive, preventive patrol work conducting intensive street searches as adding impetus to riots, and Kerner speaks critically of institutionalised racism and assembly line justice. The police have become the front line for the state in its institutionalised racism and hence a scapegoat for deeper problems. Without proper discussion with local communities concerning the sort of policing they want, the situation in both countries can only deteriorate.

It is hardly surprising, given the poverty, racism and lack of opportunity, that the hustler arises as a model for black youth. In Jamaica in the slums of Kingston he is the 'rude boy', present in Britain as the 'rudie'. Finestone (1957) in his study of Chicago delinquent boys of the early 1950s speaks of the 'cool cat' around the Chicago Area Project. The cat revolts against the low paid 'shit work' of the ghetto. Well-dressed, with style and no visible means of support, he lives on his wits by hustling. Cool and aloof, ridiculing the 'square', he is an 'operator' completely cynical about the motivations of others, his fantasy to live supported by several women working as shoplifters and prostitutes. He uses the drug of total commitment – heroin. Costume is used to convey an essential symbolic class and ethnic message. The 'ideal cat'

> would always appear in public impeccably dressed, and would be able to sport a complete change of outfit several times a day. . . . Moreover the 'cat' feels himself to be any man's equal. He is convinced that he can go anywhere and mingle easily with anyone. (Finestone, 1957, p. 791)

He is elegant, and so able to step outside race and class, very much in the way of the British mods. His coolness distances him from the stark reality of urban poverty and racism. He can be a black dandy, disdaining the 'nowhere' future and work of the ghetto – he is a sport. Krisberg (1974) shows the persistence of the model, with his Philadelphia hustlers. Again to survive, the white man's laws have to be broken, but in a cool way. When situations are difficult, he stays cool and talks his way out of trouble. Archetypal male, working-class, subcultural responses are direct attacks by violence, or disdainful distancing through being cool. Krisberg's hustlers are ignorant of black power and its leaders. As with Liebow's street corner men, the future is held at a distance just because there is no control over it. Closed off from the hustles of the wealthy, they know there is no future, but hope it will not arrive too soon. They subscribe to what Liebow calls the 'shadow system of values', attaching themselves to notions of survival, internalising failure, being made distrustful by street life. They hold conservative and non-conservative values simultaneously; they internalise a world which despises and destroys them.

'Los vatos locos' – Hispanic youth culture in the barrio

Hispanic immigrants, mainly from Puerto Rico and Mexico, and settling mainly in New York and Los Angeles, are a substantial minority in America. Ironically, they are the oldest and the newest group, the South West having been founded by Mexicans who were displaced by the settlers moving West. Many fled the Mexican revolutions of the 1910–20 period and a quarter of a million settled in Los Angeles by 1920. Selective deportation followed the depression but during the Second World War boom immigration rose, then ebbed to rise again in the 1970s. Relationships between Chicanos and the local white population have always been uneasy, and the situation was exacerbated by rioting in 1943 and 1970. Los Angeles remains a reservoir of low-paid Mexican labour, the newest arrivals from Mexico staying in the East of the city. Ironically, as shown in an excellent book by Moore (1978) one and a quarter million Mexicans have no elected representative in the city or county government.

For Mexican youth, the problems are the perennial ones of the barrio, the Mexican ghetto, poverty, housing, law enforcement, and education. Their position is not dissimilar to that of the Asians in Britain. They have a country of their own, their own language, and specific religious affiliations. The Asian people are of course a vastly more complex series of different peoples and religions, but their structural position is similar. The barrio is now several generations old. Its schools are 'factories for failure' (Rist, 1973) which prepare youth for irregular labour in marginal employment. Rather as Willis (1977) showed with his British working-class boys, the Chicano child soon abandons all hope of pleasing the teachers, evades rules and learns skills and values which prepare him or her for general labour in a casual, unskilled market. Again the context is hustling, casual labour and welfare. Something like 25 per cent of the barrio in Los Angeles are on welfare, whilst the illegal economy ranges from unlicensed, uninsured trucking to drug dealing. Barrio youth has, however, a tight, neighbourhood network to draw on, a Hispanic cultural tradition, and its own youth cultural history. The most celebrated exponents were the 'pachucos', young

129

men in zoot suits with drapes and double-soled shoes. They spoke a heavy argot, 'pachuco', sported the 'cruz del barrio' (barrio cross) tattooed on the backs of their hands and were the local heavies, fighting local Mexican 'square' kids. Known as 'vatos locos' (crazy guys), they took pride in their opposition to Anglo society. They were contemptuous of 'Gabachos' (Anglos) and their national pride reflected the strong attachment to Mexico shown by their parents. Bands of young men were common in Mexico, coming from local towns or villages, and the pachucos reflected this in an alien culture. They were involved in the Los Angeles 'Zoot Suit Riots' (Barker, 1947) where a series of race riots took place against them. Local servicemen, especially sailors, offended by the dress of 'pachucos' (oversized trousers and accessories) beat them up, cutting off their ducktail hair, destroying their obvious Mexican symbols. The mass media was instrumental in creating a moral panic against these folk devils, and the police often assisted servicemen in the beatings. 'Pachuquismo' arose as a distinct identity for Chicano youth (Paz, 1961), and a resistant subculture developed. It made a clear state-ment about ethnicity, a statement against hegemonic truisms and stereotypes concerning Mexicans, and was also a source for young men to try to disengage themselves from the poverty, large families and alcoholism which the older men were subject to. The riots were seen by Anglo society as the arrogant challenge of an ethnic group whose patriotism was considered doubtful. Pachucos were seen as filled with irrational foreign violence, and indeed the Ayres Report on the riots, put out by the Los Angeles Sheriff's Department, spoke of 'Aztec blood lust' (McWilliams, 1949). This celebration of 'la vida loca' (crazy life) was a challenge to Anglo hegemony, and the 1943 riots are still remembered with great bitterness. The wholesale blaming of Mexican youth by the media meant that in the barrio the pachucos are seen as Chicanos who refused to tolerate racism. Territoriality is important in the barrio, indeed 'mi barrio' means not only 'my neighbourhood', but also 'my gang'. Gangs are age graded into 'klikas', originating in inter-barrio conflict. They re-main salient identity groups, reinforcing neighbourhood attach-ment, so that even in prison 'homeboys' are those from the same barrio (Moore, 1978). They can remain loosely attached to the gang in later life as 'veteranos'. There is a subculture in the barrio generating gangs, all of whom are fighting groups, and most of whom use drugs, tragically enough heroin. The subculture can only be understood in its subordinate relationship to Anglo culture, the ethnic context of being a Mexican American, and the closeness of barrio life. Moore argues that because formal opportunity struc-tures are closed off even to non-delinquent aspiring youth, deviant and non-deviant values exist simultaneously, although these are mixed even in the same district. Closely knit groups co-exist with drifting individuals, but as Moore points out, a local subculture reflects the parent culture of the particular barrio. Different types dominate specific barrios. There is the new immigrant from Mexico, working and living in the barrio; there is the Chicano who is native to the district, working in the secondary labour market and unable to move out; there is the Chicano who escapes the barrio, often through the armed services, and moves to a mixed neighbourhood; finally there is the delinquent, involved in the gangs, graduating through the 'klikas' using drugs and passing from Juvenile Hall to prison. This latter group connects with Chicano factions while in prison, and on discharge joins the 'pinto' network of ex-prisoners or becomes a 'tecato' (addict) joining the tecato networks of the other barrios. Tecato-pinto groups value machismo, close blood brotherhood ('carnalismo') and 'personalismo' (long-lasting, loyal personal friendships). This group makes up the 'veteranos', tragically leading to increased isolation as addiction increases.

These were not the only subcultures. The 'low riders' of the late 1960s were a highly visible Chicano subculture of young males, whose style was cool, sharp, laid back and neatly dressed affluence, not unlike black subcultures. Cars were central, with lowered chassis and customised paint jobs, called 'cherry shorts'. A homology can be noted between the laid back, neat affluence, cherry shorts and the style of driving which involved really illegally slow driving on the L.A. boulevards in lowered seats (a 'Playboy pad on wheels'), and the use of seconals ('reds'). A major identity was constructed, making a statement about the ability to be arrogantly and coolly contemptuous of Anglo authority.

Perhaps reflecting the masculinist culture of the barrio, little is said about girls. Quicker (1974) has carried out a small study on Chicanas, arguing that as tradition declines, role changes have occurred with the girl gangs, who are now more ambivalent about the boys' gangs. It is not clear, however, whether and to what extent these gangs are separate girl gangs, or gangs attached as auxiliaries to the boys' 'klikas'.

During the 1960s the Hispanic communities became politicised, especially the gangs, as the 'movimiento' gained hold. Cesar Chavez was organising, and gangs became involved around Hispanic concerns in Los Angeles. In 1967 the Chicano student movement – the Brown Berets – was born. In the same year the Puerto Rican street gang, the Young Lords Organisation (YLO), first in Chicago, then later in New York became involved in community matters. With the YLO the 3,000 strong Chicago Latin Kings organised community programmes similar to the Black Panther Party. Peace was negotiated between gangs and school breakfasts, day care and legal assistance projects were started. In New York the YLO developed community newspapers, sanitation health, education and legal aid. There was active involvement against official racism, and a recognition of the potential solidarity in ethnic districts (Browning, 1971). Like many such organisations, cuts in grants, wrangles over aid, problems in local politics and the difficulty of organising street people in long-term projects led to the gradual disbanding of this form of community aid. Spasmodic reappearances occur, as with the quasi-official vigilante group, the Guardian Angels, who patrolled the New York subway during 1979. The visible appearance of such groups, it must be remembered, is a constant reminder that the official groups whose job it is to organise such projects are failing. The social visibility of this criticism is a constant embarrassment to official agencies, and it is hardly surprising that little is done to continue the existence of those who criticise and effectively out-professionalise the professionals.

'Inglan is a bitch' – black and brown youth in Britain

'You always get this thing like when I went for a job up the road and the man he says "You don't mind if we call you a black bastard, or a wog or a nigger or anything because its entirely a joke." . . . I told him to keep his job. Him say "I'm not colour prejudiced." . . . I don't want to work for no white man. Black people have been working for them for a long time. I don't want to work for them. I never used to hate white people. I still don't hate all of them. But its them who teach me how to hate.'
(Black teenagers, Harambee Hostel, London in
P. Gillman, 'I blame England', *Sunday Times*, 30.10.73)

Although non-white people have lived in England since 1603, they were isolated and always subject to prejudice. Elizabeth I declared herself 'discontented with the great amount of blackamoors which are crept into this realm'. However, Britain's black population, about 1.6 million people (2.9 per cent of the population), are the result of immigration during the 1950s. Massive recruitment for the health and service industries in the 1950s, combined with the McCarren Walter Act, 1952, which reduced immigration into the United States for West Indians to a mere 800 per year, meant that West Indian emigration focused on Britain. Asians were also recruited into the textile factories. English immigration became restricted after India reopened emigration in 1960. A series of Commonwealth Immigration Acts was aimed specifically at curbing non-white immigration, and Britain moved from an immigration policy based on the Old Commonwealth citizenship, offering permanent residence, to a situation of temporary work visas. The immigration doors are now closed, especially to non-white applicants, and the non-white population is made up of 43 per cent West Indian (two-thirds being Jamaican) and 57 per cent Asian (26 per cent Indian, 16 per cent Pakistani, 15 per cent African Asian). Black and white youth has never really mixed, and Britain has never really seriously dealt with its problems of race relations. Non-whites have been delegated to run-down neighbourhoods, racist attacks, police harassment, and impoverished conditions. The West Indian infrastructure produced few middle-class immigrants, but even though Asians are found to have more professional immigrants, the lower ranks of the work force are composed of 18 per cent of the white work force, 32 per cent of the West Indian, 36 per cent of the Indian and 58 per cent of the Pakistani. Exploited by these conditions, compounded by the worst educational facilities, non-whites have become an underclass, a sub-proletariat of a working class divided into indigenous and non-indigenous work forces (Sivanandan, 1976). This situation has been worsened by the exploitation of anxiety about non-whites by the white population, carried out by the neo-Nazi parties, the National Front and the British Movement.

A contributing feature to the sense of racial oppression in Britain has been the stereotyping by the police of Asians as probable illegal immigrants, and West Indians as aggressive and excitable, and probably involved in street crime. This has decreased immigrants' confidence in the police and, combined with youth unemployment, 40 per cent in some areas, which has particularly affected black and brown youth (especially if female), has led to a highly volatile situation.

'Dread in Babylon'. Rude boys and Rastafarians – Afro-Caribbean youth culture in Britain

Racism, educational disadvantage often coupled with educational ambition, the rejection of 'shit work' and increasing unemployment have formed a context for subcultural solutions open to black youth. These now have their own history in the black community. Just as the immigrant parents of black youth idealised 'Mother England' so young blacks idealise a mythical Africa. Race, we have noted, mediates the experience and lives of black people, but also raises a consciousness of structured subordination and resistance to oppression. In Britain there developed a defensive cohesion of the West Indian community against white racist society, a cultural space, allowing an alternative black life. This has been called the 'colony' and Hall *et al.* (1978, p. 351) argue that:

> Here began the 'colonisation' of certain streets, neighbourhoods, cafes and pubs, the growth of revivalist churches, mid-day Sunday hymn singing and mass baptisms in the local swimming baths, the spilling-out of Caribbean fruit and vegetables from Indian shops, the shebeen and the Saturday night blues party, the construction of the sound systems, the black record shops selling blues, ska and soul, the birth of the 'native quarter' at the heart of the English city.

There is an Asian equivalent, an Asian colonising of the city centre with Indian and Pakistani cinemas, restaurants, temples and cultural centres. The Asians brought with them the languages, religion and culture of home, of an integrated complex society, which despite political and religious divisions, had not been disrupted and rebuilt because of slavery. The colonisation by the British empire had given Asian cultures a cohesion to resist imperialism. The continued protest by West Indian youth has been written off, as is common with any youthful protest, as a generational or identity crisis. The political content of West Indian and Asian youthful struggle has too often been removed and the situation relegated to the difficulties of intra-family conflict, or the difficulties of growing up in an alien land, or successfully criminalised as in the case of mugging.

The Caribbean social economy has been reproduced in Britain, and one result was the adoption as a cultural model by West Indian youth during the 1960s of a Jamaican form of ghetto hustler – the 'rude boy' or 'rudie'. Hustling, as we have noted, is not only outside wage labour, it also supplies goods, services and entertainments to the respectable element of the black colony. Hustlers are out on the street with visible style, cool like Finestone's cats. There are those who cannot find work, and those who will not subject themselves to routine labour for white society. Rudies operated in the slums of West Kingston, living by dope dealing, pimping and gambling, hanging out in the shebeens and clubs, and whose style of 'stingy brim' hats and dark shades were sported by Jamaicans in the early 1960s. Violence and marijuana surrounded the rudie, a night cat whose music was ska, blue beat, rock steady and reggae. He followed the sporting life of horses, dominoes and women. The other major subcultural figure who contrasts with this criminal model in interesting ways is the Rastafarian locksman, his religious fervour a striking contrast to the rude boy's cool. Yet he too is a rebel, excluded by his religion, his pan Africanism and his politics. The Rastafarian movement draws upon the deep religious feelings African people have, but reverses Christianity to draw upon Biblical metaphors to make political points. It takes seriously Marcus Garvey's 1929 prophecy. 'Look to Africa, where a black king shall be crowned, for the day of deliverance is near'. It was said this would occur in Ethiopia (itself a Biblical reference for Africa), and Emperor Haile Selassie of Ethiopia was declared Ras Tafari, the living God, Lion of Judah, King of Kings, sometimes 'Jah' (an abbreviation of Jehovah). Thus a black messiah was born who would lead the Children of Israel out of Babylon (colonised ex-empires such as Jamaica) to Ethiopia, Zion, the promised land, the black man's home – Africa. For the Rastaman, black people are descended from Solomon and Sheba, the descendant of whom was Haile Selassie. The Rasta shall live with his black queen (marriage being seen as sinful), and as a true Israelite resist the ways of the white man who holds him in slavery. Capitalism is the system of Babylon and property, alcohol and gambling are disdained, but 'de herb' or 'ganja' (marijuana) is held sacred. With its aid, thought is transformed into feeling, and belief becomes knowledge. Black people are reincarnated slaves, brothers and sisters, referred to as a collective 'I and I', indicating those who know they are brethren both one and immortal. Haile Selassie's death merely confirms that God is in all men, and will be reincarnated elsewhere. The Rasta promises a 'rod of correction' for Babylon. He is an important symbol for black youth, with his long, uncut dreadlocks, his beard and woollen cap of the Ethiopian colours of red, green and gold. His patriarchy, his mysticism and poetry are as important as his belief that all black men are Rastafarians and need only to realise this. A basic cultural connection between British youth and Jamaica is the music and lyrics of reggae. Jamaican music is important in the colony: it is music for dancing and music with a political message, both essential elements of Jamaican style. American rhythm and blues greatly influenced Jamaican music in the 1950s. Its soul connections spoke from one dispossessed black population to another. It became blended into Jamaican music first in ska, then bluebeat, rock steady and reggae. Reggae has a distinctly rasta feeling, its beat based on the rhythms of 'burra' drumming used to welcome released convicts back into the West Kingston slums. Its lyrics praise Jah, preach black brotherhood and threaten revolution in Babylon. By the late 1960s, rudies were sporting a rasta style. A form of soul consciousness had been raised wedding rasta brother-hood and rudie violence. The writings of the American Black Power movement became influential, and their political message spread a consciousness of race and class oppression. The basically peaceful attitude of the rasta was fused with rasta militance. Reggae became a poetic manifesto spreading its political message to young blacks in Britain.

However, as Frith (1978, p. 219) notes, the origins of reggae are from a political culture outside Britain, and the consciousness expressed is neither youthful nor British. As Hebdige (1976b) indicates, as the demand for unskilled labour diminished, black and white school leavers came into fiercer competition for work. Reggae emphasised this division and as black consciousness increased, so did an interest in black style and identity. With the Africanisation of rasta and its exhortation of peace and harmony, found only in white hippies – a group despised by the skinheads – those working-class youths who were attracted to the music of the West Indian subculture, but who when threatened by the rise of black consciousness, took up a studied racism. The black separatism and metaphor of Rastafarianism then doubly locked out white youth. As reggae's lyrics became more political, the contradiction became insurmountable. The hostility which was in the background between black and white youth increased. The solidarity of the black community increased against police harassment, and the mutual support given by young blacks to each other in street fights was something not found among youth in the white working-class community. Robins and Cohen (1978) argue that the breakdown of stable, subcultural identity among white working-class youth, combines with the erosion of the traditional supports of their parent culture, so that they felt particularly threatened by the presence of any socio-cultural group cohesion. White groups are separated by neighbourhood, subcultural form and inter-group schisms, whilst the very element for which blacks are despised – race – unites them against a common threat, be it white gangs, the police or other authorities. This is not to argue for a simple form of cohesion among black youth, but they have a popular culture which is resistant to racism, and which makes sense of their condition to provide a supportive ideology which justifies of their oppression. It makes for a consciousness of the fact that they are schooled for low-paid, low-status work and, increasingly, for unemployment.

Rastafarianism, then, provides a space for black British youth. It has a long political history, wedded, as Campbell (1980) reminds us, to Marcus Garvey's pan Africanism, a materialist historical analysis, and celebrated in the defiance of reggae. Gilroy (1982) locates the symbols of 'dread' worn openly as transporting the difference of the 'unacceptable attribute of dark skin into open semiotic struggle characteristic of youth culture'. He indicates that, in the Rasta queen, women have begun their own distinct form of black feminist struggle. Judy Mowatt's record, 'Black Woman', made the Rasta queen a starting point for a redefinition of Rasta women and their complementary, but distinct, wage strength. Rasta politics are concerned with what is justice and equality for black people in the present, in this world, rather than an undefined future in heaven. This point is recognised and sympathised with in the black community, regardless of age, gender or status. Reggae celebrates this by offering a powerful musical experience, developed through an emphasis on the heavy dubbed-over chant, a common feature in Jamaican recordings. Often it takes the form of political verse combined with reggae, as found in the poetry of Lionel Kwesi Johnson who has a popular following because of the way he draws upon local culture and resistance. Hebdige (1976b) reminds us that West Indian music has been immensely popular among British white youth from about 1967. However, as noted, as reggae became more political, the Rasta influence insisted that a basic condition for acceptance into West Indian subcultures was being 'young, black and proud'. At the same time, black and white school leavers were coming into fiercer competition for work, and struggles occurred firstly for skilled then unskilled work. Black popular culture took note of this. Dodd (1978, p. 598) noted that

'a new revolution of the mind' is taking place in the neighbourhoods of South London. There are new images and a new aesthetic on display. The function of public space – like street corners – has visibly altered as those who derive identities from their behaviour in such places try to make it private. The police have increasingly taken on the guise of aliens confronted by a culture they do not understand and so for which they feel contempt.

But the contempt is mutual. For the streets of Brixton, once paved with hope, are now filled with the frustration, hopelessness and desperate pride of rebels and gangsters. They are the streets too of Laventille in Trinidad, West Kingston in Jamaica and South Georgetown in Guyana. The culture and meaning of black poverty is now as much of a reality in the industrial slums and housing estates of Britain as it is in the decaying urban villages of the Caribbean. The slave legacy has finally come home to roost.

The first generation of immigrants were ambitious to escape their homeland and happy to accept conditions as they found them, comparing them to those they had left behind. Their children, however, have only their contemporaries to compare their lot with, and they are not prepared to accept their stigmatised position in white society. They have developed an urban street culture, with roots in the 'rudie' hustler value system, with an overlay of Rastafarian style, politics and Caribbean culture. They look to Zion, a mythical Africa where merit and identity are not judged by pigmentation. Parents were ambitious for their children, and the British economy

137

has neither met those needs nor created opportunities for advancement. Black youth has been caught in an economic crisis where black unemployment is common, and work badly paid and demeaning. Often, because their children have rejected what work is available, strain at home can be severe, sometimes leading to children being ejected, and living in squats or youth houses. Those who continue to live at home face different problems from their parents, mostly confronting the reality that the prosperity and opportunity their parents sought is a myth cruelly dispelled by recession. Rebellion has become a solution, a subcultural style stretching from reinterpretations of Rasta, to street crime and 'voluntary unemployment'. Dodd (1978, p. 600) argues that: 'For many black adolescents growing up in the slums of Britain and the Caribbean, crime is about the only freedom they have left.'

One result of this has been the rise in street robbery, argues Dodd. It acts to depersonalise the victim (usually white, unlike the United States), and the dynamics are first of all a self-hatred, in which blackness is intrinsically involved, then hating the group who made you hate yourself, on whom you finally turn in revenge. This Dodd sees as the background to the rise of a black street subculture in Britain. Obviously the problem of personalising this type of hatred is that the wrong target is inevitably selected. The subculture functions because (Dodd, 1978, p. 600) 'it provides an appropriate social context within which males are free to engage in "character contests" to acquire a reputation and secure an identity'. However, the degree to which black youth is involved in delinquent or criminal elements is an empirical question as yet systematically unanswered. The traditional ways out of the ghetto for black people, where education has been blocked, have been through sport or entertainment. Hustling in some ways reflects these worlds. It is exciting and dramatic, and outside the dreary world of wage labour. The extent to which young blacks are involved in it is unknown, but if the figures for white working-class youth are a guide, one can safely infer that most black youth is not involved in delinquent enterprises. Voluntary unemployment is another confusing term. It is practically impossible to measure. Young people living at home may be involved in temporary voluntary unemployment because they are seeking work with a future, and are registered with private rather than public employment. Many young people now work casually, or part time, and may disguise this in order to qualify for benefits. In fact, long-term voluntary unemployment is a matter of conjecture. Before the deepening of the recession, a Commission for Racial Equality Report (1978), *Looking for Work*, compared white and black school leavers in Lewisham, London and found no evidence of voluntary unemployment. Most black and white unemployed youth were actively seeking work (only two of the black sample said they were not). Black youths were found to be less likely to have jobs fixed up when they left school, spent more time finding a job, made more applications, and were less satisfied with the jobs found. Discrimination was a major factor in this. As the recession has worsened, despair has increased among unemployed young people. As the British government increases in its determination to ´reduce welfare to force unemployed people into accepting low paid work, subsidising business interests, and reducing public sector expenditure young people are increasingly becoming a target for low paid, often temporary work, disciplined by the threat of removing benefits.

Asian youth in Britain

Asian youth has been seen as being less involved in the same alienating processes as Caribbean youth. The Asian community is made up of several different cultures, speaking different languages with important religious differences. Forty per cent are Muslim, 29 per cent Hindu and 25 per cent Sikh. Roughly speaking, Pakistani people tend to have emigrated from rural areas, Indians from urban centres, whilst East African Asians are the most Europeanised and middle class. Asian parents expect to exercise considerable control over their children, who are expected to marry a partner chosen and approved by them. Girls are under close surveillance from the local community, and informal networks control the possibilities of clandestine courtship. Sharpe (1976) noted that despite this, many of her Asian girls managed secret meetings, but her sample was mainly Indian and East African Asian. Asian youth is able to draw on its own cultures, and its own close communities, and has tended to mix little outside school with either black or white youth. Livingstone (1978) found that, regardless of area of origin or religion, Asian boys seldom joined multi-racial youth organisations, and Anwar (1976) reported that Asian parents feared the effects these might have in terms of bad company and different religious traditions.

It has been argued that Westernisation is a problem for Asian youth, who inhabit a very different world at school from that of home. Distinct youth cultural forms have not as yet shown themselves in any style recognisable to outsiders, although Bradford did have Pakistani teddy boys. Asian youth has been stereotyped either as passive, withdrawing into its own culture, or else suffering from generational conflict. However, Asian youths have recently taken a distinct stance against the effects of racism upon their communities. 'Paki-bashing' has long been a form of attack by white youth, and Asian youths who organised themselves in Bradford against racism were charged with conspiracy in 1981. Earlier, in London, Asian youths had formed vigilante groups to protect their communities against attacks on persons and property, a feature they saw the police unable or unwilling to do. In 1977, they sat down in East London to prevent fascists selling their literature, and in 1981 they attacked a skinhead concert which had several Young National Front supporters in the audience, fearing another attack on the Asian community. The future means that where young non-whites draw upon traditions of resistance in their culture to prevent racism, they are likely to be seen as criminalised, rather in the way that West Indian youth has been.

Black and brown girls

West Indians suffer from having their problems sexualised by official agencies (part of the sexualisation of black people by white) and also from being viewed as aggressive and physically violent. Black women have a long cultural tradition in the 'maroon' (escaped slave) communities in the West Indies, and African women have always been assertive rather than demure. Much has been made of West Indian family relations, which are used to present perspectives which pathologise the West Indian family. The Caribbean family structure means that women, both in the extended and immediate family, take care of the children. The inheritance of slavery, and the high degree of poverty in Jamaica meant that common law relations were both accepted and stable. Authority was shared by both partners, and both partners worked. Poverty often necessitated the man working away, and the maternal role became more important than the marital. During emigration families were split, and children arriving in Britain often found a new parent and siblings to cope with, as well as the grief of leaving the mother or mother substitute behind in the Caribbean. This helps to explain the proportion of single parenthood in West Indian family statistics, but it must be compared to the use of contraception and abortion in the indigenous population. Sharpe (1976) found close control over the daughters of West Indian families, three-quarters of her sample reporting that their parents never or seldom allowed them out with boys (although over half had boyfriends). Girls also complained that they, but not their brothers, were expected to do domestic work in the home. Reaction to pregnancy differs, but mothers feel their daughters have had more opportunities to avoid pregnancy and more opportunities for advancement. If a girl is turned out, there is not the close kin structure which she would have found in the Caribbean. Sharpe also reported that her West Indian girls placed less emphasis on marriage and a family than her English girls. Although they found school boring, they placed more emphasis on education. One study (Commission for Racial Equality, 1978) found that 75 per cent of West Indian girls obtained white-collar work in the area of Lewisham, London, but only 62 per cent of white girls; although twice as many of the white girls (17 per cent) found work in shops (public areas). West Indian girls are often seen by teachers as 'unfeminine' because they are 'too loud' or 'flaunt' their sexuality. They also 'talk back' (Carby, 1982).

Asian girls are expected to be deferential to their parents' authority, and after puberty Muslim girls are closely guarded. Nevertheless, a considerable amount of Asian women are at work. The 1971 census revealed that 40.8 per cent of Indian and 20.5 per cent of Pakistani women worked full time. Economic need is the reason for this, and one black woman in two works in Britain. Isolation is a problem for all women at home, and for Asian, especially Muslim, women it can be severe. Immigrant women have fewer contacts in their community than those born in Britain, and Wilson (1978) has written a moving account of Asian women's homesickness and isolation after marriage. When at work they are also subject to racism. Anwar (1976) notes that 85 per cent of his Asian girls over sixteen felt that women should work, and that the arranged marriage common to Asians would be a source of potential conflict. Amos and Parmar (1982) point out that arranged marriage as an institution does not mean that the girl has no say in her choice of husband, and family control varies according to the Asian community and particular family. The danger is that well-meaning white liberals then exclude Asian schoolgirls from activities they feel their parents might disapprove of, and from career advice and training. It is certainly true that a girl's reputation is important, that 'izzat', the patriarchal pride of brothers and father, acts against friendships outside a girl's immediate religious community or caste. Asian women and girls face the problems of sexism in the form of patriarchy in the family and of course outside it. A much bigger problem is racism, which prevents them obtaining the type of work they would like, and also involves the danger of racist attacks on them or their homes. Finally they also face these problems compounded by class, being of course immediately déclassé, even if middle-class, upon immigrating to Britain. The stereotype of Asian female passivity has been severely challenged by their militant opposition to poor working conditions and wages. There is a history of resistance by Asian women in India and Pakistan, and certainly two large strikes, in 1980 in Southall,

London, and earlier the long strike at Grunwicks, London, were organised and carried out by non-white women, many of them the very Asian women believed to be passive. They have created new models of womanhood for young black and brown women who have to seek work in racist and sexist conditions. Parma reminds us that to oversubscribe to the passivity of Asian women, which has no historical foundation in their own culture, is to subscribe to the new racism which argues against doing anything for them on the grounds it will go against their culture.

'Let the power fall' – racism and its effect on youth

The position of black and brown youth in terms of its relation to the political economy of Britain has become clearer during the economic crisis. Non-white youth has seen the market close against them, and no real sign of integration occur. Lack of confidence in the police has led to the development of vigilante groups. The stereotype of the passive, uncomplaining Asian withdrawing into his or her tight-knit community has been replaced by militancy. East London, especially the Bengali community, has long learned to defend itself physically, after hundreds of attacks and two murders of a racist nature. Black youth has adopted Africanisation, with a consequence that Rastafarians have been unjustly accused of high involvement in crime. Young blacks have found that the market which needed their parents does not need them. If they leave home, suspended between hustling and the labour market, they have to survive unemployment and so turn to petty crime. Hall *et al.* (1978) indicate that crime under these conditions is selected as a political revenge. Crime is then a simple survival strategy, but its effects are brutalising and destructive, so it does not contain a real solution. The police surveillance of the black community takes on a deeper political significance. What Hall *et al.* (1978, p. 332) argued five years ago is even truer today:

> Policing the blacks threatened to mesh with the problem of policing the poor and policing the unemployed; all three were concentrated in precisely the same urban areas – a fate which of course provided the element of geographical homogeneity which facilitates the germination of a militant consciousness. The on-going problem of policing the blacks has become, for all practical purposes, synonymous with the wider problem of policing the crisis.

For Hall crime conceals the wagelessness of, and the delegation to, the position of deskilled labour of black workers. To survive by hustling is to survive in a wageless world. Most hustlers are not criminal, the unemployed in the Caribbean are not down-trodden, but have developed the tough-minded pragmatism of being 'street wise'. The ways in which they have to make a living has developed a culture which is not political, but is politically aware. This has been transferred to the situation that black British youth faces today. Consequently, Rastafarian youths are marked police targets. This is justified by the quoting of police statistics on black crime, and studies, such as those by police sociologist Brown (1977, p. 8), exponent of the conventional wisdom on black crime:

> Deprived and disadvantaged they see themselves as victims of white racist society, and attracted by values and life style of alienated Dreadlocks groups drift into lives of idleness and crime, justifying themselves with half-digested gobbets of Rastafarian philosophy.

This attempt to differentiate Rastas from the respectable black population, including 'authentically religious Rastas' is part of the police drive against a section of West Indian youth culture which they quite plainly see as the dangerous classes.

The context of racism, poverty and deprivation makes sense of the move towards voluntary unemployment, as does now a recession which makes nonsense of any volition in unemployment. Ever since immigrant youth has been prepared for the labour market it has expressed dissatisfaction with its opportunities. The important thing about the criminal acts of certain aspects of black youth culture is to see it in the context in which it has arisen. It is not that work was rejected by non-white youth, but the sort of work that it was offered. Like all youth it is vulnerable, lacking a stable base to organise from. It seeks an equality and a dignity in a world which has offered oppression, humiliation and rejection. The extent to which black youth is involved in criminality is not large. The fear by the British state is that, unless occupied by make-work schemes during what may be a permanent recession, it may explode. The Rod of Correction hangs over Babylon. The hostile propaganda of the extreme right wing has left its mark. The growing resistance takes many forms, of which deviant youth cultures are only a small part. As Sivanandan argues about youth's resistance (1976, p. 366):

> That is not to romanticise their futile ambition to lay siege to the state, but to acknowledge even while acknowledging the romanticism of the act the deep dark concern out of which their commitment springs.

Black youth culture contains an inflammable rebellious element, drawing upon a heavy mixture of religion and politics, combined with a deviant, quasi-criminal hustling style which, fed constantly by oppression, could become a serious political response.

Chapter 6

'Take off eh!' – Youth culture in Canada

The location of youth cultures in Canada is a more complex question than the situation in either Britain or the United States. In Britain the presence of a clear historical class situation, with its accompanying culture of class resistance, delineates fairly clearly to youth indicators concerning their class history, present and future. Youth cultures can be argued to have a clear relationship to class, are linked to traditional class problems, and are also clearly visible stylistically. In the United States, whilst there is a general (yet locally specific) high school culture, the complexities of ethnic, working-class and minority group subcultures have a strong presence. The appropriate signs for identity are clearly there, and whilst one may, for example, differentiate West Coast punks from British punks, the former being more attracted to style, and more aggressive than the latter, both styles are native to their immediate context and reinterpret the artifice of fashion into a subculture which makes sense in the local environment. The situation is more diffuse in Canada for reasons which may be traced to complexities in the culture of Canada itself. In the United States the very real contradictions of extreme poverty in the wealthiest country in the world generates responses to attempts to create an identity in a society which claims democratic access to visible signs of success, yet plainly withholds them from the majority of its youth.

Canada is a country of vast geographical size, the second largest country in the world, but with a small population of some 25 million people, and is in many ways several countries accidentally linked by historical development, peopled by different and distinct immigrant cultures, symbolised by having two official languages. The struggles between English Upper Canada and New France have led to two distinct French and British traditions, where the French population feels distinctly at a disadvantage. There are also native and Inuit populations and both Western and Eastern im-

144

migrant cultures outside the Anglo-French population. One problem for Canada has been its sense of national identity, due to its
historical links with Britain and France, and its proximity to the
United States which, particularly in the eyes of the outside world,
has confused the sense of national identity. In some ways this has
been reflected in Canadian youth culture. It is largely derivative,
and uses elements of borrowed culture, and any oppositional force
is highly muted. The liberalism which is genuinely found in
Canada, with its very different traditions of conservatism, based on
small town and rural communities, has engulfed opposition
amongst youth. There are of course exceptions, particularly among
native youth and in Quebec, where a much deeper sense of oppression and opposition exists. Identity in Canada is ambiguous, based
outside any native ethnicity or French opposition on region or
locality. There is no distinct national flavour to youth cultures,
which are usually based on the styles of a borrowed tradition,
rather than built on the indigenous forms of local traditions. If
there is a tradition of resistance in Canadian youth culture, it is at
an individualistic rather than a collective level. The vast size of the
country acts against any distinct yet common themes, as in the folk
devil traditions of Britain, or the specific ethnically developed subcultures in America. There is certainly evidence of borrowed traditions in the larger cities, but these make no widespread media
impact with consequent societal reaction. Further, at a more banal
level, the long and severe winter which covers most of Canada
localises youth cultures to the cities, and even there public spaces
tend to be shopping malls, which do little to generate collective
gatherings and are easy to control.

Canada has a long history of importing working-class youth to
solve its labour problems. From 1869 to 1919 it imported 73,000
children from Britain into English-speaking Canada 'unaccompan-
ied by parents or guardians', a tradition intermittently followed
since the seventeenth century. These children were recruited into
farm work and domestic labour; indeed some of the first child
immigrants were fifty little girls, brought over under an extension
of the poor house scheme, who came from the Kirkdale Work-
house, Liverpool to Ontario. The system was similar to Brace's
scheme in New York to indenture children out into work in the
country, where sadly they were often exploited. The child rescue
organisations took some 1,000 children a year from the Poor Law
Union workhouses, drawn from either 'paupers', that is orphans
and illegitimate children, or 'street arabs', waifs, strays and gutter
children from the slums of Britain. Despite critical reports, these
children were not seen as a threat to middle-class morality until the
1890s. They were an essential part of farm work, and the family

145

farm without sons soon became unproductive unless it could find immigrant children. Three-quarters of the population of Ontario were involved in rural work, and far more children were sought to be indentured than could be supplied. The children had no say in the matter, either in terms of immigration or choice of work. Sutherland (1976) notes that three sorts of children were of official concern in Canada. Those described as 'neglected' - beggars, waifs, street children who could as such be brought to court for thieving, sleeping out, begging or vagrancy, including orphans who were abandoned. There were also dependent children, illegitimate children, or children who were orphaned but could not be absorbed into their extended families, and finally delinquents, that is those between seven and fourteen convicted by the courts of an offence. Boys could also be charged with 'incorrigible and vicious conduct' as from 1880, so that we note considerable concern in the latter part of the century with the large numbers of children who had run away to the towns and were involved in vagrancy, petty crime, prostitution and begging. Canada had had to deal with the problems of importing immigrant unskilled and semi-skilled labour at the same time as having to deal with an increasing urban population and the social visibility of vagrants and youthful deviants. Particular interest grew in child saving, especially the delinquent. In 1857 two acts were passed, one to provide summary trial procedures and powers to curtail pre-trial imprisonment, and the other to construct reformatory prisons for the young. The regulation of immigration procedures for children became more systematic, following Dr Barnado's model in the latter decade of the century. In 1874 an act was set up to provide industrial schools as less severe residential institutions for juveniles. J.J. Kelso developed, with the Toronto Humane Society in 1888, an Act for the Protection and Reformation of Neglected Children, and in 1891 the first Children's Aid Society was formed. Canada's first Criminal Code in 1892 provided separate trials for those under sixteen. Close associations existed between the American and Canadian child saving movements. Delinquency legislation and probation and the founding of the juvenile justice system was also advocated by W.L. Scott who, with Kelso, was instrumental in developing both the probation service and a children's court staffed by a specially trained judiciary. The passing of the Juvenile Delinquents Act 1908 was highly instrumental in this, but as Hagan and Leon (1971) point out it was resisted by those with a very immediate interest to promote. This group supported control, rather than treatment and prevention. Police Inspector Archibald of the Toronto police force took a particularly firm stand, vehemently asserting that the new proposals would work upon the sympathies of philanthropic men and women for the purpose of introducing a jelly fish and abortive system of law enforcement, whereby the judge or magistrate is expected to come down to the level of the incorrigible street Arab, and assume an attitude absolutely repulsive to British subjects. The idea seems to be that by a profuse use of slang phraseology he should place himself in a position to kiss and coddle a class of perverts and delinquents who require the most rigid disciplinary and corrective methods to ensure the possibility of their reformation. (Hagan and Leon, 1971, p. 594)

The growth of the state in Canada meant that the visible social problems concerning welfare or law and order had to be dealt with systematically. The law, as has been argued earlier, has a legitimative purpose but is also educative. It sanctions certain customs and forbids others, in an atmosphere of consensus, which in nineteenth-century Canada certainly addressed the care and control of wayward children. In the realm of juvenile legislation and family law, consensus is retained through the institutions of civil society such as family, social welfare, and juvenile legislation, and educational institutions which educate, lead and direct that consensus. We have noted that state intervention of any sort makes moral statements about the natural order of things, usually left unquestioned. Implicit in these statements are powerful images of society, which in turn condense and order views of that society. In Canada, differing cultural traditions have made this ambiguous, aided by the geographical vastness of the country, so that any common consciousness is muted. There remains an optimistic belief in the economy, and in the social democratic nature of the society, so that Canada is still seen as an emerging country with a distinct future. Consequently, there has arisen an image which generates a potent yet conservative image of what is Canadian. This is not the place to offer an exhaustive taxonomy of this imagery, but let it suffice to pursue what gives a context ideologically to the concern about legitimation which youthful, legal and normative infractions threaten.

Canada is a country which prides itself on being a land of opportunity, where the class barriers of the old country no longer hinder social advancement. Its values tend to be rugged, masculine and individualistic, but like all formerly colonised economies it carries implicitly the imperialism of the first settlers. Economic and cultural domination by Britain, France and the United States has left a distinctly uneasy sense of national identity and culture, although regional and minority cultures remain strong, forged by the threat of engulfment by outside foreign cultures. There is a subtext, which makes an appeal to a form of social Darwinism where the fit survive in a harsh climate, by hard work, thrift and endeavour. The Canadian mosaic myth (wryly seen by John Porter as a vertical mosaic) of cultural pluralism (and hence social and political pluralism) states that thanks to a just legal and educational system, and to an egalitarian social system, hard-working, respectable, ordinary people can cast off the stultifying class systems of Europe or other countries of origin, to become upwardly mobile and prosperous. This does not mean entrance into those fractions of the ruling class which dominate the corporate and government elites, but a mobility measured by income and a modest investment in the prevailing economy, the expansion of the lower middle class, and the respectable working class, their relative affluence, the dominance of the Protestant work ethic becomes mistaken for the belief that there is no 'real' class system. By implication there is also no prejudice against race (even though black slaves were first brought to Canada in 1628, and racial segregation remained by law, but not by custom, until 1964), belief or even gender. Prejudice in Canada has certainly not reached the vicious level of the United States or Britain, but it exists; in 1982 one third of Canadians favoured a white only immigration policy. A modest rise in terms of affluence, generationally, with a consequent lack of polarisation in class terms (wealth like poverty is discreetly disguised in Canada) has defused and muted class struggle. There have been distinct moments of considerable resistance in labour history, and the Royal Canadian (formerly Northwest) Mounted Police (RCMP) frequently broke up strikes in the Canadian West around World War I. The Winnipeg General Strike in 1919 was a particularly violent episode in Canada's labour history, and it probably saved the RCMP from disbandment. However, consecutive waves of immigration have assisted in dispersing any historical sense of class war. Class oppression has been left behind in the old country, in exchange for unlimited opportunities offered by a new country and a new life. Genuine resistance by working-class and minority people has been successfully crushed by the state. On the other hand, Canada's liberal welfare state has successfully staved off socialism as a valid, critical alternative, especially in the post-war period. Canadian conservatism has its own tradition, which argues for a unity of culturalism, based on a sense of community and harmony, served in turn by a democratic ruling class. In contrast the United States is seen as too multicultural, almost too open. Accordingly the free market is seen as a danger because it undermines the paternalistic parameters of social order. There is a resistance to the anarchic liberalism of the United States. Conservatism, then, offers a liveable social form; it offers a set of social relations and a sense of community, which is overlaid with the nationalism that is found in all sections of the political spectrum in Canada. The school system is, not surprisingly, remarkably uncritical of Canadian society, yet the curriculum allows considerable flexibility to individual students. Students, except during the late 1960s and early 1970s as we shall see, have been generally uncritical and nationalism, which has served as an important buffer against British and American domination in English Canada especially, becomes an optimistic belief in the Canadian nation. Even in socialist circles there is remarkably little hatred of the country's predominant culture such as one finds in both Europe and the United States. There is still a belief that economically and socially things must improve, a situation no longer believed in other parts of the West. One possible reason is that conservatism is not the blatant class war of Britain, or the fear of communism in cold war America, but harks back to the conservative community of rural and small town life, appealing to a nostalgic populism. Modest affluence and self-respect (which have different meanings for different groups) have cemented a conformity to established social norms, and a stable, established social and political order. In this sense Canada is a liberal, social democracy, but one which is determined to follow the middle path, resisting too much radicalism, and one which conceals the very real struggles going on under the surface by denying the extent to which they are embedded in the Canadian class system.

An imposition of 'Canadianism' casts a fragile and delicate veneer over a variety of ethnic and class groupings who have little else in common, and whose very diversity undermines a collective consciousness of what are objective class problems. Work is an important means to the respectable life, and if it is assumed that the system is open, then work becomes a crucial element (in place of privilege) in access to scarce resources in the new country. Failure then becomes personalised, and the system remains above approach. For older established Canadians (except native people whose devastated culture keeps them in the most impoverished groups), this means a generational rise in the standard of living and, for a fraction of them, control over the accumulation of capital. From this arises a subdued conservatism, and social identities become caught up in hard work, occupational status, individualism and masculinity. In the land of opportunity it is necessary to practise thrift and industry to achieve mobility. For the immigrant (carefully selected albeit by immigration quotas), it means a standard of living unthinkable in the old country. Consensus is not hard to shape or win, it is implicitly there as a baseline. Any adult oppositional forces in Canada are consequently individualistic rather than collective. There is a lack of class-consciousness in the adult population, because it is not seen as appropriate to the new world. There may well be embittered labour disputes, but these are fenced off from socialist opposition, although this has not succeeded in particular districts involved for a long period of time in disputes involving heavy industry. Any sense of common culture based on class origins, is at best regional, ethnic or lingual. It is hardly suprising that indigenous youth cultures have failed to develop in any large sense.

In Canada what has occurred in line with other Western democracies is an economic crisis, that is a historical moment has been reached when the economic sector is no longer able to provide income commensurate with the working population's needs. However, unlike Britain, there is no hegemonic crisis. This arises when the state is unable to provide an educative role which promotes social cohesion and maintains the legitimation of its authority and power. Whilst there were, in Canada, disruptions between English and French Canada in the early 1970s, with an ensuing growth of separatism in Quebec, there is no profound public anxiety over the future of the country's prosperity, or loss in its support of the state. Consequently, there is no deeply felt anxiety about youth, beyond a concern about youth unemployment, in the sense that there has been in either the United States or Britain. Whilst there is certainly an economic crisis in Canada (nearly 12 per cent unemployment and low levels of capital investment) public opinion polls suggest that the economy is believed by most Canadians to be merely mismanaged, with no sense of the dimensions or probable longevity of the crisis. This absence of schisms in broader society between various social formations, including inter-ethnic and inter-generational relations, at any crisis level, helps to keep any rebellious element of youth culture to the level of adolescent protest or within the cultural sphere.

Youth is appropriately rewarded for its commitment to industry, thrift and discipline which promotes these virtues through the school system, without any accompanying oppositional criticism of Canadian society. The opportunity system for youth is taken for granted, and preparation for a 'just place in society' is assisted by the nurturance of a supportive family life which loves, disciplines and assists the child. Within this context, with its accompanying mythical scenario, delinquency and deviancy become individualised as a problem. The images of deviancy invoked are those of pathology – a disturbed, maladjusted child who needs guidance towards self-control and self-discipline, or else an incorrigible wastrel who refuses to take advantage of an apparently endless opportunity system, denied in all probability to parents or grandparents. The delinquent becomes constructed as one who has failed the system, rather than vice versa. Entrance into a respectable occupation is an indicator, differentiating success from failure. Work and commitment to work separate one from the idle and unsuccessful members of the working class, or from the ungrateful immigrant. To remain in the lower depths of the work force, or among the unemployed, is seen as surrendering respectability (both self-respect and the respect of others). Those who fail deserve to be losers. Respectability separates the deserving from the undeserving poor, the 'waifs' from the 'street arabs', the working class from the lower middle class. Respectability is then a key cipher in this code.

> It is work, above all, which is the guarantee of respectability; for work is the means – the only means – to the respectable life. The idea of 'the respectable working classes' is irretrievably associated with regular, and often skilled, employment. It is labour which has disciplined the working class into respectability. (Hall *et al.*, 1978, p. 141)

Youth subcultures challenge this norm of respectability. They are accompanied by behaviour often classified as delinquent, certainly deviant, but it is the values which lie behind this, as much as the behaviour, which threaten respectability. The valued elements of leisure, pleasure and consumption are the proper rewards of hard work, thrift and investment in the prevailing order of things. There are certainly conformist youth cultures, but they are not related to school in a simple way. Everhart (1982) found that his conformists in a predominantly working-class junior high school had ambivalent attitudes to school. They were involved in a youth culture which revolved around sport, hobbies and friends, performing a minimum of what the school required, but attempting to be involved in both the formal school system and the informal aspects of youth culture, and this seems to be typical for conformist youth cultures. Youth cultures which come to the attention of authority usually attempt to gain access to hedonism and consumption by a more circuitous route. They are often irresponsible and hedonistic, and their threat is that they educate the young in ways of avoiding or neutralising forms of labour discipline. This is the basis of most status offences. Official reaction to these and to other delinquent offences is readily supported by an assumed civil consensus about the undesirability of such behaviour on moral grounds, but behind this lies an assault on values which, unchecked, challenges labour discipline. This is why juvenile legislation always contains the two elements of care and control, emphasised at different moments in history, due to structural pressures, especially economic booms or depressions.

Official statistics concerning delinquents in Canada are severely limited by three factors. Firstly, the great variation from province to province in the relative use of child welfare legislation, as opposed to juvenile justice legislation, to control behaviour disapproved of by authority. Secondly, various provinces report delinquency data differentially, making the national accumulation of data very difficult. Some provinces are more involved in informal or pre-judicial interventions than others, and the upper age limit has varied in the past. The available data still suggest that youth, predominantly males from lower income groups, figure most frequently in the official statistics (Vaz and Lodhi, 1979). That this is not the whole picture is apparent from self report studies, which indicate a higher proportion of middle-class delinquency than official statistics, and the important absence of data recording the large number of informal contacts by the authorities. The juvenile justice data for 1980 (excluding British Columbia) indicate that 35,491 juveniles came before the courts, 28,000 being found to be delinquent. (This figure comes to approximately 33,600 with the B.C. figures.) Of these, 84.5 per cent were male; 3.2 per cent under twelve, 14.9 per cent twelve to thirteen years old, and 81.9 per cent fourteen years old or older. Girls have increased over the years. In 1944 the ratio of boys to girls was 22:1, but by 1980 the ratio of those over fourteen was 5.5:1. Native youth is known to be overrepresented, yet this does not appear in the data. Youth under fourteen shows unreliable data, because it is dealt with by the welfare authorities. Sixty per cent of all delinquencies (59 per cent of males and 49 per cent of females) were offences against property, followed by liquor and traffic offences. Ninety per cent of Provincial Statute violations were for these last two. As in most countries, girls tended to be charged with immorality, liquor offences, vagrancy, disorderly conduct and truancy. Fifty per cent of charges dealt with these offences (Vaz and Lodhi, 1979) which can be constructed as 'inappropriate' female conduct. Concretely, then, there seems to be a context for youth cultures of resistance, especially in the working class, yet these have been successfully mediated, and accommodated by the stress on the individualism of failure.

Youth cultural studies are scarce, in Canada perhaps because the cultures lack the dramatic, socially visible form that they take in Britain and the United States. They tend to be derivative, and insufficiently large to form any sense of moral outrage. Elkin and Westley's (1955) study of an upper-middle-class suburb in Montreal, using a Parsonian definition of youth culture, found a remarkable conformity between adolescents and parents. Parents engaged in a social life that was not very different from that of their children, and school conformity was seen as being meaningful to future careers. This is presented as one of the arguments for youth culture as a myth, but drawing upon middle-class conformist youth would support this viewpoint. It is in this group, as Elkin and Westley remind us, that one would expect least conflict between generations. They also argue that small town and suburban settings are less likely to generate youth cultures than metropolitan areas. This may be true for small town or rural life which makes up much of Canada's social life, but in Montreal it is only true for the class base, at that particular time, of the study, rather than its location. East Montreal, with its working-class French flavour definitely has youth cultures, and the situation in Quebec has changed considerably since the 1950s. A strong nationalism has resisted the anglophone colonisation, and the French language and culture has been a central symbol in this struggle, with the result that large numbers of anglophones have left Quebec. In class terms this means middle- and lower-middle-class English groups. Consequently, with increased youth unemployment (20 per cent in Canada in 1984 with an expected rise to 30 per cent of the under twenty-four population), cutbacks, attacks on trade unions by the Quebec provincial government, with a consequent increase in delinquency, there are more elements for the formation of resistant youth cultures, although the resistance may be aimed at the dominant English culture in Canada. Montreal has, like Vancouver, the flavour of a cosmopolitan city with a distinct street life in the summer, and a cafe society. Other studies, such as Vaz (1969), who examined middle-class youth culture in five Canadian communities, found that, according to self reports, his subjects were involved in car theft, driving without a licence, staying out all night and theft, usually petty. Proportionately, more private schoolboys reported delinquent acts interestingly enough, and in this sense there was a youth culture similar to that as commonly reported for conforming youth. It was school-resistant, rather than school-rejecting. Vaz argued that the changing teenage world meant that parents were often unable to assist in contemporary youth problems, and so the adolescents turned to youth culture to assist them as a source of support and activities, although he makes no detailed analysis of what a youth culture consists of. He does emphasise various roles, 'sports star', 'grind', 'swinger', which are part of high school culture in North America, and remind us of the Schwendingers' division of 'soshes' and 'greasers'. However, this type of youth culture may be typical, but it is a far cry from working-class Montreal or McLaren's working-class Toronto of 'new suburban ghettos' (1980), as he calls the areas he taught in. McLaren, whilst not in any sense describing youth cultures, gives another picture of Canadian youth, those in the multi-deprived inner city schools. The new high-rise, suburban, working-class areas, like their counterparts in the United States and Britain, engender racial tension, vandalism and crime. There are youth squads in the local police, community youth projects and social work agencies all trying to combat the increase in youthful despair as inflation affects the young working class. McLaren describes the problems of being black, poor or on welfare in the school system. He reveals a Canada too often denied in the official attitudes to multiculturalism and poverty. The dominant cultures have at present managed to successfully instill the sense of individual success and failure, but as the comfortable, traditional, economic prosperity becomes eroded, it is doubtful whether large cities such as Vancouver and Toronto will successfully manage to conceal their problems of poverty, racism and unemployment.

An interesting study is Tanner's (1975; 1978) attempt to replicate Murdock and Phelps' (1972) British studies. These had, as mentioned earlier, argued that elements of oppositional youth culture had drawn upon elements of 'pop media culture' and 'street culture' to create a false homogeneity of activities, roles and symbols. Out of school culture, in particular the local working-class community and the mass media, influential cultural milieux formed. Tanner round self-reported delinquency to be related to low school commitment as much among middle-class as working-class boys. Working-class, school-rejecting girls were fairly delinquent; only middle-class girls failed to indicate an association between low school commitment and delinquency. Sex was a signifying factor in pop media culture associations. School-rejecting boys were involved in pop cultures more than girls, and middle-class, female school rejectors were the least involved in either delinquency or pop culture. Tanner suggests that pop media is more important to girls, and to more middle-class students, because it represents a more acceptable form of revolt. It manages to provide a vehicle for having a good time, but does not carry the stigma and after-effects of court appearances. However, Edmonton, the city in which Tanner worked, is, as he points out a relatively affluent town with a distinct belief in upward mobility, unlike the traditional British working-class neighbourhoods of the Murdock and Phelps study. Tanner also points out that rock music is a complex and diverse phenomenon, suggesting findings not unlike that of Coleman and his associates, that girls, for example, favour 'safe' pop idols, (Pat Boone, Donny Osmond), rather than the rebel imagery of Elvis Presley and Alice Cooper. We again see a similarity between American and Canadian high school cultures, which permit minimal involvement in school but are highly involved in leisure social activity that falls short of resistance and violence.

The Canadian student movement throughout the 1960s and 1970s followed much of the concern of the international student movement, especially America, over peace, civil rights and the Vietnam war. Canada offered asylum to the American draft dodgers who were involved consequently in the Canadian anti-war movement. Much of the Canadian student movement remained with an American radical tradition but was necessarily against American imperialism both abroad and within Canada. It is also necessary to differentiate within Canada the English and French student movement. A nationalist struggle occurred both economically and culturally which had different emphases in English and French Canada. Quebec students were involved more in an independence from English Canada, and also more state involvement in the economy. Quebecois people suffer a double imperialism: the historical imperialism of Britain, and later the United States, and the more immediately felt imperialism of English Canada. Canada had increased its student population by 178 per cent between 1950 and 1965, increasing the amount of lower-middle-class and, to a lesser extent, working-class entrance into university. The educational model was American, and its function was to prepare a skilled work force for the minor as well as major professions and the bureaucracies. The vast area of English Canada, with its Upper and Lower Canadian differences as well as its Eastern and Western divisions, deleted any unified student organisation, whilst Quebec was able to achieve unity through its differences with English Canada linked by two features. Firstly, there was the French language, a cohesive symbol in Quebec, and secondly the Quebecois popular culture which, due to historical exploitation, makes most Quebecois rebellious and non-conforming. Lanzon (1970) reminds us that this creates, in even the law abiding, anarchic attitudes to the police, the Protestant ethic, respectability and organised politics. The religious, political, cultural and lingual differences of Quebec created a base for the independence movement of Quebec. The Church was an important political force until the 1960s, actively running education, health and welfare services, controlling trade union activity and resisting modernisation and industrialism. This gave force to the progressive elements of French intellectual and political life in Quebec, who argued for more state responsibility in these affairs. Progressiveness became the secularisation of essential services and the resistance of anglophone economic domination and political decision making.

In an interesting paper Nesbitt Larking (1981) describes the beginnings of the student movement in Canada in the post-war period. An interest in the peace movement led to the Combined Universities Campaign for Nuclear Disarmament (CUCND) in the late 1950s. They published the magazine *Our Generation Against the Bomb* (still active as *Our Generation*). The single issue campaign for unilateral disarmament, non-violent direct action and civil disobedience was to move to a broader platform of social change and the Student Union for Peace Action (SUPA) was formed in 1964. Modelled on the American New Left model, it replaced undemocratic, bureaucratic procedures of the Old Left for a looser, uncentralised, self-determining movement. As such it was a radical organisation like many of the American movements, and took up the causes of civil rights marches, working-class community politics and native rights and was often involved in community action programmes. Cleavages and splits arose, the SUPA declining from 1967 as the emphasis on Western and Quebecois provincial issues arose. This varied from Free University movements, democratisation of the class basis of admissions to university to native people's 'red power' groups. Students were mainly concerned with the attitudes of reactionary university policy, and this led to a conservative backlash in 1970 at the University of Toronto which withdrew from the Canadian Union of Students, under the influence of conservative students. Certainly, empirical studies of students' attitudes (Ribordy and Barnett, 1979; Driedger, 1975) suggested, for example in the former study, that French students, whilst less willing to consider the legal system just or to support it, were conservative, not radical, in their opposition. Driedger's Alberta students revealed a liberal value system, which even among the left spoke vaguely of 'freedom', 'world peace', 'broadmindedness' and so forth. Laxer (1971) suggests that the liberal values of participatory democracy, suspicion of complex organisations and a perception of minority and poor people as instruments of political change characterised the beliefs of SUPA. As with their American counterparts, there was no clear analysis of the state or of socialist alternatives to the liberal system. The complex issues facing students and their relationship to the working class were neither clearly analysed, nor consequently strategised for, in terms of social change. In Quebec Belanger and Mahen (1972) suggested that two crucial periods occurred in the Quebec student movement in the 1960s. There was the so called 'quiet revolution' when Lesage's Liberal government reformed education, limited the influence of the clergy, nationalised hydro-electric power and increased state influence in the economy to bring it into line with modern capitalism, reducing the influence of the 'ancien régime'. Quebec began to move towards autonomous provincial government, lessening the influence of the federal government in Ottawa (a perennial political problem in Canada is the struggle between provincial and federal government). René Levesque became the voice of provincial government 'étatiste' opinion, and became a leading figure in the Parti Québécois and finally the premier of Quebec. It should be remembered that in 1965 the Quebecois were the third lowest income group in their own province. Their incomes in Montreal, for example, historically a colonised city, were $330 below the average, whilst Scottish Canadians were $1,319 above the average. Francophone representation in the key positions in industry had not increased since 1931, 53 per cent of the labour force worked for Anglo-Canadians or foreigners, and the language of the elites was English. As economic growth slowed, students, like many of the lower middle class, became frustrated. A few students sided with the ruling anglophone Liberal party, most became nationalists and a minority became actively involved in working-class socialist and revolutionary struggle. An activist form of community action, 'animation sociale', was developed in some areas to create interesting experiments in adult education, health and welfare. The beginning of the 1970s marked a period of considerable agitation in Quebec. The issue was Quebecois nationalism, and although there was an anglophone victory in the provincial election, it occurred against a backdrop of militant strikes, bombings, protest marches and bank robberies. The Front de Libération de Québec (FLQ) was highly influential, particularly its leading theorist Pierre Vallieres, whose *Les Nègres Blancs de l'Amerique du Nord* (1968) drew on Quebec sociology (Fanon and Sartre). The FLQ was highly active, kidnapping in October 1970 first a senior United Kingdom trade commissioner, James Cross, then Pierre Laporte, the Quebec minister of labour and immigration. Prime minister Pierre Trudeau evoked the War Measures Act in the same month, which suspended civil rights, imposed arrest without charge, imposed censorship and declared the FLQ an illegal organisation. In an interview with CBC in Ottawa (13. 10. 70) Trudeau took a strong line:

> *Trudeau:* ... 'Well there are a lot of bleeding hearts around that just don't like to see people with helmets and guns. All I can say is, "Go on and bleed". But it's more important to keep law and order in society than to be worried about weak-kneed people who don't like the looks of an army.'
> *CBC Reporter:* 'At any cost? How far will you go with that?'
> *Trudeau:* 'Just watch me.'

Some 465 people were arrested without charges being laid after the body of Laporte was discovered. In fact the FLQ never claimed credit for his murder or his kidnapping and the murder was never materially linked with that organisation. Evidence was not presented against the 465 arrested in most cases. Cross was released and his kidnappers were allowed to go to Cuba. The October Revolution provided a background which helps us understand the importance of language as a cultural symbol of extreme political importance, expecially when Quebec passed Bill 22 making French the official language of Quebec. René Levesque was to lead the Parti Québécois to victory in the provincial polls, and to pass in the 1980s some of the most repressive legislation against organised labour in Canada's history, indicating the limits of a nationalism with no connections to socialism. However, nationalism was a distinctly unifying element in all classes and Quebec became the centre of Francophone nationalism, although separatism was certainly rejected by the majority of Quebecois. For Quebecois students, then, there was a distinctly different political culture. It was more radical, more involved in cultural struggles as well as economic ones, and certainly more militant. Its traditions looked to the French student movement, rather than the United States. There is also in Quebec more fertile ground for syndicalist anarchist and socialist ideas and fractions among student movements. Quebec also had a stultifying Catholic clergy to deal with, as the struggle for abortion, symbolised in the trials and imprisonment of Dr Morgentaler, indicated. Morgentaler openly carried out abortions in Montreal, but was arrested, found not guilty by a jury, convicted by the court of appeal, sentenced by it, and this was upheld by the Supreme Court. Morgentaler was charged with another abortion offence, again found not guilty, and eventually the criminal code was amended. This example gives some sort of idea of the progressive and anti-progressive struggles in Quebec which polarised its population, and certainly influenced its youth.

Kostash (1980b), has chronicled the student movement in Canada. She traces direct action work of the 1980s, the involvement in the peace movement of SUPA, and the influence on it of the more state-led Company of Young Canadians (CYC) in its social action programmes. She reminds us that students took up the issues of the role of the university in society, in state research and in the new technocratic class structure, for which it prepared students. It was its inability to get beyond the university which was its central problem, although perhaps less so in Quebec because of wider political events which were occurring there. She also considers the Canadian 'counterculture' which, like its counterparts elsewhere, sought new forms of household arrangements and life styles, refusing traditional bourgeois life styles, and giving impetus to sexual liberation movements, although she may underestimate its maintenance of patriarchy in a new form. It was, however, a marginal impetus fairly easily controlled by the police and alternative and often traditional capitalism. She considers the native people's struggle, which was certainly influenced by the Black Power movement in the United States, as was the American native people's movement. She traces its attempts for autonomy against the cooption of the state (as with the CYC community development projects), its struggles with federal and provincial agencies, and its struggles over its own economy as with land rights. She also traces the resistance by the feminist movement to left-wing as well as traditional male chauvinism. The linking up over single issue campaigns such as the abortion caravan developed consciousness over particular forms of gender oppression outside traditional class politics. She also contrasts the Anglo-Canadian and Quebec student movements along the lines suggested earlier. The Quebecois students were more involved in workers' struggles, and in nationalist politics. The War Measures Act was aimed at Quebecois radicalism, and one thing which was revealed was the weak opposition it received throughout Canada, once again revealing to Quebec that it could not count on anglophone support even on the left.

Shragge (1982) in a thoughtful review has suggested that the left tradition in Canada has tended to be social democratic or Leninist. A strong central party is necessary to unite struggle. What the new left and the youth movements among students and the hippy groups raised was the structure of the libertarian left. Activists in the 1960s lacked a common meeting place to build alternatives and develop an articulate perspective. The strength of the 1960s for Shragge was that it was activist rather than intellectual, which he sees as a retreat for socialists today in Canada. The state was seen as a progressive veneer in the 1960s rather than being examined for its repressive aspects. The state for him is an arena for reorganising domination. As the recession bites, it should be responded to not with increased individualist competitiveness, but used to develop new forms of mutual support and cooperative forms of organisation. Whilst the theme of the 1960s was 'dropping out', the state in the 1980s is pushing youth into menial and degrading employment, or forcing it onto welfare and wagelessness. High levels of unemployment among youth will produce a significant youth culture 'whose social integration is unlikely' (Shragge, 1982). This means that a youth culture may develop 'with autonomous cultural and social forms that will be much more difficult to integrate given the reimposition of artificial scarcity' (Shragge, 1982). Serious oppositional politics can be built on a youth culture which is non-sexist, non-hierarchical and in opposition to exploitation. Shragge sees a future for cooperative movements, developed in opposition to militarism, and organised around work and community issues. Thus, it would be possible to build up an autonomous workplace and neighbourhood organisations 'without subordinating the local struggle' which were linked up with the broader oppositional politics.

Kostash comments sadly that one reason she wrote her lively and interesting account was because Canadians some fifteen years her junior seemed to have never heard of the SUPA, the FLQ, the Abortion Caravan or the campus resistances. In many ways this again illustrates the overshadowing of Canada by the United States, so that, ironically, young Canadians may know much more about the American counterculture and its political struggles than they do about those in their own country. In ways like this, dominant mainstream Canadian culture is able to smother those fractions who protest against the establishment, and reassert its stultifying control. An effective way of doing this is through the media. Because of its vastness, such primary information in Canada about other Canadians is through the imagery of the mass media, so that media stereotyping is often accepted as genuine information about the world in general and Canada in particular. Many popular programmes are American in origin and the United States still dominates popular media in Canada.

Just as the youth cultures of the 1960s tend to have become lost in Canada, contemporary Canadian youth cultures are not deeply researched. They do not, because of the vastness of the land, the small populations locally distributed, and the diversity of Canada, exist in the same way as in Britain or the United States. They tend to be imported into the large towns from abroad, and because they lack the class and ethnic origins of those cultures and their response to a particular set of contradictions, they are at a surface level. There are, then, punks in an otherwise staid Ottawa, mods in Winnipeg, but they are the surface trappings of an alien youth culture, rather than intrinsically developed from indigenous cultures. Hip hop has spread to Montreal, where it has attracted both white indigenous and black immigrant youth, but official youth provision agencies are attempting to harness this to defuse anger and hostility. Whether they will successfully wrest this from the kids remains to be seen. Otherwise youth culture is at a surface level, although there are occasional clashes with adult authority. In 1984 there was a clash between anti nuclear punks and the Royal Canadian Legion (a veterans' organisation). Both groups wished to be present on Remembrance Day at the monument of the unknown soldier, and a bitter wrangle ensued with the Legion suing the punks for using the Flanders poppy (their copyright) as a logo on peace literature and T-shirts.

Whilst Canada does have a tolerant culture, at least on the surface, it lacks the high crime rate and violence of the United States, it does not have the problems of working-class resistance and urban decay as in Britain, and it lacks the overt organised racism of both these countries. Racism exists in a defused and muted form against native people, or in the French-English struggle, although signs are showing in Toronto, for example, that relations between the police and the black community are deteriorating. It should be remembered that nearly one-third of Canadians come neither from the major English nor French traditions. There is, then, considerable scope for ethnic youth cultures to arise. By and large, however, young people have not been collectively scapegoated. There are no major 'folk devils' and moral panics, although campaigns against gay people in the media in Toronto have led to police harassment of the gay community. Delinquency has been psychologised and individualised and consequently, intervention models have not been progressive educational projects, but have drawn upon a voluntarism where the individual has been seen as 'choosing' to do wrong. Canada has not suffered from the structural backwardness of the British class system and political economy. Consequently, there has been no shift from the politics of consent to the politics of coercion as in Britain and the United States. In Britain 'folk devils', due to their overt visibility, became signs of what was 'really' wrong with Britain. These were not just delinquent folk devils, but other players in the crisis of legitimation - 'foreign agitators', immigrants, militant trade unionists, black radicals and revolting students. Youth, argue Middleton and Muncie (1982), was 'a central metaphor in the articulation of closure in consensus politics'. The affluence and classness, believed to have arrived in Britain in the 1950s, were cruelly shown to be absent in the 1960s and 1970s. Youth styles, working-class affluence or student and hippy drug use were conceptualised as symbols of the increasing permissiveness and lack of discipline in a Britain grown decadent and soft, symptomatic of its decline as a world power. Canada had borrowed its youth cultures and kept them safely within the realms of fashion. Because of its size, it has partialised them, and this, combined with lack of national media coverage, has kept them out of the public eye. Consequently, there has been no escalation of these 'folk devils' to develop moral panics about Canada's national decline. Canada retains an optimism about her economic recovery, lacking the pessimistic despair felt in Britain and the United States. There is not a popular acceptance of 'no future' as among British youth. Consequently, there is no reaction at present against youth as too affluent, too decadent, too threatening or too rebellious. Crime rates are relatively low, especially for violence and murder, and youth cultures among native or French youth are partialised from any national consciousness. Moral panics orchestrated by the new right in Canada have been around the sphere of the family, and it is abortion, homosexuality and feminism which are the targets for reactionary backlash. Inflation is increasing as is unemployment. The state is becoming more repressive but in a cautious and un- hurried manner. Civil rights are being threatened, but this is aimed at organised labour and left-wing politics, easily reconstructed as working against the national interest. As youth unemployment in- creases, there well may develop increased delinquent resistance out of sheer economic necessity. Native and black youth may well become conscious of common areas of racism and ensuing poverty, which could receive tacit support from the adult community. The highly localised youth cultures of the suburban and down town shopping areas could well take on a significance escalated by the media, the economic crisis and societal reaction into having wider consequences.

Chapter 7

The invisible girl – the culture of femininity versus masculinism

Most subcultural studies are concerned, mainly due to the male bias of their investigators, with the adolescent male delinquent, as Frith (1981, p. 7) notes,

> Because the most visible examples of delinquency have been found in gangs of boys, the concept of youth culture has been synonymous with assertive expressions of masculinity – hooliganism, violence etc. . . . It has attained another invisible prefix: (male) (delinquent) youth culture.

Girls are either invisible, peripheral or stereotyped, and as Wilson (1978, p. 66) notes,

> The history of the sociology of deviance, as far as women and girls are concerned, is a history of the uncritical adoption of conventional wisdom about the nature of women; namely that anatomy is destiny.

Subcultures are, as I have noted, central to the construction of identity outside class ascriptions. Where identity is dominated not just by occupation, age and class but by gender and race, gender is often overlooked. If subcultures are solutions to collectively experienced problems, then traditionally these have been the problems experienced by young men. Consequently, youth culture is very concerned with the problems of masculinity. Even where ethnicity complicates subcultural membership, black and brown males turn to an emphasis on masculinity. As a result, subcultures are male-dominated, masculinist in the sense that they emphasise maleness as a solution to an identity otherwise undermined by structural features. The absence of girls in subcultural studies is related not only to attitudes to femininity, but also to women's relationship to production. Here women are also seen as peripheral. As a result, as the expansion in the population has reached work age, then

163

economic production also has dropped, so that in a situation of general unemployment, women have had particular problems in finding work. Women then have to find expression in that other role assigned to them, domestic labourer. The importance of the cult of femininity (non-work-dominated identity in this case) becomes apparent. Girls have, because of the patriarchal nature of male subcultures, been seen the possessions of their boy friends. They are on sexual display, never allowed sexual independence, indeed, 'Girls must be distanced from having an independent sexual experience or identity of their own' (Dorn and South, 1982, p. 20).

Male researchers have focused on boys because of a gender identification with them, and colluded with the subjects of their studies to exclude girls from their vision. McRobbie (1980) has suggested a re-reading of the subcultural 'classics' so that 'questions hitherto ignored, or waved aside in embarrassment become central'. She is correct in stating that it is family and domestic life which is missing from subcultural studies, focusing as they do on street life. Girls in them were collectively disregarded and sexually exploited.

For boys, then, subcultures allow an exploration and an investment in forms of masculinity. Men in routinised labour, particularly in heavy industrial work, pride themselves on their ability to perform arduous work (even though they may 'skive off' from work). It is a fitting test of their masculinity, and they will emphasise this in crude sexist discussion about women and sex, and also in their parody of homosexual men. Their contempt for what is deemed unmasculine also extends to white collar workers and as such is flavoured with a class dimension. Willis (1977) illustrates the link between sexism and shop-floor culture. Manual labour in particular is given masculine qualities – 'man's work'. Work may be divested of its intrinsic significance, but patriarchy has filled it with masculine emphasis. Even the gains of trade union conflict are part of a masculine pride in struggling with the employers. Thus, as Willis (1977, p. 150) suggests:

> The wage packet is the provider of freedom and independence: the particular prize of masculinity in work. . . . The male wage packet is held to be central, not simply because of its size, but because it is won in a masculine mode in confrontation with the 'real' world which is too tough for the woman. Thus the man in the domestic household is held to be the bread-winner, the worker, whilst the wife works for 'the extras'.

This is not just true for the working-class household, but is also reflected in middle-class families. We see, then, that women have reality mediated not just by class location interpretations but also by patriarchy, the system of subordination in a world which is male-dominated in sexuality and procreative potential; a system where women's labour is organised economically, ideologically and politically by males. It is a world where sexism is the articulated, as well as the taken-for-granted, unquestioned superiority of men. In this sense women inhabit two locations: their role in their specific social class and their position in patriarchy.

This is at the basis of the construction of the psychology of femininity and the preparation for this dual role poses problems for women during their socialisation and education. There is a considerable debate on the question of domestic labour (Dalla Costa and James, 1972; Gardiner, 1976; Bland *et al.*, 1978; Himmelweit and Mohun, 1977). In brief, the class analysis of women has traditionally been based on their husband's occupation whatever 'cultural capital' they may bring to the marriage in the form of skills or money. Patriarchy recognises men as breadwinners, and women as financially dependent on them – a position reflected in women's incomes. Women work in an unwaged capacity, servicing and sustaining the family, reproducing not only the work force, but themselves as sustainers. However, women are involved in the work force in a very central way. In the United States, over the past ten years, the average male wage has not risen substantially but more women in families have gone out to work, thus increasing the income of the household. Land (1976) has argued that a quarter of a million families would be below the British official poverty 'line' if they were not supplemented by the earnings of the mother, and that one-sixth of households are substantially or completely dependent on women's earnings (this excludes pensioners) and most of these families have dependants. Women are involved in the economy as casualised temporary workers, a reserve army of labour that services the work force, works as unpaid domestic labourers, and are also consumers within the economic system. Women are judged, then, not on their occupational status but on their femininity. They are assessed in terms of their sexual desirability (described by Zetterberg (1968) as the 'secret ranking of erotic hierarchy'), and their femininity is defined by their relation to consumption (appearance, taste, fashion awareness, clothes, children's appearance, home). Work available to women in industry is deskilled, and even in the professions tends to be of low status. Whilst their income may be essential, their work is delegated to being of minor importance, both in its organisation and its form; it is 'women's work'. It often contains elements of domestic labour such as servicing men as bosses (the clerical worker as 'office wife'), and at work their source of power may not be in their function as workers, but their rank in the erotic hierarchy ('feminine wiles'), that is, their social source of power. This is illusory power in any material sense, but it is a definite source of alternative power in the personal sphere, as illustrated by the schoolgirl flirting with the male teacher, the typist with the executives, nurses with doctors, the shop-floor workers and the male overseer.

The contradictions of these roles are founded at school. Whatever the egalitarian ideology of the school, girls and boys are seldom given equal opportunities to study. There is always a schooling with marriage in mind, so that girls have an ambivalent attitude to their future, turning partially on the romanticism found in popular literature and magazines, but also on an interest in caring for people which, given women's historical alternatives, is comprehensible. Sue Sharpe (1976) reminds us that schools have a 'hidden curriculum' where work is preferred for form rather than content, and pupils are steered towards 'girls' subjects such as arts. Girls are taught to be unassertive. They tend to underachieve at the age of puberty, a time when they become self-conscious about femininity. Sharpe notes that girls report that boys dislike cleverer girls, so that socially there is a fear of success as well as a fear of failure. Girls can resolve this by emphasising the feminine role. There is some slight evidence that girls may do better in all-girls' schools, away from male competition.

Love and marriage – escape into romance

Girls receive from the mass media and from popular fiction distinct signals about the cult of femininity. Reading primers reinforce sexual roles, and comics are divided strictly along sex lines from the age of seven or eight. The themes in girls' comics are often related to isolation, competition, loneliness and emotional problems. The market aimed at the pubescent girl and the adolescent has a central theme of romanticism. Romantic attachment and dependency on men is emphasised, and advice on emotions, make-up and fashion is given as well as glamorous hints of the lives of pop stars. These are succeeded by glossy fashion magazines, aimed at specific age groups, again with advice about romance and sex, with more adult stories, but nevertheless presenting an escapist unproblematic world. Appearance is stressed, and fashion is used to construct a self which indicates to the world that the girl is from a world of fashionable femininity, where she has a relation not to class, but to a mythical world inhabited by a fashion hierarchy based on popular media figures. As girls grow older they seem to seek magazines which emphasise fashion rather than romantic stories. De Beauvoir has put this well (1972, p. 543):

to care for her beauty, to dress up, is a kind of work that enables her to take possession of her person, as she takes possession of her home through housework, her ego then seems chosen and created by herself.

Girls then have two sources of socialisation for their future, school and at home, backed up by a media interpretation of femininity which adds a sense of fatalism about marriage and motherhood. For many girls, in particular working-class girls, these are attractive and seemingly fulfilling goals. It is only after marriage the women realise its isolation and emptiness. The reality is that the average age of marriage for a woman is twenty-two, and the woman's age at the birth of the last child is twenty-six, and 42 per cent of all married women work. Schools, particularly in poorer areas where opportunities for women are restricted, prepare girls for the marriage market as much as for the job market. The future work prospects are belittled as temporary and unimportant. As Shaw (1976, p. 146), suggests.

> The meanings and consequences of sexual divisions in our society are translated into educational terms so that the different subcultures of boys' and girls' schools are but specialised versions of a wider culture, in which female futures are still defined in essentially domestic terms - a stereotyping which our educational system does little to undermine.

The organisation and form of girls' subcultures remain very much a matter of empirical investigation. As has been suggested, a prominent feature of male-dominated subcultures has been its exploration of masculinity, and its imagery, whether it is the ambiguity of mods and freaks, or the heavy machismo of greasers. Girls are present in male subcultures, but are contained within them, rather than using them to explore actively forms of female identity. The subculture may be a social focus, something to dress up for, and an escape from the restraints of home, school and work, but as yet not distinct models of femininity, which have broken from tradition, have evolved, although this may well happen when female-dominated subcultures evolve. This is unlikely at present, especially among working-class girls, because of the demands of adolescent heterosexuality and the female role. For working-class women, marriage is a role of primary importance, and economically essential. Marriage mediates against the starkness and drabness of work, it provides acceptable evidence of maturity and adulthood, and it is an important investment for the future. Its attraction may fade away with familiarity, but it is still strong enough to structure girls' choices. Working-class respectability has to be paid attention to: a girl is permitted sexual relations with her steady boyfriend, but she must guard against a reputation which will relegate her to the role of 'slag'. She develops a cynicism about boys who demand a sexual relationship without emotional commitment with a view to permanence. Girls are located in differing contradictions, as McRobbie and Garber (1976) suggest. They may be peripheral in one sphere, such as work, but they can be central in another, such as the home. Consequently, when they are mentioned in subcultural theory, they are seen as peripheral to the boys:

> Women were usually accompanied by a man and they did not
> speak anything like as much as the men. There was a small
> group of unattached females, but they were allowed no real
> dignity or identity by the men. (Willis, 1978, p. 28)

This, however, is because the largely male investigators accepted the masculinist definition of the girls' roles in these subcultures.

McRobbie and Garber (1976) argue that girls are not marginal, but structurally different, pushed by male dominance to the periphery of social activity because girls are basically involved in a different set of activities. Girls spend more time at home, according to Barker (1972), Crichton *et al.* (1962) and McRobbie (1978 a and b). Frith (1978) suggests three reasons for girls' absence from subcultures – first, parents control girls' spare time much more closely. Second, girls have to assume an apprenticeship for domestic labour which begins at home. In fact, girls often have to earn their pocket money by helping in domestic tasks. And third, girls spend a lot of time in preparation for out-of-home leisure activities. In fact Frith (1978, p. 66) argues that:

> Marriage is a girl's career and the source of the constraints on
> her leisure. This argument can be pushed further: a girl's
> leisure is her work. It is leisure activities that are the setting for
> the start of her career, for the attraction of a man suitable for
> marriage.

Where low job aspirations exist, as they do for most girls, then there is a commitment to early marriage. It is a way out, and a socially acceptable one, from educational failure and work dissatisfaction, and girls' job decisions tend to be made in terms of a short-term commitment and secondary to the long-term commitment of marriage. Romance is certainly central to girls' perceptions of the future and it is seen as a precursor to marriage. Sarsby (1972) found for a sample of fifteen-year-olds that girls sought partners who would be sensitive to them, whilst boys stressed physical attraction. Her working-class girls stressed the importance of security and support in marriage. E. Figes (1970) quotes a batch of essays written by London grammar school girls which reveal that their thoughts are very centrally on marriage, and Sharpe (1976) found that 82 per cent of her sample wanted to marry – three-quarters of them by the age of twenty-five. McRobbie and Garber (1976) suggest that one of the most important forms of subcultures amongst girls of the 1970s was the Teeny Bopper (although this phenomenon was certainly present since the early 1960s). However, it became a centre for market focus during the 1970s for the ten- to fifteen-year-old girl. It requires only the use of a bedroom, a record player and a friend. There are no exclusion rules, entrance qualifications, no risk of sexual or social failure. Frith (1978, p. 66) agrees:

> Girl culture becomes a culture of the bedroom, the place where girls meet, listen to music and teach each other make-up skills, practise their dancing, compare sexual notes, criticise each other's clothes and gossip.

This is the place that other girls are allowed to visit by their parents. Frith brings marketing evidence to show that the focus of this Teeny Bopper culture is usually a pop star, and what is purchased are magazines, then records and symbols such as T-shirts, posters and pictures. This fades as the girls go out and dance and date, but their magazines still feature pop stars rather than pop music. Attacks on Teeny Bopper idols are a cause of friction, and they are passionately defended. Robins and Cohen (1978, p. 52) note:

> Osmond baiting was, in fact, one of the most familiar weapons used by older brothers in their continuous bickering with their younger sisters. A fourteen year old boy told how 'we went by the Rainbow [Theatre] once and we started screaming out of the window "Osmonds are bent, all queers" and they were lobbing everything that come in sight. You should see one of them, she's in a state crying over the railing, going "You bastards" and the next minute she picked up a bottle and threw it at the bus'.

It is worth noting that many pop idols who are ambiguously male in this subculture are sexistly reduced to 'poofs' by males more involved in other elements of rock culture. The Teeny Bopper sub-culture is a retreat and a preparation for young girls. They can relate to their best friend (girls often emphasise the importance of their best friend, whose friendship they see as continuing after marriage) and together practise in the secrecy of girl culture for the rituals of courtship, away from the eye of male ridicule.

There is a similar pattern for boys outside the more dramatic subcultures, and who have the luxury of their own or a friend's room. They are more focussed on rock music, and other masculine pursuits. The emphasis on romance in the culture of femininity leads to courtship practices. Dancing is important in this, and Mungham and Pearson (1976) describe well the dance-hall scenario, with its heavy heterosexual machismo masking the fear of the independent woman. Girls in this setting learn an important area of their lives; that of waiting. They cannot directly initiate social encounters, but can only reject or accept what is offered. This is sometimes crudely and effectively done. One respondent told me how he went down a line of waiting girls to be brushed off with a crude 'Piss off - Dracula!' Girls become obsessed with romance in this context, realising that the only exciting event in their bleak lives may be marriage, and they have no intention of blowing this by unseemly independence. They prepare carefully for dances and discos, arrive immaculately dressed with friends, and dance well. They then have to manage the courtship rituals, from boys trying to 'split a pair' of girls, to getting off, to going steady, which means being sexual with one boy, yet guarding one's reputation against boys who, it is accepted, are after only one thing.

Girls and delinquency

Official statistics suggest girls offend less than boys (16:84 per cent) and figure largely in status offences, mainly running away, beyond parental control and sexual 'promiscuity'. Chesney Lind (1973) points out that the first juvenile court in Chicago spent a lot of time supporting the shoring up of the family. Judicial paternalism sexualises girls' offences, that is delinquency may be ignored or excused in favour of the 'immoral' sexual aspects of girls' behaviour. Girls charged with status offences received harsher treatment than those suspected of crimes, and double standards control girls who threaten parental authority yet boys are permitted to sow their wild oats. Strouse (1978) also notes that girls are brought to court and deprived of liberty for non-criminal conduct, and that the definition of misconduct in women is primarily sexual. Boys certainly offend more. Boys make up 36 per cent of the FBI's serious offences, girls 8 per cent. Larceny is the commonest charge for girls (13 per cent, 36 per cent for boys). The crime rate for girls has increased, however, girls constituting 35 per cent of all female arrests in America, boys making up only 26 per cent. Of these arrests, 41 per cent of girls and 44 per cent of boys are in the serious crimes index. Girls make up the same percentage of arrests as boys concerning vehicle theft, burglary and larceny. Arrests in America are very much a juvenile phenomenon, having increased between 1960 and 1975 by 144 per cent, boys increasing 117 per cent and girls 425 per cent. Girls increased in the property crime offences (420 per cent), although boys of course still offend more.

There is little research on girl gangs. These usually exist as all girl appendages to male gangs, and it is reported (Miller, 1975) that 10 per cent of all gangs are female, and that half of known male gangs have female branches. Usually girls perform secondary functions, providing food, support, sex and hiding weapons (Marsh and Campbell, 1978a; 1978b). Sexual roles are less traditional – it is possible to sleep with different gang members yet not be seen as 'cheap'. Brown, W.K. (1977) in his study of black gangs in Philadelphia found that whereas boys were tested through fights, girls could join by asking. They received status through street experience, gang fights with the opposing gangs' female members, carrying weapons for the boys, and also using them, and decoying and spying. They were not sexual objects, but intrinsically involved in gang activities and part of its group identity. Miller's (1973) street corner girls were known as 'bad girls' in the area, and certainly engaged in illegal behaviour, but less than their brother gangs. Their view was that you got the boys to like you by being like them, not by sexual accessibility. Girls have moved from an invisible periphery to the centre of gang activities, creating a space from male sexual exploitation, but finding themselves a role both active and supportive.

Self reports (Gold, 1966; Hindelang, 1971; Williams and Gold, 1972) also show that while girls offend less, their delinquency does parallel that of boys. Criminality has increased, including that of violence, the latter particularly among black girls. Campbell (1981) also reports increases among British girls in what were traditionally male areas of delinquency. She suggests that in the last decade, girls spend more time with boys and learn from them some of the rules of violence. She found in her study that working-class girls still aspired to be attractive wives and mothers, but also individuals to be reckoned with, who can manage. Of her non-institutionalised groups, 89 per cent had been in at least one fight, although fighting was infrequent. On the other hand, her institutionalised girls had been involved in frequent, protracted fighting, often with weapons. Coming from violent homes, they were encouraged to fight by parents. All exhibited contempt for men.

Girls in male-dominated subcultures

We have seen that the presence of girls in gangs seems to be changing. Traditionally in the more dramatic forms of male-dominated subcultures, girls were in a structurally passive situation, reflecting their position outside. In the Ted subculture of the 1950s, girls were present during social activities but absent from the street corner culture. With Mods, girls were subordinate, but mod 'cool' style allowed them to mingle in all girl groups or alone. With the bikers, they never penetrated the central masculine core, riding or owning a bike, but were always a pillion passenger. The hippy subculture still contained them in a sphere of traditional femininity, which whilst it suspended marriage, maintained long-term relationships. Attempts to make these open were often male manipulation of female radicalism to make rules permitting male escape from commitment. Hippy girls were either long-haired, wanton, wild flower children, or (McRobbie and Garber, 1976, p. 219), 'The stereotypical images we associate most with hippy culture tend to be those of the Earth Mother, baby at breast, or the fragile Pre-Raphaelite lady.' The sexual exploitation and subordination of women is emphasised in school subcultures. The boys in Sarsby's study (1972) mention that the personal qualities sought in a girl are obedience, respect and virginity. Girls have to be sexually inviting but not sexually experienced; attractive enough to raise the boy's status but not so experienced that there is no kudos in having a relationship with her. They are expected to be a surrogate wife, servicing the boy domestically. Reduced to being at the receiving end of masculine desire, they have to operate within a framework of passivity. Willis (1977, p. 44) sums it up:

> Although they are its objects, frank and explicit sexuality is
> actually denied to women. There is a complex of emotion here.
> On the one hand insofar as she is a sex object, a commodity,
> she is actually diminished by sex, she is literally worthless, she
> has been romantically and materially partly consumed.

The fear underlying this is that if a woman's desire is fully awakened, she will become a sexually active person, a subject. The male, when compared to others, may be found wanting. Thus boys will seek an idealised domestic partner, often based on an 'ideal mother' image.

Girls seem, when involved in delinquent subcultures, to be in rebellion against their traditional role (Wilson 1978). Wilson's thirteen- to fifteen-year-olds followed the cult of femininity in that they saw themselves as one-man girls, and for them love was essentially involved in sex. Their future jobs were seen merely as a step towards marriage, and they regulated their behaviour so that they avoided contact with 'easy lays' who could contaminate their own reputations. They could then be sexually active without defining themselves as 'bad'. Conventional sexual morality is implicitly maintained by the sexualising of the offences of delinquent girls. L.S. Smith (1978) found that girls involved with greasers and skinheads were not restricted in their offences to the sexual misconduct that was the concern of the courts, but committed other offences in the same pattern as the boys. Terry (1970) found that in America girls suspected of sexual misconduct were more likely than boys to be charged, and Chesney Lind (1973) found three times as many girls as boys institutionalised for sexual offences, running away and incorrigibility, even though boys commit these offences. Smith's girls were controlled in the parameters of traditional femininity through their aggression. It was this, not promiscuity which stigmatised them as 'sluts' or 'common'. They were doubly rejected, first as delinquent, then as 'sluts'. However, they resisted this, themselves condemning promiscuity, and developing a tom boy image, tough, dominant and willing to join in fights. Pushed into dependence on the delinquent group, isolated from the other neighbourhood girls they found themselves relegated to being bad examples to others. They became seriously involved in subcultural attachment, fighting, shop-lifting and drinking. Their group solidarity and active involvement during fighting meant they took central roles in the subcultures. This varies according to local subcultures. For example (Schools Bulletin, West Riding, July 1970):

Skinhead girls admire the way their boys treat them. They treat them as if they weren't there. . . . They never include them in their conversation, they have no manners and are disrespectful, but the girls respect them for being this way. It is all part of the understanding that goes with being a skinhead and being a true one. . . . The girls take as much part in the fighting as the boys and will be ready to have 'aggro' at any time.

The local male culture, then, influences subcultures, and the role girls are assigned depends on their own assertion and ability to negotiate between traditional and delinquent roles. A girl can be dissociated from the respectable working-class image of femininity, but still contained within the ideology of male supremacy. In biker subcultures, girls are fetished images which are counterparts of the male, but yet remaining the property of the male. Skinhead girls draw on an image not of a new feminine style, but feminised interpretations of working-class male imagery. This is the image utilised by working-class lesbians, the 'diesel dyke' or 'stomping dyke'. Delinquent girls in these subcultures can be seen, for Smith (1978, p. 4):

in contrast to the males whose delinquent behaviour is often seen as an extension of their role, they were seen to have

offended against their own sex role, and the traditional
stereotyped conceptions of masculinity.

Working-class girls are not exposed to any alternative concepts
of femininity, because their intimate interaction is with traditional
familial roles. Popular culture outside the home is also sexist. The
explicitness of rock and roll from Presley's pelvis on struck an
important blow against small town puritanism, but rock and roll
is a celebration of male machismo sexuality. This has a distinct
notion of a woman's place, whether in the sexuality of Rhythm
and Blues, the woman's need of a man in blues singing, or the
nostalgic, conservative ideology of country music. Musicians are
mainly men but punk, infused with feminism, has managed to
break the monopoly. Women are traditionally lyricists, singers of
sensitive work or sex objects, and again punks' satirisation has
gained a foothold against this. Fetishisation becomes satirised –
'Oh bondage, up yours' screams Poly Styrene. The sexism of popular culture is hardly surprising. It is rooted in an industry correctly
called show 'business' (once called 'the profession') whose aim is
to make money, not to criticise society. Serious women's bands
usually work outside the industry if they challenge programmed
femininity, depending on feminist and student bookings. Ratings,
airplay and exposure depend on shrewd, often corrupt business
manipulation. Whilst superstars may have artistic freedom, any
band just starting has practically none at all once it becomes a
means of living. Punk opened up through the use of shock tactics,
attacks on traditional roles, but the very nature of popularity
means that these are constrained to image rather than authentic role
explorations. However, despite this women's bands have emerged,
with a different relationship to their audience and their material
than the male 'çock rock' bands with their sexual domination.

McRobbie (1978c) has argued, as Willis has for boys, that their
own culture is the most effective agent for social control for girls.
Their anti-school subculture stresses having a good time, rather
than an achievement which would gain them a hold in male-dominated work. They resist what is for them a meaningless curriculum,
by talking back to teachers, and amongst themselves, and sometimes fighting. School imposes a passive femininity, and resistance
takes the form of assertive impertinence, seen by the school as
prerequisite to 'loose' sexuality. The romantic 'nice girl' image
found in the mainstream culture is differentially resisted or interpreted. Thomas (1980) found in an Australian study of girls' countercultures, that her working-class girls played down romance, for
toughness and freedom from vulnerability.

Working-class girls, materially, if they are to have a family, need a husband who will provide for them. They are dependent on the marriage market, and they preserve their reputations accordingly. They are permitted sexual relations with someone they love or are committed (i.e. engaged) to. Marriage holds a fascination for young working girls which, given the bleak options, is hardly surprising. It continues to be a major economic and emotional goal, despite their hard-headed realism about its problems. School for working-class girls relates to them the contradictions of their position, but home offers a less competitive position. The traditional female role is problematic, but concrete; their knowledge of it is not abstract theory, but directly experiential. Like her brother the working-class girl moves from one family to another on marriage. There is no room for a single woman in traditional working-class culture, except on the margins of sexual failure. One is not prepared by working-class life to live alone, and it is not financially viable for women. Only after marriage are its restricting aspects really experienced, where the drudgery of housework is lumped together with the more rewarding aspects of child care. The cult of romance found in mainstream culture may be differentially negotiated in working- and middle-class life (Willis, 1982). Aggression is used by working-class girls to resist authority and explicit forms of male domination. The romantic mode is used to negotiate the 'double standard'. Girls are caught up in the class trap, economic dependency, and the patriarchal trap; sexual activity offers the option of a steady relationship, or relegation to the 'loose' status. Sex is exchanged for commitment, the final end being marriage. The judicial system as we have seen reflects and encourages this. Young girls who are sexually active outside this understanding find that this part of their behaviour is sanctioned. McRobbie (1978b) reminds us of the stigma attached to the status of being seen as 'cheap':

> But the word which is richest in connotation is 'cheap'. The fear expressed in this descriptive term is that girls will cheapen themselves by dispensing their 'sexual favours' in a free and indiscriminate way. To put it another way, as vulnerable impressionable adolescents these girls could end up selling their sexuality below the 'market price', that is, outside marriage. And this cheapness is expressed in provocative clothing and heavy make-up.

One ironic spin-off of the centrality of the family in the lives of girls is found in reformatories (Carter, 1973). Girls form romantic attachments to other girls, and construct a pseudo family of husbands, wives, mothers, daughters, sisters and brothers all cast from other girls incarcerated in the institution.

The invisible girl - the culture of femininity versus masculinism

For middle-class girls, the problems of femininity are the same, but the alternatives differ. Their education prepares them for the dual role, but there may be a period between school and marriage which is more of a moratorium allowing them time for reflection. They are more likely to have careers than jobs, although these careers are expected to come second to those of the male. It is hardly surprising that the feminist movement gained support among women of higher education as it is they who have access to alternatives. There is also a feminist culture which supports the analysis of sexual politics, of women's relationship to the material world, to relating to men and to other women as viable and legitimate areas of concern. The role of the feminist woman has made inroads into working-class culture, and there is evidence from feminist teachers, social workers and youth workers that this meets with considerable support among female youth. The new concepts of assertive and independent womanhood are percolating through society, but have to deal with the patriarchal culture of traditional femininity, and its material class reinforcement. Working-class girls may rebel against male supremacy, but even in the aggressive subcultures toughness is not aimed against their men, but is a move to be accepted by machismo men. The major difficulty is that the feminine role still offers an emotional and material alternative for girls at present.

Punk women

An interesting thesis on punk women in the United States has been developed by Rothaus (1984). Her argument is that one can see in punk style discernible class variations which are 'the creative responses of youth from two different class cultures', middle and working class. Seeing America's permanent reserve army of labour as being constituted by youth aged sixteen to twenty-four, and envisaging women as a particularly vulnerable stratum within this, Rothaus sets her analysis firmly in the context of class and gender relations. Alarmingly the US Congressional Budget Office has calculated the rate of white youth unemployment as 15 per cent (twice the average of the labour force as a whole), and the non-white youth labour force as 34 per cent in a time when social welfare programmes and public sector jobs are being dismantled. Faced by downward mobility, women in the punk subculture have responded differentially - middle-class women have attempted to 'reappropriate Hollywood ideologies of femininity by fetishising its commodities of fashion and beauty' (Rothaus, 1984, p. 16). They parody 'its Aryan make-up ideals, mocking its expensively coiffed

176

hairdos with greasy, spiked hair and exchanging its precarious high heels for strapping steel-toed boots'.

One important distinction is 'dressing punk' as opposed to 'being punk'. Middle-class young women 'dress punk', and whilst their commodified style opposes traditional middle-class conceptions of femininity, punk style is seen as a possible entry into the middle-class, bohemian, musical, artistic fringes, whilst at the same time failing to challenge seriously the privileged base of punk femininity, nor the class relations of power between both middle- and working-class women and among punks themselves. By its bold assertiveness, punk feminine style permits punk women 'space' in street negotiations of sexism. Yet in the case of middle-class women this is not an emancipatory resistance, but reasserts their class position albeit in a bohemian mode. Working-class punk women, argues Rothaus, see themselves with their working-class male peers as 'being punk'. Both genders of working-class punk subculture 'used the rhetorical category of "being punk" to distinguish their experience from that of middle-class punks'. Working-class punk women do not fetishise Hollywood fashion and beauty but emphasise their class by short haircuts, plain white T-shirts with rolled-up sleeves, army fatigues and old sneakers. They do not parody Farrah Fawcett Majors, or 'new woman' professionalism, but reaffirm a non-traditional working-class cultural identity as women, distinguishing themselves from middle class punks and women.

> Their own choice of style also suggests the failure of a commodified oppositional femininity – the ideologies and class culture it represents – to resonate with or express what is meaningful in the daily lives of women who experience varying degrees of pauperisation in their economic slippage from the working class into the lumpen proletariat. (Rothaus, 1984, p. 29)

It is a resource and buffer against the drudgeries of young motherhood and the bleak prospects for employment. As such they align with working-class punk males rather than middle-class punk females. However, they have used their punk style to deal with a shared range of oppressive experiences common to all women and to combat sexual propositions by men in public, thus allowing them some 'space' to negotiate their gender relations with men. They have gained some measure of personal control over being hassled in the street, and over the expression and meaning of their gender identities. However, the particular use punk women have made of their styles has given them an apparent unity to the outside observer, but inside the subculture the punk world has reproduced their basic class antagonisms, rather than conditions which will unite women across common gender interests. The varied styles have made conspicuous their different class origins, especially to the cognoscenti, and leave unresolved the consequences that downward mobility poses for women. Rothaus is pursuing her research which is as yet unpublished.

The celebration of masculinism

I have noted above the importance of masculinity to working-class life, in terms of what one is 'manly' enough to perform as work, or capable of earning. These two elements balance each other out; if one is not doing a 'real man's' job, this can be excused by one's earning capacity. As women's wages are less than 60 per cent of men's (excluding overtime and bonuses earned in the male world), women's work remains at a low status. Work is of central importance to adolescents because it is the key to status and identity, offering the means to celebrate masculinity or femininity. Pubescent girls make particularly detailed studies of femininity (and it is incidentally the dread of street transvestites that a group of jeering teenage girls will reveal their actual gender).

Working-class boys who are involved with a specific youth subculture are placed in the contradictory predicament of attracting attention, and having to deal with consequent challenges. If they sport heavy, macho clothing (for example Hells Angels or skinheads) they are a walking challenge and have to be hard enough to live up to their image. They have to indicate that they 'deserve' the uniform. If they take up a glamrock or feminised image, they have to be either especially hard and confident, or very quick-witted in repartee. They are caught up in a situation where they are wearing a costume which transgresses traditional concepts of masculine dress, hence when challenged over effeminacy, they have to prove their masculinity, or prove by flight that they are not masculine. This is why hard glamrock boys had the sinister image of feminised hair-styles, elaborate clothes and make-up set off by scars or tattoos. They were dissociating themselves from the despised, non-familial non-masculine males – homosexuals. Interestingly enough, in highly macho surroundings, for example the military or prison, gay men who are 'out' will present themselves as outrageous queens, backing up their role-play with wit and repartee, earning themselves acceptability by 'being a good laugh' and removing themselves to a non-threatening 'mascot' role. This occurs even withing the gay subculture. For working-class youth, masculinity is a problem. It is the mark of one's independence, especially in a context such as school, where the dominant code is rational discussion. If one can handle oneself then this means that all discussion can be settled as a direct challenge. This sets one's position in the local youth hierarchy, and makes one a valuable member of local teams or fighting crews. As I have noted, teams now contain girls who are prepared to fight other girls, although as Robins and Cohen (1978, p. 96), say: 'this aggro did nothing to alter the girls' fundamental one-down position in the local youth culture – as in other areas of their lives'.

Middle-class youths subscribe to the cult of masculinity, but less directly. They do not have the neighbourhood traditions of well-known hard local families, or the mythical accounts of famous past fights. However, their competitiveness and masculinity take more subtle forms, and are institutionalised into their education and work situations. In an empirical study (Brake, 1977) comparing a semantic differential score for real, ideal and perceived concepts of self between middle-class hippies and working-class skinheads, both skinheads and hippies saw themselves as brave, strong and masculine. Indeed, both groups had assessed themselves equally on the bravery and masculinity scale. However, their interpretation of this and the acting out of it at the behavioural level was quite different. Basically the cult of masculinity is at the basis of relations with other men, and with women. Whitehead (1976) shows how, in a rural setting, the pub is used to reinforce the cult of masculinity: women are used to maintain solidarity and ambivalent rivalry between men; jokes were used to stereotype women as contemptible and as sex objects to be controlled; prestige was related to an ability to control one's wife; and that these invariably influence marital relationships. She suggests that these are a normal feature of heterosexual men in groups. Certainly, these attitudes filter down to young males, and the sexist jokes and shouts that girls and women have to put up with daily is an indication of the complex desire and hatred of that desire that men have for women.

Zaretsky (1976) argues that as industrial society organised production around an increasingly alienated labour, then personal relations became pursued as ends in themselves. Bereft of a meaning and an authority at work, men sought these at home. Obviously, responses are more complicated than this, as studies of the family suggest (Willmott and Young, 1957; Rosser and Harris, 1965; Gavron, 1966; Ball, 1968; Young and Willmott, 1973), but the home has become the focus for expressive life, leisure and consumption. This is, however, true only for men; for women the experience of home is housework. Manual labour is organised around the work group, and as Tolson (1977, p. 59) reminds us: 'Thus a man's personal experience of work is expressed through an endless drama of group interaction, and his social acceptability is defined in terms of his dramatic self-preservation.' Masculinity is important, and as such, swearing, sexist talk, a banding together against women, unite the individual into the collectivity of the work group and the company of men. They gloss over the contradictions of male chauvinism, and laugh off the unease that men feel about their need for love and for the support of women. Unhappily, this often takes the form of needing women for sexual and domestic services, but saving their deeper feelings for other men with whom there is no complication of sexual relations. This is reflected in the male bonding movies which hint at this contradiction. There is an assumption that men have true egalitarian relationships, but must assume a power relation over women. The conquest of women is in competition with other men, who are also competing for status. Stoltenberg (1975, p. 35) says:

> under patriarchy, the cultural norm of human identity is by
> definition – masculinity. And under patriarchy the cultural
> norm of male identity consists in power, prestige, privilege and
> prerogative as over and against the gender class women. . . .
> Male bonding is institutionalised learned behaviour whereby
> men recognize and reinforce one another's *bona fide*
> membership in the male gender class . . . male bonding is how
> men learn from each other that they are entitled under
> patriarchy to power in the culture. Male bonding is how men
> get that power and male bonding is how it is kept. Therefore
> men enforce a taboo against unbonding. . . .

This illustrates the importance of peer groups for males in youth cultures, and work groups in shop-floor cultures. Men develop a conflicting attitude to a family; they are a sign of masculinity, of being able to support and control it, but they are also a recognised rationalisation for failure. Domesticity is a valid tie, a valid restriction on what might have been. The material support for the family is also the condition for the recognition by the family of the male authority and influence lacking at work. Home is a retreat from work, and Tolson argues that the harmonious facade at home is important for the breadwinner to continue to work. Hence working-class men evade or deny marital tension, leaving the running of the family to the wife. This retreat to the patriarchal role, and its support in working-class male culture, means that feelings and sensitivity are not discussed. Depression, particularly for men, is explained away as 'sulking', and emotional life remains an unspoken-of area, as does sexuality.

Middle-class men have a more individualised work life. The rough machismo of working-class men, often structurally encouraged because of the necessity to preserve a patriotic militarism in the past, is replaced by a smoother but nevertheless entrenched male identity. Education and careers are both competitive structures requiring self-confidence and aggressive drive. Men are often supported at work by women who are expected to combine a quasi-domestic servicing as well as clerical and administrative skills. Tolson argues that middle-class men use their careers as indicators of identity and status, and where confidence in this is shaken, the professional man focuses his attitudes of patriarchy on his family. Where the middle-class careerist becomes disillusioned, family domesticity becomes the focus of his concern, protection and authority, and family interaction can become a focus for tension. However, the home is still central to male authority; it is his career and income that is central. The wife, like housewives in all classes, can become lonely, isolated, often too lacking in confidence to work even though she wants to, and depressed. Sexuality is often a problem, because there is a distinct emphasis on sexual success, and the concept of sex as entertainment which has increased since the 1960s has undermined male confidence, or else substituted a stud ideology of sexual domination by skill.

One effect of heterosexual male culture and the response by the feminists has been on the lives of gay people. Subcultural studies of youth never mention homosexuals, and this is hardly surprising given the masculinist emphasis of practically all youthful subcultures. Young gay people are swamped by the heterosexist emphasis they find in peer groups and subcultures. As far as popular culture is concerned they are invisible. Young people tend to be aware at the age of about ten that they are different, and by the time puberty arrives they are generally aware what this difference is. However, admitting this to themselves and especially to others is usually delayed until some supportive subculture has been found to 'come out' in. Given the obsession of most young people's subcultures, especially in the early teens, with heterosexual success and identity, it is hardly surprising that finding other homosexuals is a problem. This is the basis of differing views of feminists and gay radical men about paedophilia. For most gay men, a pubescent or adolescent seduction with a mature older man would have eased their problems considerably, whilst for most young girls a paedophiliac relationship is always exploitative. Young gay people usually do not find homosexual subcultures until they have left home. There is a subculture involving young boys in the gay world, known as 'chickens'. They can be heterosexual boys, using a sexual market-place for prostitution (see Reiss, 1961; Brake and Plummer, 1970; Harris, 1973). Most community homes and borstals have an informal information system telling runaway boys where the sexual markets are, or else a list of telephone numbers and addresses that will offer somewhere to stay for a few pounds in exchange for sexual services. They are also a haven for young homosexual boys who have run away from an unhappy home, and from a dreary, heterosexually dominated life in the provinces. There is a high status position for attractive young boys in the youth-dominated gay world, and it provides an alternative form of social mobility.

Young gay girls find the situation more difficult. There is an organisation which holds meetings and social events for homosexual teenagers, and various gay organisations offer telephone and befriending forms of counselling. Working-class lesbians, if they are aware of their homosexuality at an early age, find the pubs and clubs but because of the secrecy about homosexuality, combined with the secrecy about women's sexuality generally, young gay girls are less present on the gay scene. Middle-class gay women, like their male counterparts, can find an entry to gay subcultures through gay societies at college and university. Outside this student group, gay women find the gay world through the feminist movements, although it is probably true to say that most homosexual people are introduced by a relationship to the gay world or, in particular men, gradually become involved through local gay pubs and clubs. In general, however, for heterosexual men homosexual behaviour may take place in heterosexual peer groups in contexts which permit the disavowal of homosexual labelling. Also because of the nature of casual sex in the male gay world it is possible to find sexual outlets whilst denying any self-labelling of homosexual, or being involved with the gay community. Women, however, tend to seek deeply affectionate relationships and so tend to concentrate on establishing and maintaining a loving relationship in their early lesbian career.

We can see then that the 'absence' of girls from masculinist subcultures is not very surprising. These subcultures in some form or other explore and celebrate masculinity, and as such eventually relegate girls to a subordinate place within them. They reflect the sexism of the outside world. A sexism which still accepts the sexual division of labour and women's traditional place in the modes of production and reproduction. In some subcultures girls have won themselves acceptance, as for example in fighting teams, but again these teams operate against other girls. The male attitude when it comes to sexual relations remains traditional. However, there are the beginnings of a challenge to this, but until this finds a response in the larger, in particular the working-class community, it is unlikely to be reflected in working-class subcultures involving youth. In popular culture such as the rock industry, women are still relegated to the role of singer, usually performing sexist celebrations of sexual come-hither or sad ballads of women's lot. The culture of femininity is reflected in the various youth subcultures involving girls. Nevertheless, popular culture can hint at alternatives. Frith suggests (1978, p. 207):

> Female musicians, whether through implicit but disturbing images of what a woman could be or on the basis of an explicitly feminist culture can challenge the safe solutions to the glamorous star-as-mum.

That is not to say that girl performers are not controlled by the sexism which is a dominant form in rock. There are exceptions as Burchill and Parsons (1978) admit, but they accurately describe rock (Burchill and Parsons, 1978, p. 86):

> Rock is a pedestal sport, as in being a monarch – whenever possible a boy inherits the throne – females are not thought to be the stuff worship/idols are made for/of. Girls are expected to grovel in the mezzanine while the stud struts his stuff up there, while a girl with the audacity to go on stage is always jeered, sneered and leered up to – rock and roll is very missionary, very religious, very repressive.
> A guitar in the hands of man boasts 'cock' – the same instrument in female hands therefore (to a warped mind) screams 'castration'.

Despite the generalisation, this does help to explain why changes in girls' attitudes will come from the influence of an older age group, and through the medium of feminism. Nevertheless, the political thrust at the periphery of popular culture will at some time attack the notion of the programmed woman.

Chapter 8

No future? Subcultures, manufactured cultures and the economy

> The Americans colonised our subconscious.
>
> (Wim Wenders, *Alice in the Cities*)

Manufactured cultures and the economy – the relationship of production and consumption

> People will farm in the morning, make music in the afternoon and fuck wherever and whenever they want to.
>
> (Jerry Rubin, *Do It!*)

One problematic about the authenticity of popular culture is the extent to which it is a response to something deliberately synthetic produced for a mass market. Frith (1978) reminds us that rock music, for example, is very big business. In 1974 over four billion dollars was spent world wide on musical products. Music is the most purchased popular pastime in America, and British sales of records and tapes in 1974 was worth over £160 million. Ninety per cent of the American market is controlled by six companies (CBS, RCA, WEQ, MCA, Polygram and Capitol). Only 10 per cent of recorded music is classical, 80 per cent of purchasers are under thirty, 70 per cent of popular music is bought by the twelve to twenty-year-old age group. Profitability is further increased by the fact that many companies own both the software and the hardware. There are financial links between the firms owning and selling instruments and sound systems, and those making records, promoting concerts and radio programmes. This commercial aspect has led to scornful dismissal of popular music and its adherents. Frith (1983) traces this debate from the early Frankfurt school where Adorno and Benjamin first seriously considered popular culture, and the work of F.R. Leavis in British literary criticism. Leavis saw mass culture as standardised, escapist and passively consumed.

Because its production involved commerciality, it must therefore be denuded of authenticity. Adorno argued that this production of popular music as a commodity determined its cultural quality. Because it has to attract large number of consumers, it has to create false needs – false because they have to serve capitalism. Thus the need to consume is invented, satisfied by consumption. One reason for this line of argument was that mass culture, especially films and popular music, was seen as 'Americanised'. Non-Americans were fascinated by American music, especially jazz, films, newspapers and methods of mass production. America became a symbol of democracy, of progress, modernisation, accessibility to consumption and freedom. America itself, argues Frith, became an object of consumption and a symbol of pleasure. Most critics of mass culture took for granted the passive element of consumption by the masses. Its very accessibility meant that it became written off as inferior. One element of European criticism was elitist. Something which had such wide appeal and was mass produced must be inferior. The other criticism came from Marxists who, because of the implications of American capitalism, argued mass culture must be shoddy and banal, and its purpose was seen to divert the masses from their position of exploitation. By the 1950s the mass culture debate was in fact a debate about American mass culture. In the context of the Cold War, American culture was seen by American sociology as democratic culture, and defended as such. However, even in the 1930s there were competing interpretations of culture. Walter Benjamin (1970) discussed 'the work of art in the age of mechanical reproduction' seeing the technology of mass reproduction as a progressive force which broke the traditional authority and awe (the 'aura') of art. Artists could be seen as democratic producers, whose work was open to the mass of the people, each of whom could become an 'expert'. During the 1950s the view was popular that mass culture was a form of the 'opium of the people'. But, as Laing points out, popular music such as rock contains liberating as well as oppressive forces. Rock music certainly resulted from the music industry's attempt to develop new markets, but it also resulted from its youthful audience's attempts to find a medium expressing its own experience. It is this space which gives popular art its form and direction, and where the artist concerned can work. It was Hall and Whannel (1964) who correctly interpreted teenage culture as 'a contradictory mixture of the authentic and the manufactured – an area of self expression for the young and lush grazing ground for the commercial providers'.

One theoretical difficulty that arises in the analysis of popular culture is that of structuralism and culturalism. Culturalism, which is based on the work of Raymond Williams, E.P. Thompson and the reworking of Gramsci by the CCCS, rests on Williams's attempt to move away from the concept of popular culture as part of a superstructure erected on, determined by and having little influence on, the economic base of society. Culture is now seen as an active practice shaping and conditioning economic and political processes, as well as being conditioned and shaped by them. Culture has become conceptualised as:

> the set of practices through which men and women actively respond to the conditions of their social existence, creatively fashioning experienced social relationships into diverse and structured patterns of living, thinking and feeling. The emphasis, within this account, is placed on the notion of human agency. (Bennett *et al.*, 1981, p. 10)

The emphasis here is on the making of culture, rather than its determined conditions. Structuralism, on the other hand, claims that the spheres of culture (or ideology as it tends to be called in structuralism) within which the human subject asserts itself consist of sets of relatively autonomous determinations. These are structures of language, myth, literature, moulding forms of human interaction, in ways relatively independent of the economic, social and political context. Cultural forms for structuralists are the producers not the products, of experience. The way in which we feel and act out our lives is the product of cultural determinations, rather than the other way round. Thus, in the anthropology of Lévi Strauss, the literary criticism of Roland Barthes, the psychoanalysis of Jacques Lacan, the 'archaeology of knowledge' of Michel Foucault, the political theory of Althusser we see the elements of this paradigm. There are, however, important differences between these thinkers, and several of them would disavow the label of structuralist. Structuralism and culturalism have produced the essence for a fruitful debate.

In culturalism relations are looked at in terms of how they are lived and experienced. History shapes us in conditions which are not of our own making, yet we in turn create history. We experience the conditions of our life, define them and respond to them. Structuralism reminds us that we can only live and experience our conditions through and within the categories, classifications and frameworks of culture. In language, in particular, we construct our experience and our subjectivity and this makes it a site for a struggle for the rules of definition of the human experience. We speak of 'black' poets or 'women' writers, which shows the racist and sexist bias of an unspoken superiority assumed by white, middle-class men in the history of intellectual discourse. Language, then, is not merely a medium, but plays an active role in constructing social definitions, and making available to us the linguistic and social basis of our identity. Language is also not neutral; within it is enshrined our sense of reality and identity. Our definition of ourself is fought over by differing social interests often embedded in institutions. A sense of superiority by one person or class rests on an assumption of inferiority in the other. The power we may have over others may be only the power to despise them. Thus white people may despise black, heterosexuals despise homosexuals, men despise women and so forth. Idioms are available to us, and these already embody ideologies. Domination in this sense is invisible, and the same is true for cultural domination. The street argot of young delinquents, or the ghetto speech of young blacks, may be seen 'from above' (from the perspective of the state) as a social problem because it handicaps them in educational advantage. But 'from below' (the perspective of its users) it is more complex than a problem which requires solving by state policy; it reminds them of their subordination and can be transformed into a weapon of resistance. It is a refusal of the standard middle-class code with its connotations of an accepted and acceptable form. We see that it can be possible to combine both structural and cultural traditions, for example, to see that language structures and is structured by differential power relations. Social definitions and social categories define identity and culture, and that as such an apparently 'neutral' phenomenon such as language is historically and contemporally an important site and mechanism for cultural struggle. This is especially true for an immigrant 'melting pot' culture as in North America, which has to impose a sense of nationalism (being 'American') on disparate groups with different cultural traditions. In such a situation, nationalism must emphasise that the New Country is a better place to be in order to disarm dissent and criticism which would undermine the prevailing order.

The other problem that youth culture posits is that of leisure. The Leavisite pessimism was that routinised, mindless work destroys in youth any sense of meaningful freedom. Commercialisation of youth culture robs the young of any sense that their lives could be different. As in vulgar Marxism, the heavy hand of capitalism destroys any sense of leisure outside that synthetically produced. Frith in particular takes issue with this: leisure choice cannot be determined, it has to relate to how working people want to spend their free time. It is, after all, the control of the non-work area – leisure – that is the basis of one of the original tasks of policing. The central theme of leisure is fun, a feature often overlooked in sociological studies of mass culture. However, the form and direction of leisure, because of its unpredictable fun element, can never be determined. It becomes accommodated, commercialised

187

and marketed, but then it takes another form. It is this which makes the market unpredictable, despite commercial efforts. We have gone beyond theories of mass culture which ignore the different shape and origins of popular cultural forms. We have seen that the economics of commercialism do not rely on passive consumption. Frith argues that the capitalist leisure business relies on orderly, predictable consumption, and that it is because the audience is active, and hence unpredictable, that big business is involved in a struggle. It needs to contain rock music, for example, to a particular type of free time, which drains power from the music. Similarly the music press's political criticism becomes replaced by becoming a consumer's guide. The rock audience becomes frozen into a series of market tastes, so that if an audience feels its needs are met, rock's disturbing challenges are transformed into conventions. Finally, the anti-work elements are decollectivised to individual self-indulgence. Music, however, remains disturbing, joyous and powerful; its meanings cannot be determined. The study of popular culture, then, is related to the wider configuration of a struggle over and with hegemony. It is a battle with the state over definitions and legitimation, and broader historical changes in the political economy become reflected in it. As sets of social relations shift, then so do the contents of popular culture. Frith (1983) argues that the rock industry is a simple 'cause' which generates 'effects' in a mass audience. The rock industry itself is an effect of the shifting relations of class, sex and race, of post-war changes and of new ideas in popular art and culture. He sees rock and roll as originally performed for the proletarian weekend, but by performers who publicly displayed mastery over their working lives, as well as mastery over movement, speed, abundance and space. When rock became recorded it retained these leisure meanings but in different settings. Frith makes the interesting comment that rock and roll is the music of the American working class, but a class which is rarely symbolised as a class. Because American class experiences are mediated historically through imagery about personal success and failure, then workers' past is remembered in terms of mobility and self-sufficiency. Rock and roll captures a sense of freedom which is also rootlessness and estrangement. These accounts of loneliness and rebellion celebrate the social conditions that produce them.

We have been able to consider some aspects of the relative autonomy of popular culture, and hence youth subcultures, especially their relation to rock music. Rock music has itself changed its genre. In the decade after 1955 music was for dancing and courtship, followed by three years of blues and protest influence. It then emerged in 1967 as a youth identified music, and in the hippy counterculture developed the usage of sophisticated electronic technology, and psychedelic experience combined with this to generate new structures and meaning in rock. We see here some of the complexities of the relative autonomy of cultural forms. Complex music, as developed by the Beatles, shows the influence of musical experimentation (as, for example, carried out by Stockhausen) using electronics and large orchestras. This very complexity, as with the Pink Floyd, means that music is made in the studios, so it becomes music to listen to, as well as performance music. We see basic, simple rock and roll develop into complex progressive rock. Other factors are influential: the hippy counterculture; the mass panic over drug use; the needs of the record market and the structure of the music industry; the meaning which particular musical forms have for particular subcultures; musical education in terms of musicians' influences and interests and the use of music as ideology. We can see that in popular music there are concrete examples of structuralist and culturalist themes. Through this runs the commercial formula used by promoters to make money which, whilst successful in the mainstream and teenybopper market, becomes left behind as the youth audience seeks further innovation to express itself.

The independence that youth since the Second World War has enjoyed in terms of consumption has arisen because they have had sufficient disposable income. This is of course, changeable. Frith sees youth culture as part of the general relationship between choice and constraint involved in leisure consumption. For Frith (1983, p. 200):

> The problem is that the young since the 1920s have come to symbolise leisure, to embody the good times. Youth seems to be freer than everyone else in society . . . they are not bound like their elders by the routines and relationships of family and career. But it is because they are not really free that this matters. The truth of youth culture is that the young displace to their free time the problems of work and family and future. It is because they lack power that the young account for their lives in terms of play, focus their politics on leisure.

Youth culture and identity

Youth cultures have offered, we have argued, symbolic elements which can be used to build an identity outside the restraints of class and education. One attraction of youth cultures are their rebellious unconventionality. This has been symbolised in style and music. If white popular music has been a response to black popular music, European popular music has been a response to American music. American music is popular in Europe just because it is not European with its connotations of traditional restraint. British music is popular in America because it conjures up a mythical Britain, with a raw and committed youth culture. A constant replay of the rough and respectable dichotomy of working-class life is found in the split between suburban and street cultures among youth. Suburban culture means achievement at school, responsible family and emotional relationships, commitment to careers and the constructive use of leisure. Street culture becomes a mythical antithesis to this. It is desperate, anti-authority, raw and violent, involved in the defence of symbolic territory. It occurs outside the home, in the urban street, itself a tough environment. It is neither safe nor nice, and hence very attractive. British subcultures are explicitly more class conscious than American, and pay considerable attention to the intricacies of style. However, major divisions reflecting wider social stratifications run through youth cultures. The class and ethnic divisions are complicated by regionality in North America, by minority groups in the United States, by French and English in Canada. Westerners are not the same as Easterners and youth cultures reflect this. Divisions run further: student/ worker, skilled/unskilled, urban/rural, employed/unemployed, which underlie the further complexities of class, gender, race and sexual orientation. This is the cultural material from which identities are constructed. Because of the marginal position of young people these identities are temporary 'magical' identities, unconfined to occupation or family. In this context there is a struggle over the meaning of the subculture, as Hebdige (1979) puts it, 'a struggle over the sign'. All this occurs in the 'moment' between adolescence and adulthood with its attendant responsibilities of marriage. Youth culture emphasises a relation of unattachment, dislocated from the confinements of work and committed relationships, a genuine experiment with 'free time'. It delineates us and them, and assists youth to find the companionship of like-minded peers, and with them a relation to identity constructed from the array of signs and symbols found in subcultures. Subcultures become meaningful statements about youth's existential position. Of course youth cultural adherence varies in form – there are always those who do not fit, who rebel within the subculture, just as there are purists who define the parameters of righteousness.

We can see then that a quasi-delinquent, male-dominated, street youth subculture, dealing with unemployment and racism and mediated by local ghetto culture, is a far cry from the quasi-bohemian college culture with its roots in the middle-class intelligentsia. The attraction of subculture is its rebelliousness, its hedonism, its escape from the restrictions of work and home. It offers a place to explore fun, heterosexuality, masculinity and by definition femininity. Dominant ideology has managed to maintain hegemony as regards traditional roles and notions concerning sexuality. Despite adult fear of promiscuity, usually a projection, respectability has been maintained. Most subcultures retain traditional sexual roles, and the only ones which have developed a critique of heterosexuality are those developed out of sexist oppression, that is radical gay and feminist subcultures. Most subcultures still subscribe to romantic and monogamous views of sexuality. Young people need a space in which to explore an identity which is separate from the roles and expectations imposed by family, work and school. Youth culture offers a collective identity, a reference group from which youth can develop an individual identity. It provides cognitive material from which to develop an alternative script, kept secret from, and in rebellion with, adult authority. It represents a free area to relax with one's peers outside the scrutiny and demands of the adult world. This alternative script can be performed outside the socialising forces of work or school, before those of marriage become important. Once youth has separated itself from adulthood, and made a public dramaturgical statement about their difference from adult expectations of them, they feel free to explore and develop what they are. This is why their image is often deliberately rebellious or delinquent. It quite dramatically emphasises their difference, their individuality contained as it may be in a collectivity. Then they can feel liberated to explore another identity. This also explains why they can give up this identity, it is part of a transformation, and can be rejected as 'adolescent'. In a very real sense it is no longer them. This is also why youth cultures attract those who feel little commitment or investment in the present state of affairs. It attracts those who feel misunderstood, or that they do not fit, or rejected. Where the life of the young person reinforces this alienation or isolation, where s/he feels a misfit, the scripts being composed in subcultures become highly attractive.

Youth and the future

The future is the most expensive luxury in the world.
(Thornton Wilder, *The Matchmaker*)

Youth, its cultures and subcultures have always been seen historically as a social problem. A failure to socialise the young

adequately into its place in the work force presents serious consequences. The view that what is wrong with the country is what is
wrong with young people has taken a cruel turn. What is wrong
with young people now is that they can find no work. The state
fears that the loss of work habits and labour discipline could seriously threaten the social order. The young disaffiliated from employment attempt to make a living from hustling, or from quasi-
criminal means. Both Britain and North America fear insurrection
by the youth of minority groups who represent the most impoverished and alienated sections of youth today.

No future? Youth and unemployment

One problem which is particularly acute for youth is unemployment. The general increase in unemployment, noted throughout the
Western industrial nations, has been felt keenly by young people
since the mid-1970s. It is particularly felt by young black people.
As early as 1977, the Council for Europe National Youth Committee found that unemployment among ethnic minorities had increased by 347 per cent for males and 533 per cent for females. In
the same year the national unemployment figures for British white
males was 8.1 per cent and for British Afro-Caribbeans 16.2 per
cent. Generally in Britain unemployment had increased by 120 per
cent for whites and 350 per cent for blacks (Manpower Services
Commission Review and Plan, 1977). Obviously the situation has
worsened since then. Britain has nearly 4 million unemployed,
many of them not even showing on the unemployment statistics
because of temporary training schemes. Half of the British unemployed are under twenty-five, and some 60,000 of these have never
worked although they have left school up to five years ago. Forty
per cent of the Netherlands' unemployed are under twenty-five,
and Germany, always held up as a model for youth training in the
European Economic Community, has now abolished the minimum
wage legislation for young people. This is with the deliberate intention of forcing down youth wages. In the EEC unemployment has
exceeded 11 per cent (12.3 million people) and 42 per cent of this
number in the under twenty-five age group. In addition to this are
the hundreds of thousands in both the sixteen to eighteen-year-old
age groups in government training, and even larger groups in
higher education. The position is comparable in North America.
The situation for the young has changed under the monetarist
economics of Reagan and Thatcher. Permanent unemployment is
a feature of government policies. Incomes, whether through wages,
pensions or welfare, can only be reduced in actual spending power

by allowing increases in inflation. High labour intensity is no longer economically feasible in industrial production. This means that the majority of young people are liable to experience at least short-term periods of unemployment. Young people as a whole, not just sections of them, are being affected although clearly non-white groups and women will be particularly badly affected. Young people are being forced into dependence on families, the state, educational and training schemes and employers in a direct way. It means that incomes are so low that even very minor luxuries (say going out for a drink or to the cinema) are not possible without hustling.

Britain has produced a series of training schemes through the Manpower Services Commission for school leavers which implicitly recognises the right to further education and training, but which occurs at the same time as cuts in education. In reality youths on training schemes receive a low allowance, and employers are either subsidised by cheap labour or a grant to employ temporarily unemployed youth. The 1981 rioting certainly came as a serious shock to the British political system, and it could be argued that training schemes are seen as a substitute for work. The schemes tend to be 'make work' types of activities, and are highly gender biased. Males are trained in carpentry, building and decorating, females in sewing, community service and typing. Minority group girls from the Asian community are often occupied (by walks or watching community activities) so as not to 'interfere' with their Muslim beliefs. The problem has become one of the transformation of the labour force for the state, which never raises the contradiction of the lack of provision for employment in the economy. Presumably the hopelessness of the situation would be seen as lowering morale in the young unemployed, who are either angry or depressed.

Attitudes among young unemployed are interesting. A MORI study by the British *Sunday Times* in September 1981 found that young people who were out of work believed that violence was justified in bringing about social change, but the same number (about half) also believed that immigrants should be repatriated. A study of working-class youth by Billig and Cochrane (1982) found that only a third said they would vote for the Labour Party. Those who supported Labour were inclined to do so because things were better under the previous Labour government, rather than any belief in its policies. Views about unemployment were simplistic, many of the sample blaming immigration. Non-whites supported Labour because they feared their position would worsen under a Conservative government. Only 19 per cent of the sample felt things might improve in the future. Generally the young working-class respondents rejected traditional party politics, rather than holding consistently right-wing attitudes. They showed a populist view which condemned the elitism of politicians. There were demands for more egalitarianism and less support of the wealthier groups. What this seems to indicate among the young is a keen sense of exploitation and the concept of democracy and egalitarianism being offered only to those in employment, or those who are relatively wealthy. The problem for youth culture is that it can take either a radical right-wing rather than a radical left-wing perspective. In the case of Britain this has meant the return of the Thatcher government with a large majority, and a similar situation has happened in North America. Unable to cope with the possibility of unending periods of unemployment, youth (as has happened in Britain) can turn to a specious form of nationalism to resist change. There is a nostalgia for a mythical past rather than a belief in the future.

Unemployment in Britain, Canada and America, whilst a fertile area of research, still lacks any in-depth penetration of regional differences. Massey and Meegan (1983) remind us that the patterns of unemployment have changed in Britain between the 1930s and the 1970s. Job loss in Britain since the late 1970s has been linked to the manufacturing industry's decline, an industry less highly concentrated than the industries of the 1930s. Consequent job loss is therefore more widely spread regionally. There exist not only widely depressed areas, but also prosperous areas with large pockets of unemployment so that regional variation is considerable. This regional inequality depends on the type of work found in an area, the process of the contemporary reorganisation of industry, the types of jobs offered as well as the levels of unemployment. Some regions are areas of growth, complicating the picture, so that the employed may be undergoing a rise in the standard of living, whilst the situation of the unemployed worsens. Reorganisational decisions in the multinational corporations crucially affect the labour market. According to Taylor and Jamieson's (1983) excellent critique of youth unemployment research, the effects of unemployment are felt not only in the size, but also the shape and content of local labour markets. These labour markets determine, 'whether or not there is an unemployment problem in a particular locality and what form that unemployment may take' (Taylor and Jamieson, 1983, p. 61).

Again there exists the difference between 'worklessness', that is permanent, chronic unemployment, and unemployment of a more temporary nature, even though this may last up to two years. The unemployment picture is complicated by the underemployment rate found in part-time work. By examining these we can see the differential impact on gender, class, region and age group. Young women in the present labour market are increasingly involved in low-paid, seasonal and part-time work in a job market reduced to half the size of that of men. Presdee's interesting Australian study (Presdee, 1982) showed that between 1966 and 1976 a quarter of full-time jobs for women were eliminated in a period where the number of young men in employment increased by 1.6 per cent. For young women the market decreased by 4.8 per cent. Presdee did not find that the culture of young unemployed girls conformed to the stereotype of being bored, low in self-esteem, yet happy to be at home as housekeeper of the family. Instead the girls were frustrated and angry at not being able to work, strongly resenting domestic labour. They presented the same contradictory sentiments found in studies of their young working-class male counterparts. Fatalism was mixed with anger, resignation with revolt, ignorance with worldly wisdom, all 'underpinned by a deadening material poverty'. Patriarchal culture pressurises young working-class girls to restrict their activities to domestic labour and shopping. Often they are forced to care for very young or elderly relatives, unlike the boys who are encouraged to venture outside the home, to participate in organised leisure, or who take to the culture of the streets. Presdee's girls experienced an intensification of patriarchal oppression. He notes (Presdee, 1982, p. 13) that

> ... for unemployed young women there is not only a forced and unwelcome retreat into housework, but a retreat into the unpaid chores of the child, in many cases 'board' being paid and collected on top of the value of work in the home.

Young women are not only infantilised by unemployment, but become forcibly recruited into the domestic labour role of housewife. We become aware then that the impact of unemployment and worklessness is significantly different, experientially, between males and females. We have also noted that this is true for different social classes, and especially true for racial and ethnic groups. As Taylor and Jamieson note, both in the United States and Canada higher education has been used to 'mop up' the unemployment figures. In the United States the armed forces have been developed as a state strategy for the employment of unemployed youth. However, as the present attacks on higher education expenditure continue, such may well pose a distinct problematic for the state and the consequent employment of middle-class youth.

The state at present sees youth as having little to negotiate with in market terms. Youth labour has a value when cheap, it has no skill, experience, labour discipline, and cannot compete with adult labour. Only in certain aspects of the market where cheap youth labour is at a premium has it any value. The state intends to remove young people from the unemployment rolls and return them to state subsidised general labour as trainees in the job market. In fact the training schemes do not provide youth with a marketable skill or qualifications and certainly do not provide the protection of organised trade unions. This makes young people an exceptionally vulnerable section of the market, especially for minorities and girls, and prepares them to be grateful for low-paid, quasi-permanent labour. The defence of territory has emerged in working-class youth culture as a form of nationalism, or racism, or else a search for a space independent of family. Youth culture is emerging as a means of dealing with unemployment, offering mutual support by those in similar positions, fun, space to be free of adult authority and a defiant attitude to the state.

The state of course fears that labour discipline may be permanently lost, that the longer youth can survive without working, the less eager it will be to work. The problem for adult authority is that it is better to be unemployed on welfare, than in a tedious, empty job on low pay. The state's problem is to discipline the work force into accepting low-paid routine labour, and it can only do this by financially attacking the unemployed.

Britain has at present seven and a half million people living in abject poverty, lacking the basic necessities of warm clothing, food and heat (MORI, August 1983). The government is pledged to reduce public spending, but obviously cannot reduce the standard of living of this group. It has therefore to focus on teenagers, to maintain labour discipline, and also to recruit people forcibly into the low-paid work available, which pays the same or less than welfare. Certainly the government believes that unemployed teenagers like being unemployed and receiving state benefits. Benefits are cut to those teenagers who refuse Youth Training Schemes, making a mockery of the voluntary aspect. The next move planned is to cut the contribution to parents' housing costs, that each teenager is entitled to on reaching eighteen. Scare stories have been propagated concerning jobless youth moving to cheap lodgings in winter at holiday resorts to enjoy a life of dubious morality at state expense (*Sunday Times*, 21.8.83). The reality is that unemployed teenagers live in families where most or all of the members are unemployed, and to cut benefits would seriously affect the income of those families. We see here a major problem for the welfare state, where chronic unemployment is part of the planned government strategy. What this means in reality is that, consequently, many training and make work schemes for youth are little more than policing youth.

The future looks gloomy – many working-class young people will have to grow up working class without work. The educated and qualified student sector certainly no longer gets the jobs taken for granted in the past by those in the middle class. There is insufficient work for young people to be integrated into. There is a social and economic crisis which has given rise to an ugly nationalism in Britain, and conservatism in America. Community projects, urban aid, redevelopment have all become victims of expenditure cuts; only youth aid programmes remain. As neighbourhoods deteriorate, and as hunger reappears in a wealthy country like the United States, the 'soft' approach of community aid, 'gilding the ghetto' as it was ironically called by community workers in Britain, has to give way to harder measures of community control. The crisis has given hegemony even more legitimation, by spurious arguments for the 'common good'. Social and health services have been reduced, throwing those who need care back into the community, which usually means the unpaid care and domestic service of women. Leisure, which nowadays means not the relaxing free time after work but a grim, chronic period of non-work, is part of social control of the crisis. However, youth still manages to enjoy itself, to get things together without work, and without money. The deeper problems come in adulthood.

We have seen that the work in youth culture has widened since its early association with delinquency. The abstracted empiricism of the 1930s, 1940s and 1950s has been replaced by theoretical debates about the nature of culture, ideology and legitimation in the contemporary state. Popular culture has been rescued from being viewed as 'bad' culture. There are recognitions that a sociology of youth has to consider the wider implications of youthful participation in production and consumption. This means exploring the relationship that youth has with adulthood in contemporary society, and also concentrating on the neglected dimension of home and family. Studies of minorities cultures, girls, popular culture, which had been ignored in the past, are now recognised in the wider context of the struggle for space within hegemony, and moral panics can be seen as part of a widening sense of crisis. What is wrong with America, Canada or Britain is no longer just what is wrong with the hippies, black kids, delinquents or whatever the current folk devil is. Policy has now been forced to pay attention to young people, but at best still only develops containment strategies. The cultural rebellions between 1964 and 1972 (loosely called the 1960s) articulated a reaction against the established order of things which only a minority were able to explore. Nevertheless, many of these ideas remain, and unemployment has hardened the edge of this rebellion. It is important that these remain during the conservative backlash of the present crisis. We need to remember that cultures and subcultures are not just conveyors of alternative phenomenological forms of social reality, but real indicators of

197

material power and ideological resistance. Some subcultures are trivial, some commercial, some joyous; some are expressions of the brutalising effects of class oppression and racism. Often they are all of these, laced liberally with sexism, but a few contain the kernel of a radical and liberated culture. They are certainly a barometer of social change. They explore the relations of consent and resistance to dominant cultures. They express dissatisfaction, and youth culture can be read as a sign of this. Youth cultures are a response to the combined experience of being primarily a location in the labour force, or in the domestic labour sphere, social class and the experience of a reality mediated by the primary indicators of sex, race and class, and the secondary indicators of geographical location, neighbourhood, generation, leisure, social control and hegemony. Youth culture is an essay in experiencing this, accepting some of it and resisting other features. It is an expression of the mini-politics of rebellion against obscure social forces. During a brief period, youth steps outside the stark reality of industrial society to explore a symbolic identity, to celebrate being young, optimistic and joyous – a moment all too brief in personal biography.

Bibliography

Abbreviations used in bibliography
AJS   *American Journal of Sociology*
Annals   *Annals of the American Academy of Political and Social Sciences*
ASR   *American Sociological Review*
BJC   *British Journal of Criminology*
BJS   *British Journal of Sociology*

Aaronsen, B. and Osmond, H. (1971), *Psychedelics – the Uses and Implications of Hallucinogenic Drugs*, Schenkman, Cambridge, Mass.
Abrahams, R.D. (1963), *Deep Down in the Jungle. Negro Narrative Folklore from the Streets of Philadelphia*, University of Philadelphia.
Abrams, M. (1959), *The Teenage Consumer*, L.P.E., Paper 5, Routledge & Kegan Paul, London.
Abrams, P. and McCulloch, A. (1976), 'Men, women and communes', in Barker and Allen (eds), (1976).
Adler, F. (1975), *Sisters in Crime*, McGraw Hill, New York.
Adler, N. (1968), 'The antinomian personality – the hippy character type', *Psychiatry*, 31.
Alberoni, F. (1964), *Consumi e societa*, Il Mulino, Bologna.
Althusser, L. (1971), *Lenin and Philosophy*, New Left Books, London.
Amos, V. and Parmar, P. (1982), 'Resistance and response – black girls in Britain' in McRobbie, A. and McCabe, T. (eds), *Feminism for Girls – an Adventure Story*, Routledge & Kegan Paul, London.
Andersen, N. (1923), *The Hobo*, University of Chicago Press, Chicago.
Anwar, M. (1976), *Between Two Cultures*, Community Relations Commission, London.
Armstrong, G. and Wilson, M. (1973), 'City politics and deviancy', in Taylor, L. and Taylor, I., *Politics and Deviance*, Penguin, Harmondsworth.
Atkinson, A.R. (1975), *The Economics of Inequality*, Oxford University Press, London.
Austin, R.L. (1977), 'Commitment, neutralization and delinquency', in Ferdinand (ed.) (1977).
Bakan, D. (1972), 'Adolescence in America; from idea to social fact', in

Bibliography

Kagan, J. and Coles, R. (eds), *Twelve to Sixteen - Early Adolescence*, W.W. Norton, New York.

Balkan, S., Berger, R.J. and Schmidt, J. (1980), *Crimes and Deviance in America, a Critical Approach*, Wadsworth Publishing Company, Belmont, California.

Ball, M. (1977), 'Emergent delinquency in an urban area', in Ferdinand (ed.) (1977).

Ball, R.H. (1968), 'An empirical investigation of neutralisation theory', in Lefton, M., *Approaches to Deviance*, Appleton Century, Crofts, pp. 255-65.

Bane, M. (1982), *White Boy Singing the Blues*, Penguin, Harmondsworth.

Barker, D. (1972), '"Spoiling and keeping close" in a South Wales town', *Sociological Review*, 20.

Barker, D. and Allen, S. (eds) (1976), *Dependence and Exploitation in Work and Marriage*, Longmans, London.

Barker, G.C. (1947), 'Social functions of language in a Mexican-American community', *Acta America*, 4, pp. 189-92.

Barker, P. and Little, A. (1964), 'The Margate offenders - a survey', *New Society*, vol. 4, no. 96, July, pp. 6-10.

Barnard, J. (1961), 'Teen-age culture - an overview', *Annals*, special edn, 'Teenage culture', vol. 338, November, pp. 1-12.

Barthes, R. (1967), *Elements of Semiology*, Jonathan Cape, London.

Barthes, R. (1972), *Mythologies*, Jonathan Cape, London.

Bayley, D.H. and Mendleschohn, H. (1969), *Minorities and the Police Force*, Free Press of Glencoe, New York.

Bazalgette, J. (1978), *School Life, Work Life*, Hutchinson, London.

Bealer, R.C., Willits, F.K. and Maids, S. (1965), 'The myth of a rebellious adolescent subculture', in Burchinal (ed.) 1965.

Becker, H. (1963), *Outsiders - Studies in the Sociology of Deviance*, Free Press, New York.

Belanger, P.R. and Mahen, L. (1972), 'Pratique politique étudiante en Québéc', *Recherches Sociographiques*, vol xiii, pp. 309-42.

Belcher, J. and West, D. (1975), *Patty/Tania*, Pyramid, New York.

Bell, D. (1957), *The End of Ideology*, Free Press of Chicago.

Belson, W.A. (1975), *Juvenile Theft - the Causal Factors*, Harper & Row, London.

Benjamin, W. (1970), 'The work of art in the age of mechanical reproduction', *Illuminations*, Jonathan Cape, London.

Bennett, J. (1981), *Oral History and Delinquency. The Rhetoric of Criminology*, University of Chicago.

Bennett, T., Martin, G., Mercer, C. and Wolacott, J. (1981), *Culture, Ideology and Social Process*, Open University Press, Milton Keynes.

Berger, B. (1963a), 'Adolescence and beyond', *Social Problems*, vol. 10, pp. 294-408.

Berger, B. (1963b), 'On the youthfulness of youth culture', *Social Research*, vol. 30, no. 3, Autumn, pp. 319-432.

Berger, B. (1967), 'Hippy morality - more old than new', *Transaction*, vol. 5, December.

Berger, P. and Luckman, H. (1966), *The Social Construction of Reality – A Treatise in the Sociology of Knowledge*, Doubleday, New York.

Bersani, C.A. (1970), *Crime and Delinquency, a Reader*, Collier MacMillan, New York.

Billig, M. and Cochrane, R. (1982), 'Lost generation', *New Socialist*, November, pp. 34–7.

Bland, L., Harrison, R., Mort, F. and Weedon, C. (1978), 'Relations through reproduction', in Women's Studies Group (1978).

Blauner, R. (1969), 'Internal colonisation and the ghetto revolt', *Social Problems*, xvi, Spring, pp. 116–25.

Bodine, G.E. (1964), 'Factors related to police disposition of juvenile offenders', *Youth Development Centre*, Syracuse, mimeo.

Bordua, A.D. (1959), 'Juvenile delinquency and anomie', *Social Problems*, vi, Winter, pp. 230–8.

Bordua, D. (1961), 'Delinquent subcultures – sociological interpretations of gang delinquency', *Annals*, ccxxxviii, pp. 119–36.

Bordua, D. (1967a), 'Recent trends, deviant behaviour and social control', *Annals*, vol. 57, no. 4, January, pp. 114–63.

Bordua, D. (1967b), *The Police*, John Wiley, New York.

Borgetta, E.F. and Jones, W.C. (1965), *Girls at Vocational High*, Russell Sage Foundation, New York.

Box, S. (1971), *Deviance, Reality and Society*, Holt, Rinehart & Winston, London.

Braithwaite, J. (1981), 'The myth of social class and criminality reconsidered', *ASR*, 46, Feb., pp. 36–57.

Brake, M. (1973a), 'How the hash turned to hate – intervention in a crisis area', *Drugs and Society*, vol. 2, no. 4 January.

Brake, M. (1973b), 'Cultural revolution or alternative delinquency – an examination of deviant youth as a social problem', in Bailey, R. and Young, J. (eds), *Contemporary Social Problems in Britain*, D.C. Heath, London.

Brake, M. (1974), 'The skinheads – an English working class subculture', *Youth and Society*, Vol. 6, no. 2, December.

Brake, M. (1976), 'I may be queer, but at least I am a man – male hegemony and ascribed achieved gender', in Barker and Allen (eds) (1976).

Brake, M. (1977), 'Hippies and skinheads – sociological aspects of middle and working class subcultures', Ph.D. thesis, London School of Economics.

Brake, M. (1978), 'The homosexual in contemporary English and American novels', *British Sociological Association, Monograph on The Sociology of Literature – Applied studies*, British Sociological Association, London.

Brake, M. (1980), *The Sociology of Youth Culture and Youth Subcultures*, Routledge & Kegan Paul, London.

Brake, M. (1984), '"Under heavy manners", a consideration of racism, black youth culture and crime in Britain', *Crime and Social Justice*, 20, pp. 1–16.

Brake, M. and Bailey, R. (1975), *Radical Social Work*, Edward Arnold,

Bibliography

London.

Brake, M. and Plummer, K. (1970), 'Bent boys and rent boys', *National Deviancy Symposium*, York, January, unpublished.

Brake, M. and Polish, P. (1969), 'Art Labs and subcultures', *Report to the Young Volunteer Force and the Arts Council*, unpublished.

Brook, E. and Finn. D. (1977), 'Working class images of society', *Working Papers in Cultural Studies*, 10, University of Birmingham.

Brown, C. (1967), *Manchild in the Promised Land*, Jonathan Cape, London.

Brown, J. (1977), *Shades of Grey*, Cranfield Police Studies, Cranfield.

Brown, W.K. (1977), 'Black female gangs in Philadelphia', *International Journal of Offender Therapy and Comparative Criminology*, Vol. 21, pp. 221–8.

Browning, S. (1971), 'From rumble to revolution – the Young Lords', reprinted in *Ramparts*.

Bryan, J. (1975), *The Soldier still at Work*, Harcourt Brace Jovanovich, New York.

Buff, S. (1970), 'Greasers, dupies and hippies – three responses to the adult world', in Howe, L.K. (ed.), *The White Majority – Between Poverty and Affluence*, Vintage Books, New York.

Bugler, J. (1969), 'Puritans in boots', *New Society*, 19, November.

Bunyan, T. (1977), *The Political Police in Britain*, Quartet, London.

Burchill, J. and Parsons, T. (1978), *The Boy looked at Johnny; The Obituary of Rock and Roll*, Pluto Press, London.

Burchinal, L.G. (ed.) (1965), *Rural Youth in Crisis*, US Department of Health, Education and Welfare.

Burns, T. (1967), 'A meaning in everyday life', *New Society*, 25 May.

Burt, C. (1925), *The Young Delinquent*, University of London Press.

Campbell, A. (1976), 'The role of the peer group in female delinquency', Ph.D. thesis, Oxford University, unpublished.

Campbell, A. (1981), *Girl Delinquents*, Blackwell, Oxford.

Campbell, H. (1980), 'Rastafari – culture of resistance', *Race and Class*, vol. xxii, no. 1, Summer, pp. 1–23.

Canada, Federal Government of (1981), *The 1980 Report on Juvenile Delinquents*, Office of the Solicitor General, Ottawa.

Carby, H. (1982), 'Schooling in Babylon', in Centre for Contemporary Cultural Studies (1982).

Carney, F. (1975), 'An American army', *New York Review of Books*, 26 June, pp. 8–12.

Carr-Saunders, A.M., Mannheim, H. and Rhodes, E.G. (1942), *Young Offenders*, Cambridge University Press, Cambridge.

Carson, W.G. and Wiles, P. (1971), *Crime and Delinquency in Britain*, M. Robertson, London.

Carter, A. (1967), 'Notes for a theory of sixties style', *New Society*, 14 December.

Carter, B. (1973), 'Reform school families', *Society*, November–December, pp. 36–43.

Carter, R.M. and Lohmann, J. (1968), *Middle Class Delinquency – An Experiment in Community Control*, Berkeley, California.

Cavan, S. (1970), 'The hippy ethic and the spirit of drug use', in Douglas, J.D. (ed.) (1970).

Center for Research on Criminal Justice (1975), *The Iron Fist in the Velvet Glove - An Analysis of the US Police Force*, Berkeley, California.

Centre for Contemporary Cultural Studies, Mugging Group (1976), 'Some notes on the relationship between societal control culture and the news media', in Hall and Jefferson (1976).

Centre for Contemporary Cultural Studies (1982), *The Empire Strikes Back - Race and Racism in 70s Britain*, Hutchinson, London.

Chambliss, W. (1973), 'The saints and the roughnecks', *Transaction*, 8 Dec., pp. 124–31.

Chesney Lind, M. (1973), 'Judicial reinforcement of the female role; the family court and the female delinquent', *Issues in Criminology*, vol. 8, no. 2.

Chesney Lind, M. (1974), 'Juvenile delinquency - the sexualisation of female crime', *Psychology Today*, 8, pp. 43–6.

Chibnall, S. (1977), *Law and Order News*, Social Science Paperbacks, London.

Christoffel, T., Finkelhord, D. and Gilberg, D. (1970), *Up against the American Myth*, Holt, Rinehart & Winston, New York.

Cicourel, A.V. (1968), *The Social Organisation of Juvenile Justice*, John Wiley, New York.

Clarke, D. (1980), 'The state of cultural theory', *Alternate Routes*, vol. 4, pp. 106–56, Carleton University, Ottawa.

Clarke, J. (1976a), 'The skinheads and the magical recovery of community', in Hall and Jefferson (eds) (1976).

Clarke, J. (1976b), 'Style', in Hall and Jefferson (eds) (1976).

Clarke, J., Hall, S., Jefferson, T. and Roberts, B. (1976), 'Subcultures, culture and class - a theoretical overview', in Hall and Jefferson (eds), (1976).

Clarke, J. and Jefferson. T. (1976), 'Working class youth cultures', in Mungham and Pearson (eds) (1976).

Clarke, M. (1974), 'On the concept of subculture', *BJS*, vol. xxv, no. 4, December, pp. 428–41.

Clelland, D. and Carter, T. (1980), 'The new myth of class and crime', *Criminology*, 18, Nov., pp. 319–36.

Clinard, M. (1964), *Anomie and Deviant Behaviour*, Free Press, New York.

Cloward, R. and Fox Piven, F. (1974), *Regulating the Poor*, Tavistock, London.

Cloward, R. and Ohlin, L.E. (1960), *Delinquency and Opportunity*, Free Press of Glencoe, New York.

Coard, B. (1971), '*How the West Indian Child is made ESN in the British School System*', New Beacon Books, London.

Cockburn, R. and Blackburn, R. (1969), *Student Power*, Penguin, Harmondsworth.

Cohen, A.K. (1955), *Delinquent Boys, The Subculture of the Gang*, Collier MacMillan, London.

Cohen, A.K. (1965), 'The sociology of the deviant act; anomie theory and beyond', *ASR*, 30, pp. 1–14.

Cohen, A.K. (1967), 'Middle class delinquency and the social structure', in Vaz (ed.) *op. cit.* (1967a).

Cohen, A.K. and Short, J. (1958), 'Research on delinquent subcultures', *Journal of Social Issues*, xiv, 3, pp. 20–37.

Cohen, P. (1972), 'Subcultural conflict and working class community', in *Working Papers in Cultural Studies 2*, CCCS, University of Birmingham England.

Cohen, S. (1970), *Images of Deviance*, Penguin, Harmondsworth.

Cohen, S. (1972), *Moral Panics and Folk Devils*, MacGibbon & Kee, London.

Cohen, S. (1975), 'It's all right for you to talk – political and sociological manifestos for social work action', in Brake and Bailey (1975).

Cohen, S. (1980), Introduction to the 1980 edn of Cohen, S. (1972).

Cohen, S. and Young, J. (1973), *Mass Media and Social Problems*, MacGibbon & Kee, London.

Cohn, N. (1970), *Awopbopaloobopalopbamboom – Pop from the Beginning*, Paladin, London.

Coleman, J.S. (1961), *The Adolescent Society*, Free Press, New York.

Commission for Racial Equality (1977), *Aspirations versus Opportunities – Asian and White School Leavers in the Midlands*, CRE, London.

Commission for Racial Equality (1978), *Looking for Work – Black and White School Leavers in Lewisham*, CRE, London.

Community Development Project (1977), *Gilding the Ghetto*, Mary Ward House, London.

Cooper, C.N. (1967), 'The Chicago detached workers – current status of an action programme', in Klein (ed.) (1967).

Corrigan, P. (1976), 'Doing nothing', in Hall and Jefferson (eds) (1976).

Corrigan, P. (1979), *The Smash Street Kids*, Paladin, London.

Corrigan, P. and Frith, S. (1976), 'The politics of youth culture', in Hall and Jefferson (eds) (1976).

Cotgrove, S. and Parker, S. (1963), 'Work and non work', *New Society*, vol. xli, July.

Cottle, T.J. (1978), *Black Testimony – Voices of Britain's West Indians*, Wildwood House, London.

Council of Europe (1977), *National Youth Committee Report*, Strasbourg.

Counter Information Services (1975), *Cutting the Welfare State – Who Profits?* CIS/CDP, November, CIS, Poland Street, London.

Cousineau, D.S. and Vefvers, J.E. (1972), 'Juvenile justice – an analysis of the Y.D.A.', in Boydell, C., Grindstaff, C. and Whitehead, P., *Deviant Behaviour and Societal Recreation*, Holt, Rinehart & Winston, Toronto.

Cowell, D., Jones, T. and Young, J. (1983), *Policing the Riots*, Junction Books, London.

Crawford, P., Malamud, D.J. and Dumpson, J.R. (1950), *Working with Teenage Gangs*, Welfare Council of New York City, New York.

Crichton, A. *et al.* (1962), 'Youth and leisure in Cardiff, 1960', *Sociological Review*, 20.

Curle, A. (1972), *Mystics and Militants – A Study of Awareness, Identity, and Social Creation*, Tavistock, London.

Dalla Costa, M. and James, S. (1972), *The Power of Women and the Subversion of the Community*, Falling Wall Press, Bristol.

Daniel, S. and McGuire, P. (eds) (1972), *The Paint House – Words from an East End Gang*, Penguin, Harmondsworth.

David, J. (1936), *The Lost Generation*, Collier, New York.

Davis, B. (1969), 'Non swinging youth', *New Society*, 3 July.

Davis, F. (1967), 'Focus on the flower children – why all of us may be hippies one day', *Transaction*, vol. 5, no. 2, reprinted in Douglas, J.D. (ed.) (1970).

Davis, F. and Munoz, L. (1968), 'Heads and freaks – patterns and meaning of drug use among hippies', in Douglas, J.D. (ed.) (1968).

De Beauvoir, S. (1972), *The Second Sex*, Penguin, Harmondsworth.

De la Mater, J. (1968), 'On the nature of deviance', *Social Forces*, 46, pp. 455–65.

Denzin, N.K. (1970), *The Research Act in Sociology*, Butterworths, London.

Distler, L.S. (1970), 'The adolescent and the emergence of a matristic culture', *Psychiatry*, 16 March.

Dodd, D. (1978), 'Police and thieves on the streets of Brixton', *New Society*, 16 March.

Dorn, N. and South, N. (1982), 'Of males and markets – a critical review of youth culture theory', *Research Papers*. No. 1, Middlesex Polytechnic, Enfield.

Douglas, J.D. (ed.) (1970), *Observations of Deviance*, Random House, New York.

Douglas, J.D. (1972), 'The absurd and the problem of social order', in Douglas and Scott (eds) (1972).

Douglas, J.D. and Scott, R.A. (eds) (1972), *Theoretical Perspectives in Deviance*, Basic Books, New York.

Douglas, J.W.B. (1971), 'Delinquency and social class', in Carson and Wiles (1971).

Douglas, M. (1970), *Purity and Danger*, Penguin, Harmondsworth.

Douglas, M. (1972), 'Self evidence', *Proceedings of the Royal Anthropological Institute*, pp. 27–43.

Downes, D. (1966), *The Delinquent Solution*, Routledge & Kegan Paul, London.

Downes, D. (1968), 'Review of D Hargreaves, "Social relations in a secondary school"', *BJC*, 12, pp. 399–401.

Driedger, A. (1975), 'In search of cultural identity factors; a comparison of ethnic students', *Canadian Review of Sociology and Anthropology*, vol. 12, no. 12, May, pp. 150–62.

Driver, C. (1964), *The Disarmers*, Hodder & Stoughton, London.

Dubin, R. (1950), 'Deviant behaviour and social structure', *ASR*, 24, pp. 147–64.

Durkheim, E. (1951), *Suicide*, Free Press of Glencoe, Chicago.

Easton, B., Kazin, M. and Plotke, D. (1979), 'The people's temple and the left', *Socialist Review*, vol. 9, no. 2, pp. 44–60.

Edwards, R., Reich, M. and Weiskoff, T. (eds) (1972), *The Capitalist System – A Radical Analysis of American Society*, Prentice-Hall, Englewood Cliffs, New Jersey.

Ehrenreich, B. (1983), *The Hearts of Men*, Doubleday, New York.
Eisen, J. (1970), *Altamont - The Death of Innocence in Woodstock Nation*, Avon, New York.
Eisenstadt, S.N. (1956), *From Generation to Generation*, Free Press of Glencoe, New York.
Elkin, F. and Westley, W.A. (1955), 'The myth of adolescent culture', *ASR*, vol. 20, pp. 680-4.
Empey, L.T. (1978), *American Delinquency - Its Meaning and Construction*, Dorsey Press, Holmwood, Illinois.
Empey, L.T. and Rabow, J. (1961), 'The Provo experiment in delinquency rehabilitation', *ASR*, 26, October, pp. 679-95.
Engels, F. (1962), *Conditions of the Working Class in England in 1844*, Allen & Unwin, London.
England, R.W. jnr (1967), 'A theory of middle class delinquency', in Vaz (1967a).
Eppels, E. and Eppels, E. (1960), *Adolescents and Morality*, Routledge & Kegan Paul, London.
Erikson, K. (1966), *Wayward Puritans, A Study in the Sociology of Knowledge*, John Wiley, New York.
Everhart, R. (1982), *The in between Years*, Routledge & Kegan Paul, London.
Eysenck, H.J. (1970), *Crime and Personality*, Paladin, London.
Feldman, E. and Gartenburg, M. (eds) (1959), *The Beat Generation and the Angry Young Men*, Citadel, New York.
Ferdinand, T.N. (ed.) (1977), *Juvenile Delinquency - Little Brother Grows Up*, Sage, Beverly Hills.
Figes, E. (1970), *Patriarchal Attitudes*, Faber & Faber, London.
Figueora, P. (1969), 'School leavers and the colour barrier', *Race*, April, pp. 506-7.
Finestone, H. (1957), 'Cats, kicks and colour', *Social Problems*, vol. 5, pp. 3-13.
Finestone, H. (1976), *Victims of Change - Juvenile Delinquents in American Society*, Greenwood Press, Connecticut.
Firth, R. (1951), *Elements of Social Organisation*, Routledge & Kegan Paul, London.
Fischer, C.S. (1972), 'Urbanism as a way of life - a review and an agenda', *Sociological Methods and Research*, vol. 1, no. 2, November, pp. 187-243.
Fischer, C.S. (1973), 'On urban alienation and anomie', *ASR*, 38, June, pp. 311-26.
Fischer, C.S. (1975), 'Towards a subcultural theory of urbanism', *AJS*, 80, no. 6, pp. 1319-41.
Flacks, R. (1970), 'Social and cultural meanings of student revolt', *Social Problems*, vol. xvii, Winter.
Flacks, R. (1971), *Youth and Social Change*, Markham Press, Chicago.
Fletcher, C. (1966), 'Beats and gangs on Merseyside', in Raison (1966).
Folb, E.A. (1980), *Running down some Lines - The Language and Culture of Black Teenagers*, Harvard University Press.
Foote, N. (1951), 'Identification as the basis for a theory of motivation', *ASR*, February pp. 14-41.

Ford, C.S. (1942), 'Culture and human behaviour', *Scientific Monthly*, vol. 44, pp. 546-57.

Ford, J., Box, S. and Young, D. (1967), 'Functional autonomy, role distance and social class', *BJS*, 18, pp. 370-81.

Fox, J. (1969), 'The scapegoat kids', *Sunday Times*, 21 September.

Fox, R.G. and Spencer, M.J. (1972), 'The Young Offenders Bill - destigmatizing juvenile delinquency', *Criminal Law Quarterly*, 14, pp. 172-219.

Fox, Piven, F. and Cloward, R.A. (1982), *The New Class War - Reagan's Attack on the Welfare State and its Consequences*, Pantheon, New York.

Friedenberg, E.Z. (1966), 'Adolescence as a social problem', in Becker, H. (ed.), *Social Problems; A Modern Approach*, John Wiley, New York.

Friedlander, S.L. (1972), *Unemployment in the Urban Core*, Praeger, New York.

Frith, S. (1978), *The Sociology of Rock*, Constable, London.

Frith, S. (1980), 'Music for pleasure', *Screen Education*, 34, Spring.

Frith, S. (1981), *Downtown. Young People in a City Centre*, Leicester, National Youth Bureau.

Frith, S. (1983), *Sound Effects*, Constable, London.

Fyvel, T.R. (1963), *The Insecure Offenders, Rebellious Youth in the Welfare State*, Penguin, Harmondsworth.

Gagnon, J. (1977), *Human Sexualities*, Scott Forman, Illinois.

Galbraith, J.K. (1974), *The New Industrial State*, Penguin, Harmondsworth.

Gans, H. (1962), *The Urban Villagers*, Free Press, New York.

Gardiner, J. (1976), 'Political economy of domestic labour in capitalist society', in Barker D and Allen (eds) (1976).

Gavron, H. (1966), *The Captive Wife: Conflicts of Housebound Mothers*, Routledge & Kegan Paul, London.

Gayford, J. (1972), 'Wife battering, a preliminary of 100 cases', *British Medical Journal*, 25 January, pp. 194-7.

Gelles, J. (1972), *The Violent Home - A Study of Physical Aggression between Husbands and Wives*, Sage, London.

Geoffrey, S. and Grafton, T. (1967), 'Hippies in college - teeny bopper to drug freaks', *Transaction*, vol. 5, pp. 27-32.

Giallambardo, R. (1972), *Juvenile Delinquency - A Book of Readings*, John Wiley, New York.

Gibbons, D. (1970), *Delinquent Behaviour*, Prentice-Hall, Englewood Cliffs, New Jersey.

Giddens, A. (1976), *New Rules of the Sociological Method*, Hutchinson, London.

Gilroy, P. (1982), 'You can't fool the youths - race and class formation in the 1980s', *Race and Class*, vol. xxiii, no. 2/3, Autumn 1981/Winter 1982, pp. 207-23.

Gilroy, R. (1982), 'Police and thieves', in Centre for Contemporary Cultural Studies (1982).

Ginsburg, A. (1956), *Howl*, City Lights Press, San Francisco.

Giosca, V. (1969), 'LSD subcultures, acidity versus orthodoxy', *American Journal of Orthopsychiatry*, 39, pp. 428-36.

Glaser, B.G. and Strauss, A. (1971), *Status Passage - Formal Theory*, Routledge & Kegan Paul, London.

Glaser, D. (1966), 'Criminality theories and behavioural images', *AJS*, 61, March.

Gleason, R. (1970), 'Rock for sale', in Eisen (1970).

Gleason, R. (1971), 'Like a rolling stone', in Gaviglio, G. and Raye, M. (eds), *Society as it is*, Macmillan, New York.

Glessing, R.J. (1970), *The Underground Press in America*, University of Indiana Press.

Gold, M. (1966), 'Undetected delinquent behaviour', *Journal of Research in Crime and Delinquency*, 3, January, pp. 27-46.

Gold, M. (1970), *Delinquent Behaviour in an American City*, Brooks/Cole, Belmont, California.

Gold, M. and Reimer, M.J. (1974), 'Changing patterns of delinquent behaviour among Americans 13-16 years old; 1967-72', *National Survey of Youth. Report no. 1*, Institute for Social Research, University of Michigan (mimeo).

Goldman, N. (1963), 'The differential selection of juvenile offenders for court appearance', *Social Forces*, October.

Gordon, M. (1947), 'The concept of the subculture and its applications', *Social Forces*, October.

Gordon, M. (1951), 'A system of class analysis', *Drew University Studies No. 2*, August.

Gordon, R.A. (1967), 'Issues in the ecological study of delinquency', *ASR*, 32, December, pp. 927-44.

Gramsci, A. (1973), *Prison Notebooks*, Lawrence & Wishart, London.

Greely, A. and Casey, J. (1963), 'An upper middle class deviant gang', *American Catholic Sociological Review*, xxiv, Spring, pp. 33-41.

Greenberg, D. (1979), 'Delinquency and the age structure of society', *Contemporary Crises*, California.

Greer, H. (1965), *Mud Pie - The CND Story*, Max Parrish, London.

Griffen, C. (1981), 'Cultures of femininity and romance revisited', *Proceedings of SISWO*, Conference on Youth, Culture and Education, Amsterdam, Holland.

Griffiths, J. (1978), *The Politics of the Judiciary*, Fontana, London.

Hagan, J. and Leon, J. (1971), 'Rediscovering delinquency; social history, political ideology, and the sociology of law', *ASR*; vol. 42, August, pp. 587-98.

Hall, S. (1969), 'The hippies, an American moment', in Nagel, J. (ed.), *Student Power*, Merlin Press, New York.

Hall, S. (1981), 'Cultural studies - two paradigms', in Bennett, T., Martin, G., Mercer, C. and Wolacott, J. (eds), *Culture, Ideology and Social Process*, Academic Press, London.

Hall, S. (1982), 'Culture and the state', in *Popular Culture, The State and Popular Culture*, 1, Block 7, unit 28, Open University, Milton Keynes.

Hall, S., Critcher, C., Jefferson, T. and Roberts, B. (1978), *Policing the Crisis*, Macmillan, London.

Hall, S. and Jefferson, T. (eds) (1976), *Resistance through Rituals*, Hutchinson, London. Originally published as, *Working Papers in Cultural*

Studies 7/8, (1975), Centre for Contemporary Cultural Studies, University of Birmingham.

Hall, S. and Whannel, P. (1964), *The Popular Arts*, Penguin, Harmondsworth.

Han, Wan Sang, (1969), 'The conflicting themes – common values versus class differential values', *ASR*, 34, pp. 679–90.

Hannerz, U. (1969), *Soulside; Inquiry into Ghetto Life and Community*, Columbia University Press, New York.

Hannerz, U. (1980), *Exploring the City*, Columbia University Press, New York.

Hargreaves, D. (1967), *Social Relations in a Secondary School*, Routledge & Kegan Paul, London.

Harrington, M. (1962), *The Other America*, Macmillan, New York.

Harris, D. (1972), 'The black ghetto as "internal colony" a theoretical critique and alternative formulation', *Review of Black Political Economy*, vol. 2, no. 4, Summer.

Harris, M. (1973), *The Dilly Boys*, Croom Helm, London.

Harrop, P. and Zimmerman, M. (1977), *Report on Greater London Council Elections 1977*, Department of Government, June, University of Essex, Colchester.

Haskell, M. and Yablonsky, L. (1971), *Crime and Delinquency*, Rand McNally, New York.

Hebdige, D. (1976a), 'The meaning of mod', in Hall and Jefferson (1976).

Hebdige, D. (1976b), 'Reggae, rastas and rudies', in Hall and Jefferson (1976).

Hebdige, D. (1979), *Subcultures – The Meaning of Style*, Methuen, London.

Helmreich, W.B. (1973), 'Black crusaders, the rise and fall of political gangs', *Society*, 11, November/December, pp. 44–50.

Herskovitz, H., Levene, M. and Spivak, G. (1959), 'Anti social behaviour of adolescents from higher socio-economic groups', *Journal of Nervous and Mental Diseases*, cxxv, November, pp. 1–9.

Hill, W.W. (1935), 'The study of transvestites and hermaphrodites in Navajo culture', *American Anthropologist*, vol. 37, June.

Himmelweit, S. and Mohun, S. (1977), 'Domestic labour and capital', *Cambridge Journal of Economics*, vol. 1, no. 1, March.

Hinckle, W. (1967), 'The coming of the hippies', *Ramparts*, New York.

Hindelang, M.J. (1970), 'Commitments of delinquents to their misdeeds; do delinquents drift?', *Social Problems*, vol. 17, no. 4, pp. 502–9.

Hindelang, M.J. (1971), 'Age, sex and the versatility of delinquent involvements', *Social Problems*, 18, pp. 522–35.

Hines, V. (1973), *Black Youth and the Survival Game in Britain*, Zulu Publications, London.

Hiro, D. (1973), *Black British, White British*, Penguin, Harmondsworth.

Hirschi, T. (1969), *The Causes of Delinquency*, University of California Press.

Hjelmslev, A. (1959), 'Essais linguistiques', *Travaux du cercle linguistique de Copenhagen*, vol. xiii, pp. 59ff.

HMSO (1975), *Parliamentary Select Committee on Violence in Marriage*, Session 1974–5, Report HC 533, i, HMSO, London.

HMSO (1976), *Public Expenditure*, Command, HMSO, London.
Hodges, E.F. and Tait, C.T. (1965), 'A follow up study of potential delinquents', *American Journal of Psychiatry*, 120, pp. 449-53.
Hofstadter, R. (1955), *The Age of Reform*, Knopf, New York.
Hollingshead, A.B. (1949), *Elmstown's Youth*, John Wiley, New York.
Holmes, J.C. (1960), 'The philosophy of the beat generation', in Krim (ed.) (1960).
Holt, J. (1969), *How Children Fail*, Penguin, Harmondsworth.
Holtz, J.M.A. (1975), 'The "low riders" – a portrait of an urban subculture', *Youth and Society*, vol. 6, no. 6, June, pp. 495-512.
Horton, J. (1964), 'The dehumanisation of alienation and anomie – a problem in the ideology of sociology', *BJS*, 15, pp. 238-300.
Horton, J. (1966), 'Order and conflict theories of social problems as competing ideologies', *AJS*, vol. 71, May.
Houghton, M. and Head, D. (1974), *Free Ways to Learning*, Penguin, Harmondsworth.
Houriet, R. (1973), *Getting Back Together*, Abacus, London.
Humphrey, P. and John, G. (1972), *Police, Power and Black People*, Panther, London.
Illich, I. (1973), *Deschooling Society*, Penguin, Harmondsworth.
Illinois Institute for Juvenile Research (1972), *Juvenile Delinquency in Illinois*, Illinois Department of Mental Health, Chicago.
Irwin, J. (1973), 'Surfing – the natural history of an urban scene', *Urban Life and Culture*, 2, pp. 131-60.
Jefferson, T. (1976), 'The Teds – a political resurrection', in Hall and Jefferson (eds) (1976).
Jephcott, P. (1967), *A Time of One's Own*, Oliver & Boyd, Edinburgh.
Jephcott, P. and Carter, M.P. (1954), 'The social background of delinquency', University of Nottingham, unpublished.
John, G. and Humphrey, D. (1971), *Because They're Black*, Penguin, Harmondsworth.
Johnston, J. (1973), *Lesbian Nation*, Simon & Schuster, New York.
Johnston, N., Savitz, L. and Wolfgang, M.E. (1967), *The Sociology of Punishment and Correction*, John Wiley, New York.
Johnston, N., Savitz, L. and Wolfgang, M. E. (1970), *The Sociology of Punishment and Correction*, 2nd edn, John Wiley, New York.
Johnstone, J.W. (1961), *Social Structure and Patterns of Mass Media Consumption*, Ph.D. Thesis, University of Chicago, unpublished.
Jones, G.S. (1971), *Outcast in London*, Oxford University Press.
Jones, L. (Baraka, I.A.) (1963), *Blues People*, Morrow, New York.
Keill, C. (1966), *Urban Blues*, University of Chicago Press.
Keniston, K. (1972), *Youth and Dissent*, Harcourt, Brace & Jovanovich, New York.
Kerouac, J. (1957), *On the Road*, New American Library, New York.
Kerouac, J. (1959), 'Beatific – on the origins of a generation', *Encounter*, vol. 13, August, pp. 57-61.
Kerr, M. (1958), *The People of Ship Street*, Routledge & Kegan Paul, London.
Kettle, M. and Hodges, A. (1982), *Uprising*, Pan, London.

Kitsuse, J.I. and Dietrich, D. C. (1959), 'Delinquent boys - a critique', *ASR*, April, pp. 208-15.

Kitzinger, S. (1978), 'West Indian adolescents - an anthropological perspective', *Journal of Adolescence*, pp. 35-46.

Klein, M.W. (ed.) (1967), *Juvenile Gangs in Context*, Prentice-Hall, Englewood Cliffs, New Jersey.

Klein, M. (1971), *Street Gangs and Street Workers*, Prentice-Hall, Englewood Cliffs, New Jersey.

Klein, M. and Meyerhof, B.G. (eds) (1963), *Juvenile Gangs in Context, Research, Theory and Action*, University of Southern California, Youth Studies Center, mimeo.

Knapp, D. and Polk, K. (1971), *Scouting the War on Poverty*, D.C. Heath, Lexington.

Kobrin, S. (1967), 'The Chicago area project', in Johnston *et al.*, (1967).

Kochman, T.H. (ed.) (1972), *Rapping and Styling Out - Communication in Urban Black America*, University of Illinois Press, Chicago.

Komarovsky, M. (1967), *Blue Collar Marriage*, Vintage Books, New York.

Kostash, M. (1980a), 'The New Left', *This magazine*, vol. 14, no. 6, December, pp. 30-5.

Kostash, M. (1980b), *Long Way from Home*, James Lorimer, Toronto.

Kozol, J. (1972), *Free Schools*, Penguin, Harmondsworth.

Krim, S. (1960), *The Beats*, Fawcett Publications, Greenwich, Connecticut.

Krisberg, B. (1974), 'Gang youth and hustling', *Issues in Criminology*, vol. 9, Spring, pp. 115-29.

Krisberg, B. and Austin, J. (1978), *The Children of Ishmael*, Mayfield, Palo Alto.

Kroeber, A.L. and Kluckhohn, S. (1952), 'Culture - critical review of concepts and definitions', *Papers of the Peabody Museum of American Anthropology and Ethology*, vol. 47, no. 1.

Kuhn, M. (1964), 'The reference group reconsidered', *Sociological Quarterly*, Winter, pp. 6-21.

Kushnik, L. (1982), 'Parameters of British and North American racism', *Race and Class*, vol. xxiii, no. 2/3, Autumn 1981/Winter 1982.

La Colectiva de la Gente (1975), *Palabra*, Barrio Youth Conference, East Los Angeles College, unpublished, see also Balkan *et al.* (1980).

Laing, D. (1969), *The Sound of our Time*, Sheen & Ward, London.

Laing, D. (1978), 'Interpreting punk rock', *Marxism Today*, pp. 123-8.

Laing, D. (1979), *An Introduction to the Marxist Theory of Art*, Sheen & Ward, London.

Laing, R.D. (1966), *The Divided Self*, Penguin, Harmondsworth.

Land, H. (1976), 'Women - supporters or supported?', in Barker and Allen (eds) (1976).

Lander, B. (1954), *Towards an Understanding of Juvenile Delinquency*, Columbia University Press, New York.

Lanzon, A. (1970), 'The New Left in Quebec', in Roussopoulos, D.J. (ed.), *The New Left in Quebec*, Black Rose, Montreal, pp. 113-30.

Laufer, R.S. and Bengston, V.L. (1974), 'Generations, ageing and social stratification; on the development of generational units', *Journal of Social Issues*, vol. 30, no. 3.

Bibliography

Laxer, J. (1971), 'The student movement and Canadian independence', *Canadian Dimension*, vol. 6, 3-4, pp. 27-34/69-70.

Leamer, L. (1972), *The Paper Revolutionaries - The Rise of the Underground Press*, Simon & Schuster, New York.

Leary, T. (1968), *The Politics of Ecstasy*, Putnam, New York.

Lee, A.M. (1945), 'Levels of culture as levels of social generalisation', *ASR*, August.

Lee, A.M. (1949), 'A sociological discussion of consistency and inconsistency in inter-group relations', *Journal of Social Issues*, 5, pp. 12-18.

Lemert, E. (1951), *Social Pathology*, McGraw Hill, New York.

Lemert, E. (1967), *Human Deviance, Social Problems and Social Control*, Prentice-Hall, Englewood Cliffs, New Jersey.

Leon, J.S. (1977), 'The development of juvenile justice in Canada - a background for reform', *Osgoode Hall Law Journal*, 15, pp. 71-106.

Lerman, P. (1967a), 'Argot, symbolic deviance and subcultural delinquency', *ASR*, vol. 1, 32, pp. 209-24.

Lerman, P. (1967b), 'Gangs, networks and subcultural delinquency', *AJS*, vol. 1, 33.

Levine, M. and Levine, A. (1970), *A Social History of the Helping Services*, Appleton, New York.

Lewis, O. (1952), 'Urbanisation without breakdown', *Scientific Monthly*, 75, July, pp. 31-41.

Lewis, R. (1972), *Outlaws of America - The Underground Press and its Context*, Penguin, Harmondsworth.

Lichtmann, R. (1970), 'Symbolic interactionism and social reality - some Marxist queries', *Berkeley Journal of Sociology*, January.

Liebow, E. (1967), *Tallys Corner*, Little, Brown, Boston, Mass.

Lindesmith, A.B. (1947), *Opiate Addiction*, Principa Press, Indiana.

Linton, R. (1942), 'Age and sex categories', *ASR*, 7, pp. 589-603.

Lipton, L. (1960), *The Holy Barbarians*, W.H.Allen, London.

Little, A., Mabey, C. and Whittaker, R.G. (1968), 'The education of immigrant pupils in Inner London Primary Schools', *Race*, ix, pp. 439-52.

Livingstone, P. (1978), 'The leisure needs of Asian boys aged 8-11 in Slough', *Scout Association*, London.

Lukes, S. (1974), *Power*, MacMillan, London.

Lydon, M. (1971), 'Rock for sale', in Ramparts (eds) (1971).

McAll, G.J. and Simmons, J.L. (1966), *Identities and Interactions*, Free Press, New York.

McCabe, P. and Schonfield, R. (1973), *Apple to the Core - The Unmaking of the Beatles*, Sphere, London.

McCord, J. and McCord, W. (1959), 'A follow up of the Cambridge-Somerville youth study', *Annals*, pp. 89-96, pp. 321-33.

McDonald, L. (1969), *Social Class and Juvenile Delinquency*, Faber & Faber, London.

McEarchern, A.W. and Bauzer, R. (1963), 'Factors related to disposition in juvenile police contacts', in Klein and Meyerhof (eds) (1963).

McIntyre, A. (1967), 'Winch's idea of a social science', *Proceedings of the Aristotlean Society*, Supplement.

McLaren, P. (1980), *Cries from the Corridor, The New Suburban Ghetto*,

Methuen, Toronto.
McRobbie, A. (1978a), '"Jackie" – an ideology of adolescent femininity', Centre for Contemporary Cultural Studies, reprinted in Waites, B., Bennett, T. and Martin, G. (eds) (1981), *Popular Culture*, Croom Helm, London.
McRobbie, A. (1978b), 'Working class girls and the culture of femininity', M.A. thesis, University of Birmingham, unpublished.
McRobbie, A. (1978c), 'Working class girls and the culture of femininity', in Women's Studies Group (1978).
McRobbie, A. (1980), 'Settling accounts with subcultures – a feminist critique', *Screen Education*, Spring, 34.
McRobbie, A. and Garber, J. (1976), 'Girls and subcultures – an exploration', in Hall and Jefferson (eds) (1976).
McWilliams, C. (1949), *North from Mexico*, Greenwood Press, New York.
Mailer, N. (1961), 'The white negro', in Mailer, N., *Advertisements for Myself*, André Deutsch, London.
Mankoff, M. (1972), 'Societal reaction and career deviance – a critical analysis', *Sociological Quarterly*, 12, pp. 204-18.
Mannheim, H. (1948), *Juvenile Delinquency in an English Middletown*, Routledge & Kegan Paul, London.
Mannheim, K. (1952), *Essays on the Sociology of Knowledge*, Routledge & Kegan Paul, London.
Manpower Services Commission (1977), Review and Plan, HMSO, London.
Marcuse, H. (1964), *One Dimensional Man*, Routledge & Kegan Paul, London.
Marris, P. and Rein, M. (1967), *Dilemmas of Social Reform, Poverty and Community Action in the United States*, Atherton Press, New York.
Marsh, A. (1977), 'Who hates the blacks?', *New Society*, 23 September.
Marsh, P. (1978), *Aggro – The Illusion of Violence*, Routledge & Kegan Paul, London.
Marsh, P. and Campbell, A. (1978a), 'The youth gangs of New York go into business', *New Society*, 46, pp. 67-9.
Marsh, P. and Campbell, A. (1978b), 'The sex boys on their own turf', *New Society*, 46, pp. 133-6.
Marsh, P., Rosser, E. and Harre, R. (1978), *The Rules of Disorder*, Routledge & Kegan Paul, London.
Marx, K. (1951), *The 18th Brumaire of Louis Napoleon*, Moscow Publishing House, Moscow.
Marx, K. and Engels, F. (1970), *The German Ideology*, Lawrence & Wishart, London.
Massey, D. and Meegan, R. (1983), 'The new geography of jobs', *New Society*, 17 March, pp. 416-18.
Matza, D. (1961), 'Subterranean traditions of youth', *Annals*, 338, pp. 102-18.
Matza, D. (1962), 'Position and behaviour patterns of youth', in Paris, E. (ed.), *Handbook of Modern Sociology*, Rand McNally, New York.
Matza, D. (1964), *Delinquency and Drift*, John Wiley, New York.
Matza, D. (1966) 'The disreputable poor', in Bendix, R. and Lipsett, S.M., *Class, Status and Power*, Routledge & Kegan Paul, London.

Matza, D. (1969a), 'Reply to Charles Valentine's "Culture and Poverty"', *Current Anthropology*, 10, (2-3), April-June, pp. 192-4.

Matza, D. (1969b), *Becoming Deviant*, Prentice-Hall, New Jersey.

Matza, D. and Sykes, G. (1957), 'Techniques of neutralisation', *ASR*, 22, December, pp. 664-70.

Matza, D. and Sykes, G. (1961), 'Juvenile delinquency and subterranean values', *ASR*, 26, pp. 712-19.

Maxine, D. (1936), *The Lost Generation - A Portrait of American Youth Today*, MacMillan, New York.

Mayo, M. (1977), *Women in the Community*, Routledge & Kegan Paul, London.

Mays, J. (1954), *Juvenile Delinquency*, Jonathan Cape, London.

Mays, J.B. (1964), *Growing up in the City*, Liverpool University Press.

Mays, J.B. (1967), *Crime and the Social Structure*, Faber & Faber, London.

Mays, J.B. (1972), *Juvenile Delinquency, the Family and the Social Group*, Longmans, London.

Mead, M. (1928), *Coming of Age in Samoa*, Penguin, Harmondsworth.

Melly, G. (1972), *Revolt into Style*, Penguin, Harmondsworth.

Merton, R.K. (1938), 'Social structure and anomie', *ASR*, *3*, October, pp. 672-82.

Merton, R.K. (1957), *Social Theory and Social Structure*, John Wiley, New York.

Middleton, R. and Muncie, J. (1982), 'Pop culture, pop music and post war youth countercultures', in *Politics, Ideology and Popular Culture*, Popular Culture, Block 5, Unit 20, Open University Press, Milton Keynes.

Miller, A. (1973), 'On the road - hitching on the highway', *Transaction*, vol. 10, no. 5.

Miller, W.B. (1958), 'Lower class culture as a generating milieu of gang delinquency,' *Journal of Social Issues*, 14, pp. 5-19.

Miller, W.B. (1962), 'The impact of a "total-community" delinquency control project', *Social Problems*, Fall, pp. 168-91.

Miller, W.B. (1966), 'Violent crimes in city gangs', *Annals*, March, pp. 364-97.

Miller, W.B. (1973), 'The Molls', *Society*, vol. II, November-December, pp. 32-5.

Miller, W.B. (1975), *Violence by Youth Gangs as a Crime Problem in Major American Cities*, US Government Printing Office, Washington.

Mills, C.W. (1957), *The Power Elite*, Oxford University Press, London.

Mills, R.W. (1970), *The Young Outsiders - A Study in Alternative Communities*, Tavistock, London.

Mitchell, J. (1971), *Women's Estate*, Penguin, Harmondsworth.

Monod, J. (1967), 'Juvenile gangs in Paris - towards a structural analysis', *Journal of Research in Crime and Delinquency*, vol. 4, August, pp. 168-91.

Moore, J.W. (1978), *Homeboys; Gangs, Drugs and Prison in the Barrio of Los Angeles*, Temple Press, Philadelphia.

Moore, R. (1975), *Racism and Black Resistance in Britain*, Pluto Press, London.

?I (1981), *Survey on Attitudes among Young Unemployed*, Market

Opinion Research International, London.

MORI (1983), 'Breadline Britain', *Sunday Times*, August, Market Opinion Research International, London.

Morris, T. (1957), *The Criminal Area*, Routledge & Kegan Paul, London.

Morse, M. (1965), *The Unattached*, Penguin, Harmondsworth.

Moynihan, D.P. (1965), *The Negro Family – The Case for National Action*, US Department of Labor, Washington, D.C.

Mungham, G. and Pearson, G. (eds) (1976), *Working Class Youth Cultures*, Routledge & Kegan Paul, London.

Murdock, G. (1973), 'Culture and classlessness – the making and un-making of a contemporary myth', *Symposium on Work and Leisure*, University of Salford.

Murdock, G. (1974), 'Mass communications and the construction of meaning', in Armistead, N. (ed.), *Reconstructing Social Psychology*, Penguin, Harmondsworth.

Murdock, G. and McCron, R. (1973), 'Scoobies, skins and contemporary pop', *New Society*, vol. 23, no. 247.

Murdock, G. and McCron, R. (1976), 'Consciousness of class and consciousness of generation', in Hall and Jefferson (eds) (1976).

Murdock, G. and Phelps, G. (1972), 'Youth culture and the school revisited', *BJS*, 23, 2, June, pp. 478–82.

Musgrove, F. (1964), *Youth and the Social Order*, Routledge & Kegan Paul, London.

Musgrove, F. (1969), 'The problems of youth and the social structure', *Youth and Society*, 11, pp. 28–58.

Musgrove, F. (1974), *Ecstasy and Holiness, Counter Culture and the Open Society*, Methuen, London.

Nairn, T. and Quattrocchi, A. (1968), *The Beginning of the End*, Panther, London.

National Criminal Justice Information and Statistics Service (1976), *Criminal Victimization in the US – A Comparison of the 1973 and 1974 Findings of the Law Enforcement Assistance Administration*, Washington, D.C.

Nesbitt Larking, P. (1981), 'French and English Students in the 60s, a comparative analysis of student discontent', unpublished paper, Carleton University, Ottawa.

Nuttall, J. (1969), *Bomb Culture*, Paladin, London.

Nye, I. (1956), *Family Relationships and Delinquent Behaviour*, John Wiley, New York.

O'Brien, J.E. (1971), 'Violence in divorce prone families', *Journal of Marriage and the Family*, 33, November, pp. 692–8.

O'Connor, J. (1973), *The Fiscal Crisis of the State*, St Martins, New York.

Palmer, T. (1971), *The Trials of Oz*, Blond & Briggs, London.

Park, R.E., Burgess, E. and McKenzie, R.D. (1925), *The City*, University of Chicago Press.

Parker, H.J. (1974), *View from the Boys, A Sociology of Down Town Adolescents*, David & Charles, Newton Abbott.

Parkin, F. (1968), *Middle Class Radicalism*, Manchester University Press.

Parkin, F. (1971), *Class Inequality and Political Order*, MacGibbon & Kee, London.

215

Parkinson, T. (ed.) (1961), *A Casebook on the Beat*, Crowell, New York.

Parmer, P. (1982), 'Gender, race and class', in Centre for Contemporary Cultural Studies (1982).

Parsons, T. (1942), 'Age and sex roles in the United States', reprinted in Parsons (1964), pp. 89–103.

Parsons, T. (1950), 'Psycho analysis and the age structure', reprinted in Parsons (1964).

Parsons, T. (1964), *Essays in Sociological Theory*, Free Press, Chicago.

Partridge, W.L. (1973), *The Hippy Ghetto – The Story of a Subculture*, Holt, Rinehart & Winston, New York.

Patrick, J. (1973), *A Glasgow Gang Observed*, Eyre-Methuen, London.

Paz, O. (1961), *The Labryinth of Solitude; Life and Thought in Mexico*, Grove Press, New York.

Pearce, F. (1973a), 'Crime, corporations and the American social order', in Taylor and Taylor (eds) (1973).

Pearce, F. (1973b), 'How to be immoral, pathetic, dangerous and sick all at the same time', in Young, J. and Cohen, S. (eds), *Mass Media and Social Problems*, Constable, London.

Pearce, F. (1976), *Crimes of the Powerful*, Pluto Press, London.

Pepinsky, H. (1976), 'Police patrolmen's role – offence reporting behaviour', *Journal of Research in Crime and Delinquency*, vol. 12, no. 1, January.

Perkus, C. (ed.) (1974), *COINTELPRO*, Monad, New York.

Phillipson, C.M. (1971), 'Juvenile delinquency and the school', in Carson and Wiles (1971).

Piccone, P. (1969), 'From youth culture to political praxis', *Radical America*, 15, November.

Piliavin, I. and Briar, W.S. (1964), 'Police encounters with juveniles', *AJS*, vol. 70, September, pp. 206–14.

Pine, G. (1965), 'Social class, social mobility and delinquent behaviour', *Personnel and Guidance Journal*, April, pp. 770–4.

Piven, F.F. and Cloward, R. (1974), *Regulating the Poor – the Functions of Social Welfare*, Tavistock, London.

Pizzorno, E. (1959), 'Accumulation, loisirs et rapports de classe', *Esprit*, June.

Plant, M. (1975), *Drugtakers in an English Town*, Tavistock, London.

Platt, A. (1968), *The Child Savers – The Invention of Delinquency*, University of Chicago Press.

Plummer, K. (1975), *Sexual Stigma – An Interactionist Account*, Routledge & Kegan Paul, London.

Polk, K. (1957), 'Juvenile delinquency and social areas', *Social Problems*, v, Winter, pp. 214–17.

Polk, K. and Halferty, D.S. (1966), 'Adolescence, commitment and delinquency', *Journal of Research in Crime and Delinquency*, vol. 3, no. 2, July, pp. 82–96.

Polsky, N. (1971), *Hustlers, Beats and Others*, Penguin, Harmondsworth.

Powell, E.H. (1962), 'Beyond Utopia – the "Beat generation" as a challenge for the sociology of knowledge', in Rose, A.M., *Human Behaviour and Social Processes – An Interactionist Perspective*, Routledge & Kegan

Paul, London, pp. 360–77.

Power, M.J. (1962), 'Trends in juvenile delinquency', *The Times*, 9 August.

Power, M.J. (1965), 'An attempt to identify at first appearance before the courts, those at risk', *Proceedings of the Royal Society of Medicine*, vol. 58, 9, pp. 704–5.

Power, M.J., Benn, R.T. and Morris, J. (1967), 'Neighbourhoods, schools and juveniles before the court', *BJC*, 12, 2, pp. 111–32.

Powers, E. and Wilmer, H. (1950), *An Experiment in the Prevention of Delinquency*, Columbia University Press, New York.

Powers, M. and Sirey, E.C. (1972), 'A commentary', *BJC*, 12, pp. 402–3.

Presdee, M. (1982), 'Invisible girls – a study of unemployed working class young women', *Tenth World Congress of Sociology*, unpublished paper, Mexico City.

Pryce, K. (1979), *Endless Pressure*, Penguin, Harmondsworth.

Quicker, J.C. (1974), 'The chicana gang – a preliminary description', *Pacific Sociological Association*, unpublished.

Quinney, R. (1977), *Class, State and Crime, on the Theory and Practice of Criminal Justice*, McKay, New York.

Rainwater, L. (1966), 'The problem of lower class culture', *Pruitt-Igoe Occasional Paper 8*, Washington University, Washington.

Rainwater, L. (1970a), *Behind Ghetto Walls; Black Families in a Federal Slum*, Aldine, Chicago.

Rainwater, L. (1970b), *Soul*, Transaction books, Aldine, Chicago.

Raison, T. (1966), *Youth in a New Society*, Hart-Davis, London.

Ramparts (eds) (1971), *Conversations with the New Reality*, Harper & Row, Canfield Press, San Francisco.

Reckless, W.C. (1961), *The Crime Problem*, Appleton-Century Crofts, New York.

Reckless, W.C. and Dinitz, S. (1972), *The Prevention of Juvenile Delinquency – An Experiment*, Ohio State University, Columbia.

Reich, C.A. (1970), *The Greening of America*, Random House, New York.

Reich, C. and Wenner, J. (1972), *Garcia – The Rolling Stone Interview*, Straight Arrow, San Francisco.

Reid, I. (1977), *Social Class Differences in Britain*, Open Books Ltd, London.

Reiss, A. (1961), 'The social integration of queers and peers', *Social Problems*, 9, pp. 102–19.

Reiss, A. and Rhodes, A. (1961), 'Delinquency and the social class struggle', *ASR*, 26, pp. 720–32.

Report of the National Advisory Commission (1968), *Kerner Commission*, Bantam Books, New York.

Resistance through Rituals (1975), *Working Papers in Cultural Studies*, also published as Hall and Jefferson (eds) (1976).

Reuter, E.B. (1936), 'The adolescent world', *AJS*, xliii, 1, pp. 82–4.

Reuter, E.B. (1937), 'The sociology of adolescence', *AJS*, xliii, 3, pp. 414–27.

Rex, J. and Moore, R. (1967), *Race, Community and Conflict*, Oxford University Press and Institute of Race Relations, London.

Reynolds, D.J. (1976), 'When pupils and teachers refuse a truce – the secondary school and the creation of delinquency', in Mungham and Pearson (eds) (1976).

Ribordy, F.X. and Barnett, A.N. (1979), 'La conscience du droit chez les étudiants anglo et franco ontariens', *Canadian Journal of Criminology*, vol. 21, April, pp. 184-96.

Ricoeur, P. (1963), 'Structure et hermétique', *Esprit*, November.

Ricoeur, P. (1972), 'The model of the text - meaningful action considered as a text', *Social Research*, April.

Riesman, D. (1951), *The Lonely Crowd*, Yale, New Haven.

Rigby, A. (1973), *Alternative Realities*, Routledge & Kegan Paul, London.

Rist, R.C. (1973), *The Urban School; A Factory for Failure*, MIT Press, Cambridge, Mass.

Robertson, G. (1974), *Whose Conspiracy?* National Council for Civil Liberties, London.

Robins, D. and Cohen, P. (1978), *Knuckle Sandwich*, Penguin, Harmondsworth.

Rock, P. and Cohen, S. (1970), 'The teddy boy', in Bognador, V. and Skodalsky, V., *The Age of Affluence*, 1951-61, MacMillan, London.

Rodman, H. (1965), 'The lower class value stretch', in Ferman, L., *Poverty in America*, University of Michigan Press, Ann Arbor.

Ross, A.M. and Hill, H. (1967), *Employment, Race and Poverty*, Harcourt Brace Jovanovich, New York.

Rosser, C. and Harris, C.C. (1965), *The Family and Social Change. A Study of Kinship in a South Wales Town*, Routledge & Kegan Paul, London.

Roszak, T. (1970), *The Making of a Counter Culture*, Faber & Faber, London.

Rothaus, L.G. (1984), 'Punk femininity; style and class conflict', paper presented at American Popular Culture Association, Toronto, Department of Education, University of Madison-Wisconsin, unpublished.

Rowbotham, S. (1973), *Woman's Consciousness, Men's World*, Penguin, Harmondsworth.

Rubin, J. (1970), *Do It!*, Simon & Schuster, New York.

Runciman, W.G. (1966), *Relative Deprivation and Social Justice*, Routledge & Kegan Paul, London.

Rutter, M. (1971), 'Why are London children so disturbed?' *Proceedings of the Royal Society of Medicine*, 66, pp. 1221-5.

Ryan, W. (1976), *Blaming the Victim*, Vintage Books, New York.

Sainsbury, P. (1955), *Suicide in London*, Institute of Psychiatry, London.

Sarsby, J. (1972), 'Love and marriage', *New Society*, 28 September.

Saussure P. (1960), *Course in General Linguistics*, Peter Owen, London.

Scarman, Rt. Hon. Lord (1981), *The Brixton Disorders - Report of an Enquiry*, Cmnd. 8427, HMSO, London.

Schofield, M. (1965), *The Sexual Behaviour of Young People*, Longmans, London.

Schofield, M. (1973), *The Sexual Behaviour of Young Adults*, Longmans, London.

Schur, E. (1973), *Radical Non Intervention*, Prentice-Hall, Englewood Cliffs, New Jersey.

Schwendinger, H. and Schwendinger, J. (1967), 'Delinquent stereotypes of probable victims', in Klein (ed.) (1967).

Schwendinger, J. and Schwendinger, H. (1976a), 'The collective varieties of youth', *Crime and Social Justice*, 5, Spring/Summer, pp. 7-25.

Schwendinger, H. and Schwendinger, J. (1976b), 'Marginal youth and social policy', *Social Problems*, vol. 4, no. 2, pp. 184-91.

Schwendinger, J. and Schwendinger, H. (1982), 'The paradigmatic crisis in delinquency', *Crime and Social Justice*, Winter, pp. 70-9.

Scott, J. and Vaz, E.W. (1967), 'A perspective on middle class delinquency', in Vaz (ed.) (1967a).

Scott, M.B. and Turner, R.H. (1965), 'Weber and the anomie theory of deviancy', *Sociological Quarterly*, vi, pp. 223-40.

Scott, P. (1967), 'Gangs and delinquent groups in London', *British Journal of Delinquency*, 1, pp. 525-6.

Scott, R.A. (1972), 'A proposed framework of analyzing deviancy as a property of social order', in Douglas and Scott (eds) (1972).

Shanley, F.J. (1967), 'Middle class delinquency as a social problem', *Sociology and Social Research*, 11, January, pp. 185-98.

Shanley, F.J., Lefever, D.W. and Rice, R.E. (1966), 'The aggressive middle class delinquent', *Journal of Criminal Law, Criminology and Police Science*, June, pp. 145-57.

Sharpe, S. (1976), *Just Like a Girl*, Penguin, Harmondsworth.

Shaw, C.R. (1930), *The Jack Roller*, University of Chicago Press.

Shaw, C.R. and McKay, H. (1927), *Juvenile Delinquency and Urban Areas*, University of Chicago Press.

Shaw, J. (1976), 'Finishing school - some implications of sex segregated education', in Barker and Allen, (eds) (1976).

Shibutani, T. (1955), 'Reference groups as perspective', *AJS*, ix, May, pp. 562-9.

Shibutani, T. (1966), *Improvised News - A Sociological Study of Rumour*, Bobbs-Merrill, New York.

Short, J. and Strodbeck, F.L. (1965), *Group Processes and Gang Delinquency*, University of Chicago Press.

Shragge, E. (1982), 'The left in the 80s', *Our Generation*, vol. 15, no. 2.

Simmons, J.L. (1965), 'Public stereotypes of deviants', *Social Problems*, Fall, pp. 223-32.

Simon, G. and Trout, G. (1967), 'Hippies in college - from teeny boppers to drug freaks', *Transaction*, vol. 5, pp. 27-32.

Singer, M. (1979), 'Coming out of the cults', *Psychology Today*, 12, 72.

Sivanandan, A. (1976), 'Race, class and the state, the black experience in Britain', *Race and Class*, Institute of Race Relations, London.

Skolnik, J. (1969), *Justice without Trial*, John Wiley, New York.

Skolnik, J. (1970), *The Politics of Protest*, Simon & Schuster, New York.

Smart, C. (1976), *Women, Crime and Criminology*, Routledge & Kegan Paul, London.

Smart, C. and Smart, B. (1978), *Women, Sexuality and Social Control*, Routledge & Kegan Paul, London.

Smith, C. (1966), 'Young people at leisure', *Bury Department of Youth Work Report*, University of Manchester.

Bibliography

Smith, D.H. (1970), *Marijuana - The New Social Drug*, Prentice-Hall, Englewood Cliffs, New Jersey.
Smith, D.H. and Gay, G. (1972), *Heroin - it's so good don't even try it once*, Prentice-Hall, Englewood Cliffs, New Jersey.
Smith, D.H. and Luce, J. (1971), *Love Needs Care*, Harper & Row, San Francisco.
Smith, D.J. (1977), *Racial Disadvantage in Britain*, Penguin, Harmondsworth.
Smith, E.A. (1962), *American Youth Culture*, Free Press, New York.
Smith, L. Shacklady (1978), 'Sexist assumptions and female delinquency', in Smart and Smart (1978).
Spector, M. (1971), 'On "Do delinquents drift?"', *Social Problems*, 18 March, pp. 420-2.
Spinley, M. (1953), *The Deprived and the Privileged*, Routledge & Kegan Paul, London.
Sprott, W.J., Jephcott, P. and Carter, M. (1954), *The Social Background of Delinquency*, University of Nottingham.
Stack, C.B. (1974), *All Our Kin - Strategies for Survival in a Black Community*, Harper & Row, New York.
Sterling, J.W. (1962), 'The juvenile offender from community to court - two stages of decision', unpublished paper read at Illinois Academy of Criminology, 31 November.
Stern, S. (1971), 'Altamont - Pearl Harbor to the Woodstock Nation', in Ramparts (eds) (1971).
Stewart, J. (1971), 'Communes in Taos', in Ramparts (eds) 1971.
Stimpson, G. (1969), 'Interview with skinheads', *Rolling Stone*, 26 July.
Stoltenberg, J. (1975), 'Towards gender justice', *Social Policy*, May/June.
Strouse, J. (1978), 'To be a minor and female - the legal rights of women under 21', in Krisberg and Austin (1978).
Sugarman, B. (1967), 'Involvement in youth culture, academic achievement and conformity in school', *BJS*, June, pp. 151-64.
Sutherland, E.H. and Cressey, D.R. (1966), *Principles of Criminology*, J.P. Lippincott, Philadelphia, (7th edn).
Sutherland, N. (1976), *Children in English Canadian Society - Framing the Twentieth Century Consensus*, University of Toronto Press.
Swingewood, A. (1977), *The Myth of Mass Culture*, MacMillan, London.
Tabb, W.K. (1970), *The Political Economy of the Black Ghetto*, W.W. Norton, New York.
Tabb, W.K. (1974), 'Marxist exploitation and domestic colonisation', *Review of Black Political Economy*, vol. 4, no. 4, pp. 69-89.
Tanner, J. (1975), 'Commitment to school and involvement in youth cultures; an empirical study', M.A. thesis, unpublished, University of Alberta, Edmonton.
Tanner, J. (1978), 'Youth culture and the Canadian high school - an empirical analysis', *Canadian Journal of Sociology*, 3 (1).
Taylor, I. (1970), 'Soccer consciousness and soccer hooliganism', in Cohen, S. (1970).
Taylor, I. (1981), *Law and Order - Arguments for Socialism*, Macmillan, London.

Taylor, I. (1982), 'Monetarism and popular protest, the challenge for sociology of the 1981 summer riots in Britain', *Departmental Working Paper, 82-6*, Department of Sociology, Carleton University, Ottawa.

Taylor, I. and Jamieson, R. (1983), 'Young people's response to the job crisis in Canada – a framework for theoretical and empirical research', unpublished paper, Department of Sociology, Carleton University, Ottawa.

Taylor, I. and Taylor, L. (eds) (1973), *Politics and Deviance*, Penguin, Harmondsworth.

Taylor, I. and Wall, D. (1976), 'Beyond the skinheads – comment on the emergence and significance of glamrock', in Mungham and Pearson (eds) (1976).

Taylor, I., Walton, P. and Young, J. (1973), *The New Criminology*, Routledge & Kegan Paul, London.

Taylor, I., Walton, P. and Young, J. (1975), *Critical Criminology*, Routledge & Kegan Paul, London.

Taylor, L. (1968), *Deviance and Society*, Michael Joseph, London.

Taylor, S. (1978), 'Racism and youth', *New Society*, 3 August, pp. 249-50.

Tennent, T.G. (1971), 'School attendance and delinquency', *Educational Research*, 13, 3, pp. 185-90.

Terry, R.M. (1970), 'Discrimination in the handling of juvenile offenders by social control agencies', in Garabedian, P. and Gibbons, D. *Becoming Delinquent*, Aldine Press, New York.

Teselle, S. (1972), *Family, communes and Utopian Society*, Harper & Row, New York.

Thomas, C. (1980), 'Girls and counter school cultures', *Melbourne Working Papers*, Department of Education, University of Melbourne.

Thompson, E.P. (1969), 'Time, work discipline and industrial capitalism', *Past and Present*, no 38.

Thornberry, T. (1973), 'Race, socioeconomic status and sentencing in the juvenile justice systems', *Journal of Criminal Law and Criminology*, 64, pp. 90-8.

Thrasher, F.M. (1927), *The Gang*, University of Chicago Press.

Titmuss, R. (1962), *Income Distribution and Social Change*, Allen & Unwin, London.

Tittle, C.R., Wayne, J. Villemez, J. and Smith, D.A. (1978), 'The myth of social class and criminality', *ASR*, 43, October, pp. 643-56.

Tolson, A. (1977), *The Limits of Masculinity*, Tavistock, London.

Townsend, P. and Abel-Smith, B. (1965), *The Poor and the Poorest*, Routledge & Kegan Paul, London.

Truzzi, M. (1972), 'The occult revival as popular culture, the old and nouveau witch', *Sociological Quarterly*, 13, Winter.

Tylor, E.B. (1871), *Primitive Culture*, John Murray, London.

Urry, J. and Wakeford, J. (1973), *Power in Britain*, Heinemann, London.

US Congressional Budget Office (1982), *Improving Youth Prospects: Issues and Options*, Washington, D.C., February.

Valentine, B.L. (1978), *Hustling and Other Hard Work; Life Styles in the Ghetto*, Free Press, New York.

Valentine, C.A. (1968), *Culture and Poverty*, University of Chicago Press.

Bibliography

Valentine, C.A. (1971), 'Deficit, difference and bi-cultural models of Afro-American behaviour', *Harvard Educational Review*, 31 (2), pp. 135-57.

Vallieres, P. (1968), Les Nègres Blancs d'Amérique du Nord, Editions Parti Pris, Montreal.

Vaz, E.W. (ed.) (1967a), *Middle Class Delinquency*, Harper & Row, New York.

Vaz, E.W. (1967b), 'Middle class delinquency in the middle class youth culture', in Vaz (1967a).

Vaz, E.W. (1969), 'Delinquency and youth culture in upper and middle class boys', *Journal of Criminal Law, Criminology and Police Science*, vol. 60, no. 1.

Vaz, E.W. and Lodhi, A.Q. (1979), *Crime and Delinquency in Canada*, Prentice-Hall, Toronto.

Veness, T. (1962), *School Leavers, Their Expectations and Aspirations*, Methuen, London.

Walton, P. (1973), 'Societal reaction and radical commitment – the case of the Weathermen', in Taylor and Taylor (eds) (1973).

Warren, M. Q. (1970), 'The community treatment project', in Johnston *et al.* (1970).

Weber, M. (1970), *The Protestant Ethic and the Spirit of Capitalism*, Allen & Unwin, London.

Weir, S. (1976), 'Youngsters in the Front line', *New Society*, 27 April, pp. 189-93.

Weissman, H. (1969), *Community Development in the Mobilization for Youth*, Association Press, New York.

Werthman, C. and Piliavin, I. (1967), 'Gang members and the police', in Bordua, D. (ed.), *The Police*, John Wiley, New York.

West, D.J. and Farrington, D. (1973), *Who Becomes Delinquent?* Heinemann, London.

West, G.W. (1980), 'Education, moral reproduction and the state', Ontario Institute for Studies in Education, Toronto, unpublished paper.

Westergaard, J. and Resler, H. (1975), *Class in Capitalist Society*, Heinemann, London.

Westhues, W. (1972), 'Hippiedom – some tentative hypotheses', *Sociological Quarterly*, Winter, pp. 81-9.

Westley, W. and Elkin, F. (1955), 'The myth of adolescent culture', *ASR*, xx, December, pp. 680-4.

Westley, W. and Elkin, F. (1967), 'The protective environment and adolescent socialisation', in Vaz (1967a).

West Riding Education Committee (1970), *Schools Bulletin*, July.

White, C.E. (1981), 'The peripheralization of blacks in capitalist America – the crisis of black youth', *Catalyst*, vol. 3, no. 1-2, pp. 115-31.

Whitehead, A. (1976), 'Sexual antagonisms in Hertfordshire', in Barker and Allen (eds) (1976).

Whyte, W.F. (1943), *Street Corner Society, The Social Organisation of a Chicago Slum*, University of Chicago Press, Chicago.

Widgery, D. (1973), 'What went wrong?', *Oz*, no. 48.

Wieder, D.L. and Zimmerman, D.H. (1974), 'Generational experience and the development of the freak culture', *Journal of Social Issues*, vol. 30, no. 2.

Wiener, R. (1976), *Drugs and Schoolchildren*, Longmans, London.

Wilder, T. (1957), *The Matchmaker*, Harper & Row, New York.

Wiles, P. (1976), *The Sociology of Crime and Delinquency in Britain, Vol. 2*, Martin Robertson, London.

Wilkins, L. (1964), *Social Deviance*, Tavistock, London.

Willener, A. (1970), *The Action Image of Society - On Cultural Political-isation*, Tavistock, London.

Williams, A. and Gold, M. (1972), 'From delinquent behaviour to official delinquency', *Social Problems*, Fall, 20, pp. 209-29.

Williams, R. (1961), *The Long Revolution*, Chatto & Windus, London.

Williams, R. (1973), *Culture and Society, 1780-1950*, Penguin, Harmondsworth.

Willis, P. (1970), 'Subcultural meaning of the motor bike', *Working Papers in Cultural Studies*, University of Birmingham.

Willis, P. (1972), 'Pop music and youth groups', *Phil. D. thesis*, Centre for Contemporary Cultural Studies, University of Birmingham, unpublished.

Willis, P. (1977), *Learning to Labour*, Saxon House, London.

Willis, P. (1978), *Profane Culture*, Routledge & Kegan Paul, London.

Willis, P. (1982), 'Male school countercultures', in *The State and Popular Culture*, Open University, Milton Keynes.

Willmott, P. (1966), *Adolescent Boys in East London*, Routledge & Kegan Paul, London.

Willmott, P. and Young, M. (1957), *Family and Kinship in East London*, Penguin, Harmondsworth.

Wilson, A. (1978), *Finding a Voice - Asian Women in Britain*, Pluto Press, London.

Wilson, D. (1978), 'Sexual codes and conduct - a study of teenage girls', in Smart and Smart (1978).

Wilson, E. (1977), *Women and the Welfare State*, Tavistock, London.

Wilson, J.Q. (1963), 'The police and their problems, a theory', *Public Policy*, xii, pp. 198-216.

Winckle, W. (1971), 'The coming of the hippies', reprinted in Ramparts (eds) (1971).

Wirth, L. (1938), 'Urbanism as a way of life', *AJS*, 44, July, pp. 187-243.

Wolfe, T. (1969), *The Electric Cool-Aid Acid Test*, Bantam, New York.

Wolfgang, M.E. and Ferracuti, F. (1967), *The Subculture of Violence*, Tavistock, London.

Wolfgang, M.E., Figlio, S. and Sellin, T. (1972), *Delinquency in a Birth Cohort*, University of Chicago Press.

Women's Studies Group (1978), *Women take Issue*, Centre for Contemporary Cultural Studies, Hutchinson, London.

Woods, P. (1977), *Youth, Generations and Social Class*, Open University Press, Milton Keynes.

Wright, N. (1977), *Progress in Education*, Croom Helm, London.

Wright, P. (1968), *The Coloured Worker in British Industry*, Oxford University Press, London.

Bibliography

Yablonsky, L. (1967), *The Violent Gang*, Penguin, Harmondsworth.
Yablonsky, L. (1971), *The Hippy Trip*, Pegasus, New York.
Yinger, J.M. (1960), 'Contraculture and subculture', *ASR*, vol. 55, pp. 625–35.
Young, J. (1971), *The Drugtakers*, Paladin, London.
Young, J. (1973), 'The hippies – an essay in the politics of leisure', in Taylor and Taylor (eds) (1973).
Young, M. and Willmott, P. (1973), *The Symmetrical Family. A Study of Work and Leisure in the London Region*, Routledge & Kegan Paul, London.
Youth in the Ghetto (1964), *Harlem Youth Opportunities Unlimited Report*, Department of Youth and Education, New York City.
Zaretsky, E. (1976), *Capitalism, the Family and Personal Life*, Pluto Press, London.
Zetterberg, H. (1968), 'The secret ranking', in Truzzi, M. (ed.), *Sociology and Everyday Life*, Prentice-Hall, Englewood Cliffs, New Jersey.

Index

Althusser, L., 4, 66, 67
Angry Brigade, 60-3
Anomie, 48-53
Anti-school culture, 60-3

'Ban', 56
Bane, M., 125
Barrio, 129-32
Beats, 87-90
Becker, H., 18
Berger, B., 26
Black culture and youth, 124-5
Black Panthers, 11
Black power, 108
Black youth, 6, 11, 32, 80, 116-44
Blues, 124-6
Bohemian youth, 83-115
'Bombing' graffiti, 127
Braithwaite, J., 43, 44
Brake, M., 8, 62, 66, 71, 84, 93, 97, 179
Break dance, 78, 123, 126
Bricolage, 14, 68, 72, 76, 77
Brown youth, 132-43

Canadian youth culture, 144-62
Centre for Contemporary Cultural
    Studies (CCCS), 8, 58, 62, 65-70,
    134, 142
Chicago School, 34-43, 84
City, social ecology of, 34-43, 59-63
Civil Rights Movement, 107-8
Clarke, J., 14, 68
Class, social, 3-11, 37-9; and youth
    culture, 39-43, 67

Clothing, 13, 117, 128
Cloward, R. and Ohlin, L. E., 8, 51, 52
Cohen, A. K., 2, 11, 38, 50-2, 66; and
    Short, J., 52
Cohen, P., 7, 8, 67
Cohen, S., 63, 64
Coleman, J., 41, 61, 85
Company of Young Canadians, 158
Consumers, youth as, 71
'Cool cats', 117, 128
Counterculture, 90-103; in Britain,
    90-7; in Canada, 158; in USA,
    97-103
Cults, religious, 103-5
Culturalism, 185-6
Cultural rebels, 23, 83-115
Culture, anti-school, 60-3
Culture, 1, 184-9; and class, 3-11;
    corporate and hegemonic, 67; and
    identity, 15-18; see also Black
    culture

Dance, 123, 126, 170
Delinquency, statistical presence of, 43
Delinquent girls, 171-4
Delinquent subcultures in UK, 60-82
Delinquent subcultures in USA, 30-57
Delinquent youth, 23
Delinquescent subculture, 61
Deviancy amplification, 64
Differential association, 46, 47
Differential identification, 46-8
'Dirty dozens', 126
Disaffiliation, 36, 89

225

Index

Disco, 125
Dissociation, 100, 123, 126
Dodd, D., 137, 138
Double articulation of parent culture and youth subculture, 67-8
Downes, D., 7, 37, 58, 61

Education and anti-school culture, 60-3
Eisen, J., 97
Elkin, F. and Westley, A., 152
Engels, F., 42
Ethnographic studies, British, 64-5
Existentialism, 87, 89
Expressivity, 100

Fatalism, 63
Femininity, 171-6
Finestone, H., 117, 128, 134
Fischer, C., 9
Focal concerns, 7; of beats, 89; of hippies, 99
Folk devils, 63-4, 76, 161
Freaks, 90-103
French Canada, 150, 153, 156, 157
Frith, S., 71, 163, 168, 183, 184, 188

Gangs, 32, 36, 64; girls, 131
Gay youth, 173, 175, 178-83
Ghetto, 76, 120-9
Girls: black and brown, 140-3; Canadian, 152; Chicanas, 131; culture, 169; and delinquency, 170-1; in masculine cultures, 171-6; punk, 176; and romance, 166-70; skinhead, 173
Glamrock, 76, 178
Graffiti, 127
Gramsci, A., 5, 59, 67
Glaser, B. and Strauss, A., 19

Hall, S., 4, 8, 92, 134, 142
Hargreaves, D., 61
Harlem Youth Opportunities Unlimited (HARYOU), 33, 119
Heads, 90-163
Hebdige, D., 68, 70, 72, 137
Hegemony, 5, 68
Hip hop, 126

Hippies, 90-103; women, 172
Hipster, 88, 117, 128
Hispanic youth, 32, 118, 129-32, 137-8
Homeboys, 137-8
Homology, 15, 68, 78, 94
Hustling, 117, 121, 128

Identity, 15-18; differential 46-8; and youth culture, 189-91
Ideology: and class, 3-11; and ideological state apparatuses, 4
Image, 12, 13
Individualism, 100

Jones, L. (Baraka, I.), 21, 125

Keill, C., 21, 124
Kostash, M., 157, 160

Labelling, 63-4
Lacan, J., 4
Laufer, R. and Bengston, V., 90
Leisure, 12
Lemert, E., 18
Lesbian youth, 173, 175, 182
Lévi-Strauss, C., 68
Liebow, E., 9, 126, 128
Low riders, 79, 131

Mannheim, K., 25, 26
Marsh, P., 77
Marxism, 3, 4
McRobbie, A., 168, 174, 175; and Garber, J., 168, 169, 172, 175
Masculinism, 178-83
Masculinity, 29, 57, 62, 65-6, 164, 173, 178-83
Matza, D., 34, 53-7, 79, 86; and Sykes, G., 10
Merton, R. K., 49, 50
Middle-class delinquency, 40, 43-6, 83-115
Miller, W. B., 7
Mobilisation for youth, 118
Mods, 14, 64, 74-5; girls, 12
Moral panics, 63-4
'Movement', 100
Mungham, G. and Pearson, G., 71, 170
Murdoch, G., 8, 27, 40, 62, 71

National deviancy conferences, 64
National Front, 81, 133
Neighbourhood, British working-class, 38, 39–67; *see also* Barrio, Ghetto
Nesbitt Larking, P., 155

Pachucos, 130
Parent subculture, double articulation with youth culture, 67–8
Parkin, F., 67
Parsons, T., 39–41
Passive resistance, 99
Politically militant youth, 23, 105–15
'Pop media' culture, 66
Popular music, 41, 73
Presley, Elvis, 41, 73
Punk, 69, 76–80; girls, 176–8

Quebec, 153, 156, 157, 158

Racism, 76, 90, 120–4, 127–8, 142, 143
Radical youth, 105–15, 156, 157
Rapping, 126
Reference groups, 47
Reich, C., 91
Respectable youth, 23
Respectability, 151
Rockers, 64, 74, 75
Rock music, 125, 182, 183, 188
Rodman, H., 10
Romance, 166–70
Rothaus, L., 176, 177, 178
Rudies, 128, 132, 134

Saussure, P., 12
Schwendinger, J. and H., 29, 46, 66
Scott, R., 17
'Scratching', 125
SDS (Students for a Democratic Society), 108, 109
Semiology, 12
Semiotics, 12, 13, 68
Sexism, 90, 102, 140, 172, 173–5, 178–83
Shaw, C. and McKay, H., 34, 35, 36, 38
Shragge, E., 159
Signs, 8, 12, 13, 68
Skinheads, 71, 75, 173

Smith, L. S., 173
Social ecology of city, 34–43, 59–63
Social reality, 15–18
Societal reaction, 18, 63–4
Status passage, 19
Stradom formations, 45, 66
Street people, 65, 66, 95, 102
Structuralism, 186
Student Union for Peace Action, 156
Style, 11–15, 72–82
Subcultural analysis 1–3, 18–21
Subculture: as analytical tool, 1–29; and anomie, 48–53; and delinquency, 21–7; social reality and identity, 15–18; and style, 11–15
Subjectivity, 100
Subterranean values, 22
Symbionese Liberation Army, 111
Symbols, cultural, 18

Tanner, J., 154
Taylor, I. and Jamieson, R., 193, 195
Taylor, I., Walton, P. and Young, J., 19, 37
Techniques of neutralisation, 53–4
Teddy boys, 14, 73–4; girls, 172
Teeny bopper culture, 169
Thrasher, F., 35, 36
Tittle, C., 43
Transitional phases of youth, 26

Unemployment and youth, 192–8; black youth in UK, 133; in USA; 120, 121, 126; and girls, 141, 193, 195; and youth values, 193, 195

Valentine, B., 121
Valley girls, 79
Value stretch, 10
Values: of girls, 168–9, 172, 195; subterranean, 10; of unemployed youth, 193, 195
'Vatos locos, los', 129–36
Vaz, E., 153

Weatherpersons, 111
West Indian youth, 133–9
Whyte, W., 35, 39
Williams, R., 1, 185

Index

Willis, P., 13, 15, 28, 62, 63, 64, 65, 70, 93, 165, 172, 174
Withdrawal, 89
Wolfgang, M., 43
Working-class youth culture: American, 30–77; British, 58–82

Yippies, 101
Young, W., 10, 20, 53, 55, 90, 195

Young Lords Organisation, 119, 132
Youth: politically militant, 23; respectable, 23; as a social problem, 21–7
Youth culture: Asian, 139–42; Black, 116–44; British, 58–142; Canadian, 144–62; and identity, 189–91; rise of, 21–7
Youth uprisings in Britain, 80–2